Modern Swedish Design

Modern Swedish Design
Three Founding Texts

By Uno Åhrén, Gunnar Asplund, Wolter Gahn,
Ellen Key, Sven Markelius, Gregor Paulsson,
and Eskil Sundahl

Edited and with introductions by
Lucy Creagh, Helena Kåberg,
and Barbara Miller Lane

Essay by Kenneth Frampton

The Museum of Modern Art, New York

Modern Swedish Design: Three Founding Texts is made possible by the Barbro Osher Pro Suecia Foundation, Kerstin and Pontus Bonnier, Stockholm, and The International Council of The Museum of Modern Art. Additional support is provided by the Consulate General of Sweden in New York, Estrid Ericsons Stiftelse, and the Department of Art History, Uppsala University.

Produced by the Department of Publications, The Museum of Modern Art, New York

Edited by Jennifer Liese
Designed by Amanda Washburn
Production by Elisa Frohlich
Printed and bound by Editoriale Bortolazzi-Stei s.r.l., Verona
This book is typeset in Berthold Akzidenz Grotesk (front and back); Consort Medium Condensed and Century Book (Key); Caslon Old Face and Adobe Caslon Pro (Paulsson); and Bauer Bodoni, Poster Bodoni, and Fette Fraktur (*acceptera*). The paper is 120 gsm Planoplus

Published by The Museum of Modern Art, 11 W. 53 Street, New York, New York 10019

Distributed in the United States and Canada by D.A.P./ Distributed Art Publishers, Inc., New York
Distributed outside the United States and Canada by Thames & Hudson Ltd, London

Library of Congress Control Number: 2008925655
ISBN: 978-0-87070-722-3

Cover: Kurt von Schmalensee. Model apartment no. 6, Stockholm Exhibition, 1930

Page 10: back cover of *acceptera* (Stockholm: Tiden, 1931)

Printed in Italy

Illustration Credits

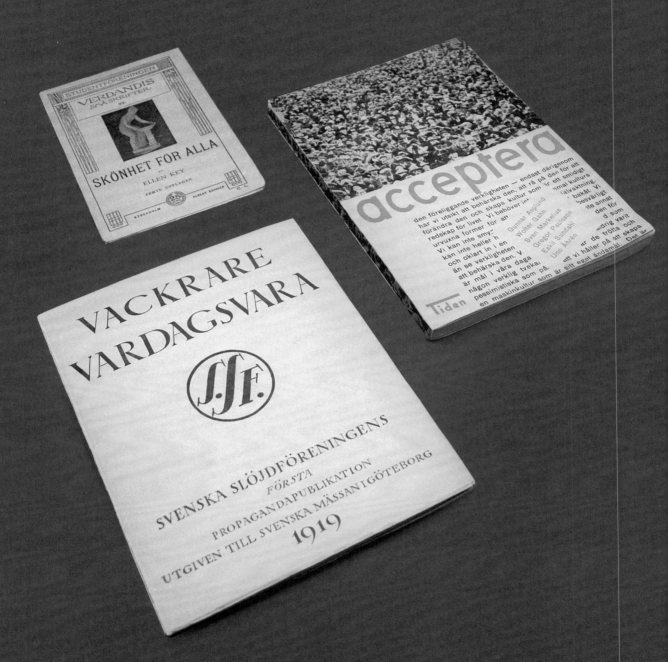

Preface

The history of architecture and design encompasses far more than bricks and mortar, drawings and models, and beautiful objects. Alongside this expressive material production are the allied rich histories of ideas and theories articulated in the writings of critics, art historians, artists, and architects. Indeed, for those concerned with the history and theory of architecture and design, it is impossible to divorce objects from the intellectual and social contexts from which they emerged. Every era since at least the Florentine Renaissance, when Leon Battista Alberti published his observations on art and architecture, has produced remarkable discourses. One thinks of Abbot Marc-Antoine Laugier's "Essay on Architecture" from the mid-eighteenth century; the forceful and moralizing prose of John Ruskin, which profoundly shaped the British Arts and Crafts movement in the nineteenth century; and, spanning the twentieth century, the widely disseminated works of Frank Lloyd Wright, Le Corbusier, Robert Venturi (whose *Complexity and Contradiction in Architecture* was published by this museum), and Rem Koolhaas, each of whom defined some of the key debates of their times. These writings communicate well beyond their time and place of origin, in no small part for having been printed in books; publication bestows both longevity and the potential for far-reaching influence, attracting not only the professional but anyone interested in the arts and society.

This volume is part of a series presented by The Museum of Modern Art's International Program that is intended to give English-speaking readers access to fundamental art-historical texts written in other languages. *Modern Swedish Design: Three Founding Texts* presents the first English translations of seminal texts that informed and responded to the development of modern Swedish design. The Swedish design movement has exercised a wide influence on modern architecture and interior furnishings internationally since the early twentieth century, yet the intellectual background from which it emerged has remained less well known. *Modern Swedish Design* promises to make the modern movement in Sweden—from artist Carl Larsson's influential renderings of his cottage, with its simple bright interiors, to IKEA, the phenomenally successful international home products retailer founded in 1943—more fully appreciated.

This publication encapsulates the movement's essential arguments, which developed over several decades from the late nineteenth century to the 1930s, a period that parallels the beginnings of modernism. The earliest text is by the noted philosopher and critic Ellen Key, who argues in "Beauty in the Home," an essay published in 1899, for the transformation of the domestic environment as a means to social reform. Key's writings were an inspiration to the influential art historian Gregor Paulsson, whose *Better Things for Everyday Life* appeared in 1919. The third text is *acceptera*, a book-length manifesto written in 1931 by Paulsson and a group of leading young modern architects, most notably Gunnar Asplund and Sven Markelius, who set forth progressive ideals of modern design for the noble goal of social well-being.

These authors, effective advocates for progressive social and artistic reform, shared a belief in the transformative power of a well-designed environment. Their essays are characterized by a fervent conviction that when the aesthetic realm is attuned to contemporary realities, an environment will be a catalyst for necessary social, cultural, and economic improvement. They also engage in the principal concerns of their time: the reader will recognize in these texts some of the central debates of the modern movement—regarding the relationship between art and industry, beauty and technology, and the individual and society, for example. Interestingly, the authors' ideas about taste, design, production, and the role of the domestic environment, the latter of which was a central concern, are set against a backdrop of ambitious exhibitions. While the exhibitions are not the focus of this volume, they were conceived with similar intent—to demonstrate, educate, and persuade.

Modern Swedish Design offers insights not only into Swedish history, but also into how the intellectal and critical discourse of that country relates to significant debates that took place simultaneously in Scandinavia, England, the Continent, and the United States. The Museum of Modern Art was founded in 1929 and presented its first architecture exhibition in 1932, just one year after *acceptera* was published. That landmark exhibition, *Modern Architecture— International Exhibition*, organized by Henry-Russell Hitchcock and Philip Johnson, included a recently constructed building by Eskil Sundahl and one by Markelius and Uno Åhrén (see p. 129; figs. 4 and 5), thereby representing three of the six authors of *acceptera*. Ever since, the institution has been committed to educating people about the art of our time as reflected in its collection, exhibitions, and publications, whose reach includes the modern movement that unfolded in Scandinavia.

The Museum is grateful for the opportunity to collaborate with Lucy Creagh, Helena Kåberg, and Barbara Miller Lane—three scholars who provide insightful introductions and annotations to the primary texts. The editors' astute commentaries provide the historical contexts in which Key, Paulsson, and the other authors of *acceptera* developed their influential ideas. Their introductions also convey the lasting relevance of the primary texts, a discussion that is developed further in Kenneth Frampton's essay. Frampton describes how the ideas put forth in these writings—which were not overly radical nor utopian—infused Scandinavia in the 1930s and mid-century in such a way that the modern experiment became not only possible, but a pervasive if arguably fleeting way of life in Scandinavia and beyond. In all, this publication provides an opportunity to reassess the history of modern Swedish architecture and design and its attendant writing and to pursue a deeper understanding of the polemics surrounding the social and aesthetic changes that so forcefully characterize the modern movement. With the International Program's commitment to support such scholarly activities, it is with great pleasure that we bring these founding texts and their engaged analysis to the English-speaking reader.

—Peter Reed, Senior Deputy Director
for Curatorial Affairs,
The Museum of Modern Art

Acknowledgments

The editors owe special thanks to Amelie Heinsjö at the Consulate General of Sweden in New York, who helped us get the project off the ground, and to Solfrid Söderlind and Kerstin Wickman for their support in its early stages.

This publication has been supported by the Barbro Osher Pro Suecia Foundation, Kerstin and Pontus Bonnier, Stockholm, and The International Council of The Museum of Modern Art. Jay Levenson, Director of MoMA's International Program, ensured critical support. Additional support has been provided by the Consulate General of Sweden in New York, Estrid Ericsons Stiftelse, and the Department of Art History, Uppsala University.

We are grateful to the family of Gregor Paulsson for permission to translate and publish *Vackrare vardagsvara*, and to the families of Uno Åhrén, Gunnar Asplund, Wolter Gahn, Sven Markelius, Gregor Paulsson, and Eskil Sundahl for their permission to translate and publish *acceptera*.

David Jones skillfully translated the Paulsson and *acceptera* texts, and Anne-Charlotte Harvey not only provided a superb translation of Ellen Key's "Beauty in the Home," but also offered unstinting help on other translation issues. Her translation is dedicated to her father, Eric Hanes (1911–2004), "whose life and works embodied Key's aesthetic with grace and clarity, and who would have approved of making her ideas more widely known in this world."

Many friends and colleagues have offered advice, critical readings, or support in obtaining funding or rare documents. Our thanks for their invaluable aid to Nicholas Adams, Ronny Ambjörnsson, Michael Asgaard Andersen, Fredric Bedoire, Kimberley Elman Zarecor, Eva Eriksson, Michelle Facos, Katja Grillner, Hans Hayden, Per Hedström, Matilda Herdland, Torun Herlöfsson, Frederike Huygen, Hedda Jansson, Karin Linder, Johan Mårtelius, Mary McLeod, Verne Moberg, Erik Mørstad, Eva Rudberg, Elisabet Stavenow-Hidemark, Dick Urban Vestbro, and Christina Zetterlund.

Anders Åman kindly permitted us to quote from the list of notes on the illustrations to *acceptera* published in the facsimile edition of 1980. Other colleagues have helped us track down and identify elusive images in *acceptera*: David Cast, Jeffrey Cohen, Robert Jonathan Esau, Paul Groth, Sabine Hartmann of the Bauhaus Archiv, Maria Ihrsén, Kathleen James-Chakraborty, Bo Legelius, Andrew Saint, Michael Sanz, and Henrik Widmark. For their kind help in locating manuscripts, archival material, rare books, and other illustrative material, we are grateful to Jonas Malmdal, Arkitekturmuseet; Ulrika Sundberg, Nordiska museets bildförmedling; Eva Karlsson, National-museum; Anita Christiansen; and the Archives at Svensk Form, all in Stockholm; and the Bryn Mawr College Library in Bryn Mawr, Pennsylvania.

The unflagging support of Peter Reed, Christopher Hudson, Kara Kirk, and David Frankel and the design, production, and research expertise of Amanda Washburn, Elisa Frohlich, Gina Rossi, and Margaret Raimondi at The Museum of Modern Art, along with the brilliant editorial work of Jennifer Liese, have made the book possible.

Finally, we thank our wonderfully supportive families, especially Henry Willoughby, Siv and Bengt Kåberg, and Jonathan Lane.

—Lucy Creagh, Sydney
Helena Kåberg, Uppsala
Barbara Miller Lane, Bryn Mawr

General Introduction

Lucy Creagh, Helena Kåberg, and Barbara Miller Lane

This volume presents three founding texts of Swedish modernism from the early twentieth century, translated and annotated in English for the first time. These writings, by pioneer reformers Ellen Key, Gregor Paulsson, and his five fellow authors of *acceptera*—Uno Åhrén, Gunnar Asplund, Wolter Gahn, Sven Markelius, and Eskil Sundahl—played central roles in the development of modern thought on architecture, design, and society in twentieth-century Sweden. While the authors' ideas and visions share many similarities with those of the French, German, American, and British founders of modern movements, they are also distinct from those of reformers abroad. Many of the differences resulted from the specific economic and political contexts in which Swedish modernism developed.

"Only when there is nothing ugly available for sale, when beautiful things are as inexpensive as ugly ones now are, can beauty for everyone be fully realized," wrote Ellen Key in "Beauty in the Home" at the turn of the twentieth century. Indeed, each of these texts presents beauty as an elevated expression of purpose, and each promotes a reformed version of industrialization as a means to bring about a new era in which "better things for everyday life," as Paulsson's title put it some twenty years later, would be available for all. Manufacturers, artists, architects, and craftspeople would unite to produce "a new visage" for "our new age," as the *acceptera* authors proclaimed a decade hence. Each of these texts sought design reform in every area of life, from the simplest household objects to the dwelling to the cityscape. Each also mounted powerful campaigns against buildings and manufactured products that were imitative of historical styles. For Key and Paulsson, contemporary industry was at fault in producing false and useless imitations; for the authors of *acceptera*, historical styles had become an obstruction to beauty.

Each text, however, has a different emphasis, which was of course shaped by the times in which it was written. Key's "Beauty in the Home" (1899) stresses that the beautification of the home can be achieved by turning to the simplest of models—some derived from early Swedish architecture, some from craft traditions, some from the potential of machine production, and some from nature itself. The essay was directed to the individual reader, to women and workers, and sought to educate them in redesigning the home. Further, Key argues for "utility" in the home, proposing that "each man-made thing must ... serve its purpose with simplicity and ease," and "the only thing worth striving for is harmony between the useful and beautiful." In his *Better Things for Everyday Life* (1919), Paulsson also wrote about purpose ("truth . . . means fitness for the purpose"), but to a greater extent than Key he emphasized the essential role of machine production in bringing about new forms, specifically through standardization and the creation of types by artists and craftspeople. His book was intended for manufacturers as well as for designers and artists. He also championed strong alliances between designers and industry. *Acceptera* (1931) was a response to the Stockholm Exhibition of 1930; a manifesto of Swedish modernism presented in a bold marriage of written and graphic form, it emphasizes architecture and city planning, subjects that Key and Paulsson also considered, though in texts not included here. Having grown partially out of earlier articles in specialist journals, *acceptera* was nevertheless addressed to a wide popular audience. The *acceptera* authors were more explicitly egalitarian and socialist, though these leanings are present in Key and the earlier Paulsson text, too.

While initially addressed to different audiences, all three texts were works of persuasion, intended to play a widespread and significant role in the re-education of popular taste. And all were effective: over time, regardless of initial intent, they came to be known to a broad audience. Each author promulgated his or her ideas not only through the publications translated here (each issued in a relatively inexpensive soft-cover edition) but also through public lectures, articles in newspapers and magazines, and popular exhibitions. Key helped put together two exhibitions on the design and furnishing of small apartments in 1899; Paulsson was involved in Svenska Slöjdföreningen (The Swedish arts and crafts society) when it sponsored the 1917 Home Exhibition, which was devoted to the design and furnishing of minimal dwellings. Thirteen years later he organized the Stockholm Exhibition of 1930 in collaboration with the other *acceptera* authors and with the sponsorship of Svenska Slöjdföreningen. These exhibitions engaged large audiences for their time (the 1930 exhibition was of course the best known) and prompted extensive newspaper coverage. In one way or another, the ideas of these design reformers reached a great many people.

While popular, each of the texts translated here is strikingly erudite. In addition to the Scandinavian languages, the authors appear to have read German, English, and French fluently; philosophical and literary allusions to works in English, German, and Swedish abound; technical and economic arguments are cited from American, French, British, and German sources. At the same time, the writing is strongly contextual: contemporary Swedish and other Scandinavian authors are referred to by allusion to their arguments or reputations, occasionally without much further identification. Like other Swedish intellectuals of their times, the design reformers included here were very well educated, closely familiar with those who shared their expertise or interests but also in touch with business and political leaders, and simultaneously convinced of their ability to address people from all spheres of society.

The ideas expressed in these texts are essential to any study of modern twentieth-century society and the birth and development of modern architecture, design, and city planning. Throughout the world today, the products inspired by modern Swedish design principles are well known and admired for their attention to utility and everyday beauty. This is partly because these authors were influential not only in Sweden but also internationally: during the troubled first half of the twentieth century, many looked to Sweden as a social and political model as well as a beacon for socially engaged modern architecture and design. This interest was particularly pronounced in Britain and the United States from the 1920s onward, where Sweden was often singled out as providing the Anglo-Saxon world with a more palatable, less extreme vision of modernism than that of Germany or France. Many of the writers included here lectured and wrote in German and English and presented their ideas at international symposia; some were members of international organizations that promoted modernism, such as CIAM (Congrès Internationaux d'Architecture Moderne) and the design team for the postwar United Nations Headquarters in New York.

Notwithstanding such international cross-pollination, Swedish modernism arose in a specific Swedish context. Unlike the developers of modern design in Germany, Great Britain, or the United States, Swedish proponents of modern design ideals were able to cultivate their principles in a climate of relative calm—Sweden experienced neither political revolution nor the full impact of the world wars that shockingly transformed other societies in the early twentieth century. Some of the differences between the development of modernism in Sweden and elsewhere can be accounted for by this comparatively placid history, but other factors—economic, political, and intellectual, as well as the long-term persistence of crafts traditions in Sweden—were equally formative.

Sweden in the late nineteenth century was marked by a sudden convergence of events that in other countries took place more gradually and separately. Large-scale industrialization occurred here only in the 1880s and 1890s, "late" in comparison especially to Britain, but also to the United States and Germany. In Sweden, however, industrialization built on a long tradition of manufacturing that has often been termed "proto-industrial." Iron and steel, wood products, and some textile making depended on small mills and "works," while other crafts products were often made at home or in the village. Such production was widely dispersed among many small urban and rural centers. This proto-industrial structure eased the transition to full industrialism, making it perhaps less jarring, and permitted the long-term survival of "crafts" traditions into the modern period, and into modern design.

Because full industrialization came late to Sweden, it coincided with the so-called Second Industrial Revolution, a phase in which older sources of power like steam and coal were rapidly supplemented by electricity and the internal combustion engine, while railroad networks improved distribution. Hence, the brutal economic and social dislocations typical of industrialization everywhere—urbanization, the growth of a large and impoverished working class, the crisis in housing conditions for the poor, class violence—were, while acute and catalytic for the emerging modern reform movement, shorter lived and less severe in Sweden. This is not to suggest, however, that Sweden was immune to struggle. In fact each of the texts translated here was written during periods of great social and economic crisis and at least partly in response to a troubled labor market and severe housing shortages.

Not long before the pace of industrialization began to accelerate, political reforms gave power to broad segments of both the urban and rural populations. At the same time, powerful workers' organizations began to form. The version of socialism that developed in Sweden in the 1880s and gained increasing political power beginning in the 1920s was so-called revisionist (i.e., non-Marxian) socialism—a non-revolutionary and democratic socialism that blends demands for social justice with a desire to respond to individual needs, wants, and rights. After the Second World War, modern architecture and design received the patronage of the new welfare state. In the 1940s, '50s, and '60s, under the leadership of Social Democrats or social democratic coalition governments, the government introduced large new housing and "new towns" programs that built on the teachings of prewar reformers.

Of course the new design programs also diverged from the specific mandates of the writer-reformers included in this volume, for instance replacing the severe simplicities of *acceptera* with more natural materials and more playful forms. And how could this divergence be otherwise? What these authors promoted was essentially a design philosophy, applicable at any given point in history, the essence of which is to analyze and take advantage of *current* conditions to fulfill the needs of all in the *current* society. Living, as we do today, in a different society with different technologies, many of the specifics of these authors' proposals are inapt for us. Their overall approach, however—which we might call "design for the times"—is not only of design-historical importance, but inspirational for our times as well.

In asserting the significance of these Swedish design writings and making them available to an English-speaking readership, our hope is to stimulate awareness and new scholarship. The editors came to this project with this shared intent but from different backgrounds: Creagh is an Australian architect and architectural historian whose research focuses on Swedish theory and practice in the mid-twentieth century; Kåberg, a Swedish art historian and museum curator with a special interest in international perspectives on Swedish architecture and design; Lane, an American historian concerned with the links between German and Scandinavian architecture. We have found each of our perspectives to be absolutely essential to our interpretation of the texts. Separated by continents but joined together by the pleasures of electronic mail, we have collaborated closely on every aspect of the manuscript.

Our initial interest in this project arose through our efforts to include the history of Swedish modernism in teaching English-speaking students. These efforts were constantly frustrated by the absence of translations from the Swedish. Our first concern, therefore, has been to make these texts available to teachers and students who do not read Swedish, but who want to understand the role of Swedish architecture and design in the general and international development of modernism. To this end, we have included in our annotations and bibliography as many relevant English titles as possible, as well as works in languages that are more accessible than Swedish to English readers. A second goal has been to stimulate new scholarship on the history of Swedish architecture and design—on both its specifically Swedish development and its international relationships. We hope that this volume will interest a general audience, but also that it will encourage a more international approach among scholars, perhaps also prompting additional translations from the Swedish.

Two further notes for the close reader—first, on translation. The qualities of the original texts—their erudition, allusiveness, their mixture of high philosophy and cheerful wit, their frequent references to economic, social, and political events and personalities well known at the time—present some problems to the English translator, and to the modern reader. In our introductory essays to each text, we have provided a great deal of interpretation, and in the notes to the translations we have endeavored to supply as many as possible of the less obvious references to philosophical, literary, political, and economic texts, events, and people. Working with our translators, we have tried to render early twentieth-century Swedish prose into contemporary language, while at the same time retaining the flavor of the originals and the differences in tone among them. And finally, a note on the design of this volume: Ellen Key's *Skönhet för alla* (Beauty for all), in which "Beauty in the Home" was first published, was part of the popular Verdandis småskrifter (Verdandi booklets) series and shared its layout and design with the other volumes in that series. Its cover, partially designed by Key's friend the painter Carl Larsson, has been reproduced in this volume. In the original publications of *Better Things for Everyday Life* and *acceptera*, illustrative material added a crucial visual dimension to the written arguments. These two books were works of design in their own right. In order to retain the strong visual dimension and design qualities of the original publications, The Museum of Modern Art has here reproduced their design and typeface qualities and their illustrations in full, in arrangements that are as close as possible to the original.

The Untimely Timeliness of Swedish Modernism

Kenneth Frampton

While we cannot make anything without waste, this is distinguishable
from an ideology of waste.   —Tomás Maldonado[1]

The paradoxical timeliness of this anthology, which touches on the evolution of Swedish
material culture from the late nineteenth century through 1931, acquires its current
pertinence from the persuasive way in which these essays successively expound on the
beneficial impact of environmental design on the overall quality of everyday life. Indeed,
the origin of today's sustainable approach to the mediation and furnishing of the built
environment may be said to date back to the last half of the nineteenth century, when
the bourgeois ideal of a total, all-encompassing artwork came to be given a broader,
more inclusive social dimension. The three texts assembled here comprise Ellen Key's
"Beauty in the Home" (1899), Gregor Paulsson's *Better Things for Everyday Life*
(1919), and the manifesto *acceptera* (1931), written by the designers of the didactic
Stockholm Exhibition, which had been realized in the previous year.
    Key's feminist manifesto is dedicated to rendering the home as the cradle
of a new egalitarian culture, and thus may be readily compared to the writings of
the American domestic reformers Harriet Beecher Stowe and Christine Fredericks.
Key's position, however, was not only progressively liberative and in favor of industrial
production but also nostalgic to a degree for the values of an agrarian, preindustrial
life, as in her advocacy of simple, handcrafted furniture and textiles. Key had a profound
influence on the art historian Gregor Paulsson, whose essay picks up the theme of
environmental reform where Key leaves off, greatly widening the scope of its reformist
agenda. Paulsson adopts Key's Socratic mode of arguing, for after recognizing
that tastes differ, he would go on to question not only why one person should want
magnificence and another simplicity but also what specific kinds of magnificence and
simplicity would apply in each instance. A similar didactic line would seem to obtain
in his contribution to *acceptera*, collectively written with Gunnar Asplund, the lead
architect of the Stockholm Exhibition, and four other architects who had participated
in its design. In effect, this exhibition had succeeded in humanizing the radical
constructivist syntax of the Soviet avant-garde, transforming its language into a
modern set piece that was as generously open and popular in its general atmosphere

as it was functional in its tectonic detail. *Acceptera* advanced the same ethos at a theoretical level while responding to those who still found its functional manner cold and severe. This exercise in total design, ranging from tableware to the micro-urban environment, was brilliantly characterized by the Finnish architect Alvar Aalto, whose appraisal, dating from May 1930, captured the way in which the exhibition bestowed upon its functionalist language an accessibly warm and ludic humanism. He wrote: "The deliberate social message that the Stockholm Exhibition is intended to convey is expressed in the architectural language of pure spontaneous joy. There is a festive elegance, but also a childlike lack of inhibition about it all. . . . This is not a composition of glass, stone, and steel, as a visitor who despises functionalism might imagine; it is a composition of houses, flags, flowers, fireworks, happy people, and clean tablecloths."[2]

Aalto's characterization finds its counterpart in the Danish architect Jørn Utzon's 1989 recollection of being taken to the exhibition at the age of twelve, whereupon his family began redoing the family home. As he recalled, "The concept was space and light. All the heavy impractical furniture was moved and simple things were brought in. We developed new eating habits; healthy, green, and lean. We began to exercise, get fresh air, cultivate light and the direct way of doing things. . . . I believe at this time we learned to see and this quite naturally was of great importance. The empty, dead, museumlike feeling about architecture disappeared and it became a living reality."[3]

A less intimate reaction to the significance of the exhibition was registered by the British critic P. Morton Shand when, in the August 1930 issue of the *Architectural Review*, he wrote of the way in which the exhibition could be seen as an apotheosis of the Swedish Arts and Crafts movement, which had long exercised an influence on the British scene:

> The Gothenburg Exhibition of 1923 revealed Sweden to an astonished world, not merely as an "artistic" nation, but as almost the only one that really counted as far as design and craftsmanship were concerned. . . . The perfectly edited Swedish pavilion at the Paris Exposition des arts décoratifs of 1925 confirmed this suddenly acquired reputation. . . . And now, just when the boom in "Swedish grace" is at its very zenith, Sweden calmly proceeds to jettison this halcyon godsend. . . . In the Stockholm Exhibition this process of spiritual renunciation—the act of craftsmen nerving themselves to take the first hesitant and half-dismayed steps toward an unexpected apotheosis—can actually be seen at work. . . . For the 1930 Stockholm Exhibition has at least taught us that the future of the machine as an integral organ of modern culture is assured; and its technical perfection as an art-form is only a matter of time.[4]

The section of *acceptera* dealing with modern furnishings was devoted not only to achieving the delicate transition between craftwork and machine production but also to distinguishing between meeting the everyday necessities of modern life and the human desire for luxury as an end in itself. It is highly probable that Paulsson was the author of this section, and in concluding that "every form of production that has no counterpart in our needs must come to an end," he anticipates, as it were, the ecological anxieties of our age.[5] At the same time he went on to recapitulate the profoundly democratic aims of the *acceptera* circle, to the effect that: "We are looking for forms that are suitable and natural for our age, we are looking for a close link with the fine arts and with the finest gifts of nature, we want to give people the better homes they need, which will leave them with some energy to cultivate their intellectual gifts."[6] Further evidence of the Swedish penchant for establishing a balance between nature and culture may be found in Paulsson's 1931 essay "White Industry," published, once again, in the *Architectural Review*.[7] For Paulsson, the putative "whiteness" of Swedish industry stemmed from its dependence on hydroelectric power rather than coal.

While environmental culture on both sides of the Atlantic was influenced in various ways by Stockholm 1930—one thinks of the exhibitions staged in Chicago (1933), Paris (1937), and New York (1939)—England was particularly susceptible to Swedish modernism throughout the 1920s and '30s, and Sweden would continue to exert an influence on the British scene during and after the Second World War. This much is evident from the mutual Anglo-Swedish adoption of the so-called New Empiricism in 1948, following Asplund's shift toward an organic brick-faced aesthetic with his state Bacteriological Laboratories of 1937.[8] Irrespective of this retrenchment to a more traditional tectonic language, the 1951 Festival of Britain was a reiteration of Stockholm 1930 at a smaller scale, consciously combining in the name of social accessibility the constructivist syntax of the Dome of Discovery and the Skylon with the festive tropes of flags, fountains, canopies, and flowers, interspersed with one café terrace after another. It is surely no accident that the Festival of Britain, which celebrated the rise to power of the Labor Party in 1950, should echo in its rhetoric the triumph of the Swedish Welfare State, as this was anticipated by the Stockholm Exhibition.

If the decade that followed the First World War and the 1917 October Revolution was when the "unfinished modern project" first acquired its avant-gardist character, Stockholm 1930 was the moment when this cultural rupture was rendered as a socially accessible synthesis, one which by 1944 had been developed into the Swedish Welfare State by such committed intellectuals as Gunnar and Alva Myrdal, figures with whom Paulsson would have had much in common.

It is a far cry from this maturation of Swedish social democracy in 1944, or even its state in 1974, to the last two decades of our globalized market economy, where capital flows around the world at ever-increasing speed, perennially focused on the maximization of profit in the shortest possible time. This whirlwind has effectively deprived the fields of environmental planning and design of a comprehensive social and civic vision. As a result we have not only passed the tipping point of climate change but have also, despite our techno-scientific, digital, and informatic prowess, become incapable of evolving a residential land settlement pattern and way of life that in terms of basic resources, land use, and public transport makes any kind of ecological or economic sense. The texts in this volume testify to a point in the evolution of the modern project, to which, in all likelihood, we shall eventually have to return.

Notes

1. A sharp aphoristic comment made in conversation with the author in the late 1960s.

2. Alvar Aalto, "The Stockholm Exhibition 1930," in Göran Schildt, ed., *Alvar Aalto in His Own Words* (New York: Rizzoli, 1998), p. 72.

3. Richard Weston, *Utzon* (Hellerup, Denmark: Edition Blondal, 2002), p. 16. From an interview with Henrik Sten Møller, "Jørn Utzon on Architecture," *Living Architecture* 8 (1989): p. 172.

4. P. Morton Shand, "Stockholm, 1930," *Architectural Review*, August 1930, pp. 67, 69, 70, 72.

5. *Acceptera*, in the present volume, p. 257.

6. Ibid., p. 334.

7. Gregor Paulsson, "White Industry," *Architectural Review*, March 1931, pp. 78–84.

8. See Eric de Maré, "The New Empiricism: Antecedents and Origins of Sweden's Latest Style," *Architectural Review*, January 1948, pp. 9–11.

1. Hanna Hirsch Pauli. Untitled (Ellen Key). 1903. Pastel on paper, 24 ¹/₄ x 30 ³/₈" (61.5 x 77 cm).
Stockholms arbetareinstitut, Stockholm

An Introduction to Ellen Key's "Beauty in the Home"

Barbara Miller Lane

Ellen Key (1849–1926; fig.1), Swedish philosopher, socialist, feminist, pacifist, peda-gogue, and design theorist, was one of the most influential intellectuals of her time. She was famous not only throughout the Scandinavian countries, but in continental Europe and the United States as well. More than forty books and hundreds of essays and jour-nal articles flowed from her pen. Most of these works grew out of the many hundreds of lectures she gave: in the Scandinavian countries, in France, Italy, Finland, and most extensively in Germany. Her major publications were translated not only into English but into almost all European languages before the First World War.[1] By 1900 she was able to make a living (though a frugal one) from her books and lecture tours.[2] A great many of Key's works dealt with aesthetics—with the importance of the love of beauty in all realms of life.[3] In an early essay ("Beauty," 1897–98) she speaks of a "religion of beauty" and calls for "a visionary prophet . . . to preach fanatically . . . the laws of beauty and the evan-gelism of the personality."[4] The "prophet," of course, was Key herself. She foretells a new era, a "Third Empire" of reason, social justice, creativity, peace, and beauty.[5] She predicts that when a new art has conquered industry, "making everyday life festive and beautiful, for rich and poor," the beauty of the home will spread outward to society, to architecture and city planning. Then, "under . . . modern social conditions, beautiful cities, monuments, and buildings [will] be created."[6]

In "Beauty in the Home," translated here into English for the first time, Key asserts that the new aesthetic sensibility must begin in the domestic setting.[7] The beauti-ful, she writes, is that which is practical, useful, informed by its purpose, and expressive of the soul of its user or creator. All people, she adds, need to create beautiful surround-ings for themselves, and this creation begins in the home. If beauty exists in the home, Key writes, lives will be transformed, and so, ultimately, will every aspect of society. The new aesthetic would not be restricted to the wealthy, or to artists and connoisseurs. Ordinary people—farmers and workers—would achieve it more easily in fact because their taste had not been corrupted by fashion and because they possessed fewer *things*. Every worker, Key once wrote, is a potential artist.[8]

Key also believed that every woman is a potential artist. The new taste and the new aesthetic would be created principally by women, partly because of their devotion to utility—"that whatever is useful is worthy of respect, all women realize"—but also in their role as nurturers and artists of the home, "of which [the woman] is the soul."[9] The mother, in particular, is the fountainhead of change, Key believed, as both the artist of the home and the educator of the children within it. By educating a new generation, mothers would found a new era, beginning with "the century of the child" (the title of Key's most famous book, published in 1900).[10] Outside the home, Key said, women also had a special role to play: they were the source of nurturing, caring, and indeed passion, within society. Their tasks were those of "motherliness," which she saw as the fostering of creative individuality and the reeducation of taste among all walks of life.[11]

In addition to writing on design and on art education, Key was an outstanding liberal and an early proponent of women's political rights.[12] A committed yet idiosyncratic socialist, she insisted that social justice be combined with personal self-expression and creativity.[13] There was a strain of anarchism in her thought too, stemming partly from her powerful commitment to individualism, and partly from her rebellious and contentious nature.[14] She was a leading pacifist before, during, and after the First World War. She condemned Christianity, saying that it and asceticism were the enemies of beauty, art, and culture. She developed a personal religion, prophetic of modern existentialism, in which holiness is immanent in nature, in ordinary people, and in everyday life.[15]

Many of the origins of Key's ideas lie in her childhood and youth. As a girl growing up at the family estate in Sundsholm, she learned to care deeply for the condition of the poorer farmers; she taught their children and involved herself in the "folk high school" movement.[16] Key loved the Swedish countryside, with its age-old handcraft and folk traditions (fig. 2). She also admired traditional rural buildings, especially the typical red-painted farmsteads of the provinces and the simple rustic classicism of her own home and others like it (figs. 3 and 4).[17] As a teenager, she began to gather artifacts for historian and ethnographer Artur Hazelius (1833–1901), who was collecting and re-creating early buildings, furniture, and fabrics; these collections ultimately became the world-famous museum at Skansen (fig. 5).[18] Later, in "Beauty in the Home," Key came to see the traditional architecture and crafts of rural Sweden as potential models for a new kind of design.

The love of painting that informs all Key's writings also began at an early date. In 1873, on the way to the Vienna World's Fair with her father, she visited the most important art museums of Europe (in Berlin, Dresden, Florence, Paris, London, Kassel, and Vienna). She repeatedly revisited these museums, as well as those of Copenhagen, Rome, and Munich. Like the German museum director Alfred Lichtwark (1852–1914), whom she came to admire, she believed that looking at works of artistic genius offered unique educational benefits for children and untutored people.[19] Key took this idea further, though, arguing in her publications and speeches that even reproductions of good paintings were better for the viewer than ugly originals.

Educated almost entirely at home, Key early on formed a lifelong habit of voracious reading and self-education. In addition to her admiration for English women novelists, and for the greatest works of German Romanticism, she was deeply influenced by the writings of Herbert Spencer, John Stuart Mill, Charles Darwin, and Auguste Comte. Thus her early philosophical stance can be characterized as strongly rationalist and positivist, yet based on a fundamental attachment to a rural way of life, and with an undercurrent of Romantic beliefs.

When around 1875 she moved to Stockholm and began to act as informal secretary to her father, Emil Key (1822–1892), a landowner and member of the newly

2. Cushion. Skåne, early nineteenth century. Wool embroidery on handwoven cloth, 22 $\frac{1}{4}$ x 19" (56.5 x 48.5 cm). Nordiska museet, Stockholm

3. Key's childhood home in Sundsholm, Småland. Eighteenth century. Photograph: collection Ellen Keys Strand, Ödeshög

4. Farm laborer's cottage, Södermanland, now in the Skansen outdoor museum, Stockholm. Early nineteenth century. Skansen, Stockholm

5. Mora Cottage, Mora, Dalarna, now in the Skansen outdoor museum, Stockholm. Eighteenth century. Photograph: collection Nordiska museet, Stockholm

reformed Swedish Parliament, she was especially eager to work with him on liberal issues such as education and the political rights of women and farmers.[20] She became a forceful proponent of political reforms and acquainted herself with Stockholm's leading liberal politicians and intellectuals. In the 1880s she drew progressively closer to avant-garde artists and literary figures: to the painters among The Opponents and the writers of the Young Sweden movement. Both groups rebelled against traditional taste and espoused Naturalism; for the artists, this meant plein air painting and a new appreciation of the northern landscape; for the writers, often, a concern with women and the working classes.[21]

In 1883 Key's family suffered financial reverses, the family estate was lost, and she was forced to support herself in Stockholm.[22] While teaching at the new Stockholms arbetareinstitut (Stockholm workers' institute, founded in 1880), she began to lean toward socialism. Sweden's industrialization began in the last decades of the nineteenth century—late, as compared to England, France, Germany, and the United States. Stockholm especially experienced large-scale population growth, absorbing a rapidly increasing number of new immigrants, without much new building. The living conditions of Stockholm's poor toward the end of the century were considerably worse than in most of the rest of Europe. Working-class families with as many as eight children often crowded into a single room.[23] The poorest people lived in the decaying wooden structures of Stockholm's outer periphery.

In this context, Key transferred her early concern for Sweden's rural poor to the working classes of Swedish cities. Inspired by reformist ideas not unlike those of Jane Addams, Key formed an association called Tolfterna (The twelves) that brought middle-class professional women together with working-class women to help them improve their way of living.[24] In 1885 she cofounded Nya Idun (New Idun), an organization for women artists and intellectuals that she led until 1900.[25] During the same years, she befriended leading Social Democrats. In 1889 Key forcefully (and famously) defended socialist leaders who had been imprisoned by the Swedish government for atheist writings, among them August Palm (1849–1922) and Hjalmar Branting (1860–1925), founders and first leaders of the nascent Social Democratic Party. After the formal establishment of the party in 1889, she appeared with Branting at party meetings, where she spoke about working conditions for women. An admirer and disciple was Gustaf Steffen (1864–1929), prominent Swedish political economist and social democratic representative to the Riksdagen, often seen as one of the progenitors of the Swedish "middle way" in politics and social policy.[26]

Key's lectures at the Workers' Institute were open to the public; soon she also began to lecture at workers' unions and clubs in Stockholm, and to student groups at Swedish and Finnish universities. Her lectures gained her great fame: she was, by all accounts, a bewitching speaker. Her talks—vivid, extemporaneous, presented with a modest (almost shy) demeanor and in a low voice—commanded attention from huge audiences of artists, architects, philosophers, literary figures, politicians, students, and workers.[27] By the early 1890s, Key was a central figure in Stockholm's intellectual life. She wrote regularly for radical periodicals, lectured widely, and began to publish her lectures and articles as books. She had already read and appreciated Kierkegaard and Nietzsche and would promote Nietzsche's ideas among Stockholm's intellectuals. She and her intimates gathered together at her apartment on Valhallavägen or at the home of artist Hanna Pauli (1864–1940) for weekly conversations about socialism, pacifism, education, philosophy, religion, and art (fig. 6).[28] Often discussed among Key's artist and literary friends were the writings of the eighteenth-century aesthetic philosopher Carl August Ehrensvärd (1745–1800). She and her circle subscribed to Ehrensvärd's belief that Swedish artists and architects had a special mission to achieve an almost primitive

6. Hanna Hirsch Pauli. *Vänner* (Friends). 1900–07. Oil on canvas, 6' 8 ³/₈" x 8' 6 ³/₈" (204 x 260 cm).
Nationalmuseum, Stockholm

simplicity.[29] They also shared Key's view that Sweden must begin to play a leading role
in educating continental Europe and the rest of the world in a new aesthetic.[30]

Key and her friends were in touch with the Swedish crafts revival and reform
movements of the time, and they were aware of the English Arts and Crafts move-
ment. They knew and admired the revival of Swedish crafts promoted by Föreningen
Handarbetets Vänner (The association of friends of textile art) and attended Erik
Folcker's lectures on English wallpapers sponsored by Svenska Slöjdföreningen (The
Swedish arts and crafts society) in 1892.[31] They read the English art periodical *The
Studio* as soon as it began publication in 1893. (Key probably read William Morris and
John Ruskin at about this time.[32]) And they went to the new Swedish exhibitions, most
notably the major Stockholm Exhibition of May 1897, where watercolors of "the home"
by the painter Carl Larsson (1853–1919) were displayed. Key reviewed the Stockholm
Exhibition, highlighting the paintings of her close friend. Larsson published these paintings in an enormously successful series of books beginning in 1899; it is from the first
of this series, *Ett hem* (A Home), which Key quotes in "Beauty in the Home."[33]

In his paintings and books, Larsson depicted an ideal home, furnished with colorful, simple, and somewhat rustic-looking pieces designed by him and his wife, Karin,
and decorated with textiles created by Karin, who was inspired by traditional crafts.
Larsson peopled the dwelling with an idealized version of his own family (Karin and
their eight children), leading an idealized life, plain and unpretentious, close to the soil
and to local traditions. In Larsson's home, children worked and played, the family put
on theatricals, light flooded in. Perpetual sunlight seemed to illuminate the life of the
home, and strong colors predominated (figs. 7, 8, and 9). Key's own emphases on color
and light are very similar to Larsson's, and, as she writes in "Beauty in the Home," she
strongly approved of his depiction of family life.

Acting on her commitment to workers' education, Key joined with artists Gerda Bergh (1864–1919) and Richard Bergh (1858–1919) and art historian Carl G. Laurin (1868–1940) to organize furnishing and decoration exhibits at the Workers' Institute in the spring and fall of 1899, calling them the "Blue Room" and the "Green Room."[34] The "Blue Room" attempted to show a typical Swedish interior made tasteful by simplifying its contents and decorations. Plain white curtains, straw mats on the floor, tableware by designer Alf Wallander (1862–1914), and reproductions of works by artists (including Albrecht Dürer, Jean-François Millet, and Larsson) combined to display a "simple and purposeful form."[35] The "Green Room," intended as the model for a more humble worker's dwelling, was papered with an English wallpaper "in a pattern of small poppies" against a "background of yellow, green, and red tones" (figs. 10, 11, and 12).[36] The furniture, designed by architect Carl Westman (1866–1936), was stained green in a "mixture of Swedish country and modern English styles"; the pattern of the wood was permitted to show through the stain. The sideboard was bright red, like much of the furniture in the Larsson home. As in the "Blue Room," vases of flowers, bookcases, and art reproductions enhanced the interior. The exhibition showed, Key said, that the best effects could be achieved "with inexpensive materials and little effort," by employing harmonious colors and simple, practical furniture.[37]

About five thousand people visited the "Green Room" exhibition, and this success encouraged Key to expand the short essay published in 1897 into the much longer work translated here. In 1899 she collected the expanded essay and three earlier short writings on related subjects into *Skönhet för alla* (Beauty for all). Verdandi,

7. Carl Larsson. *Köket* (The kitchen). 1898. Watercolor on paper. Seen here as published in Larsson, *Ett hem* (Stockholm: Bonnier, 1899)

8. Carl Larsson. *Namnsdag på härbret* (Name day in the storehouse). 1898. Watercolor on paper. Seen here as published in Larsson, *Ett hem* (Stockholm: Bonnier, 1899)

9. Carl Larsson. *Sommarmorgon* (Summer morning). 1908. Watercolor on paper. Seen here as published in Larsson, *Åt solsidan* (Stockholm: Bonnier, 1910)

10. Couch, table, and stove in the "Green Room" at Stockholms arbetareinstitut, Stockholm, September 1899. Photograph: collection Nordiska museet, Stockholm

11. Sideboard in the "Green Room" at Stockholms arbetareinstitut, Stockholm, September 1899. Photograph: collection Nordiska museet, Stockholm

12. Bed, window, washstand, and closet in the "Green Room" at Stockholms arbetareinstitut, Stockholm, September 1899. Photograph: collection Nordiska museet, Stockholm

an influential radical students' organization based at Uppsala University, published the book, with a cover by Larsson.[38] The essays in *Beauty for All* differ greatly in tone and subject matter. "Vardagsskönhet" (The beauty of everyday life) (first published in *Julbloss*, 1891) speaks of the importance for the individual soul of sensing a connection to nature and creative work in art, music, and literature. "Festvanor" (Domestic celebrations) (*Idun*, 1896) argues that domestic festivals (Christmas, New Year's, May Day, birthdays, name days, and other traditional household gatherings) awaken the understanding of each new generation to continuities, providing a kind of religious appreciation of everyday life. In "Skymmningsbrasan" (Twilight fire) (*Idun*, 1895, written in 1870) Key writes of the experience of light and the role of the hearth in the dwelling.[39] The tone of these three essays, as of many of her other works, is often ecstatic, mystical, and prophetic.

"Beauty in the Home" is much more down-to-earth. Full of specific advice, it is a do-it-yourself manual for people of humble means, people seeking to establish some kind of judgment in the face of bad taste in home decoration. In the Swedish home of 1899, Key believed, "the most garishly cheap German taste" prevailed: ugly, ostentatious, crowded, dark, and gloomy.[40] Manufacturers instead should be guided by artists and craftsmen who would impart "beautiful form and appropriate decor to all things, from the simplest and smallest . . . to the largest."[41] We are told to avoid dark colors in upholstery and wall coverings, to mistrust pictures on the walls, to despise artificial flowers, doilies, knickknacks, imitative styles, any appearance of ostentation—or, indeed, of wealth. The home and its furnishings must be close to nature, made as far as possible of natural materials, not from industrial products at least insofar as these imitate

13. Yngve Rasmussen. Strand, Key's home on Lake Vättern. 1910. Ellen Keys Strand, Ödeshög

14. Key's bedroom in Strand. Ellen Keys Strand, Ödeshög

something that they are not. We must not use certain kinds of varnish, but choose others that are lighter and more natural looking. Light colors are always good, but strong, bright, and cheerful ones must complement them. There is a discussion of the ideal number of guests to seat at dinner and finally a list of good buildings and paintings the reader should know about, in order to improve her taste.

Underlying these sometimes amusing and sometimes distracting instructions is a central vision that stresses simplicity, naturalness, and the path to a new kind of self-expression for each individual in society. Out of this vision will come a new way of life for each, and ultimately for all. References to light occur over and over again, not only as advice in decorating, but also as metaphors of enlightenment and transformation. To achieve the moral and social progress that will begin in the home, to move on to the century of the child and the millennial empire of justice and beauty, we must "let the sunshine come flooding in"![42]

The editors have chosen to translate "Beauty in the Home" as it was published in its 1913 edition, the final version during Key's lifetime and the one most widely read. The essay did not change very much between 1899 and 1913: the major change was the addition, in 1904, of a long passage praising the home of Carl and Karin Larsson.[43] The list of organizations, buildings, paintings, and sculptures of which Key approved was also added to and emended in each new edition, but the text as a whole was never rewritten after 1904.[44] Thus "Beauty in the Home" is very much a product of the turn of the century, and of Key's life before she became a peripatetic traveler and an internationally famous author.

That there was never after 1904 a revised edition of *Beauty for All* nor a new edition after 1913 during Key's lifetime probably has to do not only with Key's busy schedule in her fifties and sixties, but also with her preoccupation with her house at Strand, on Lake Vättern, built according to her specifications by her architect and brother-in-law, Yngve Rasmussen, in 1910.[45] Key occupied Strand almost continuously from December 1910 on. Here she put some of her ideas about design into practice (figs. 13 and 14). There were strong colors on the walls, simple mats and runners on the floors, a mixture of relatively plain-looking (but by no means rurally inspired) furniture, and reproductions of Symbolist paintings on the walls. (Her favorite was Arnold

Böcklin's *Island of the Dead*.)[46] The exterior bore a certain resemblance to Sundsholm, her childhood home.[47] In keeping with Key's wishes, Strand was used as a vacation place for working-class women after her death.[48]

From about 1900 to 1909, Key's lectures outside of Sweden magnified her fame. At this time too she began an enormous correspondence with foreign intellectuals, a correspondence she carried on until the end of her life.[49] She also started to attract disciples from abroad, of whom perhaps the most well known to scholars are the German poet Rainer Maria Rilke, Austrian novelist and librettist Stefan Zweig, Lou Andreas-Salomé (German journalist, companion to Nietzsche and Rilke), and Mamah Bouton Borthwick and her lover Frank Lloyd Wright. Borthwick was one of Key's earliest visitors at Strand; she translated four of Key's works into English (from German), and she and Wright arranged for their publication in the United States.[50]

Ellen Key had a genius for gathering up the most progressive ideas of her contemporaries—artists, crafts enthusiasts, designers, writers, politicians, labor leaders, reformers of all types—and welding them together through the force of her own intellectual passions into novel and persuasive arguments. Within Sweden, she was powerfully influential for a time. Among the younger generation of architects, housing planners, and design theorists, Carl Westman, Ragnar Östberg, and Gregor Paulsson owed her a great deal (figs. 15 and 16).[51] In the longer term, her insistence that individualism and socialism must be joined together probably played some part in the evolution of Swedish social thought; certainly this idea provided a foundation for the social conscience so prevalent in later Swedish design and architecture.[52] Her significance for twentieth-century educational theories has often been noted. Her ideas about feminism are still significant, and still hotly debated. The further dimensions of her importance are difficult to measure. Scholars have only recently begun to scale the veritable mountain of material—her own letters, speeches, essays, journal and newspaper articles, and books, as well as comparable publications and manuscripts from her admirers and detractors—involved in studying her work. Thus there is much in Key's life and thought that remains obscure. Still it is clear that Key's belief that the home, the dwelling, could be the source of creative change in both the arts and in society had a decisive and long-lasting impact on Swedish design theory, applied arts, and architecture.

15. Carl Westman and Elin Anderssen. Pressens Villa, Saltsjöbaden. 1901–02. Main hall. Photograph: collection Nordiska museet, Stockholm

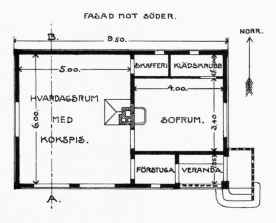

16. Ragnar Östberg. Proposal for workers' housing. 1905. Plan as published in Östberg, *Ett hem, dess byggnad och inredning*, Studentföreningen Verdandis småskrifter no. 131 (Stockholm: Bonnier, 1906)

Notes

1. Translated into all European languages except Italian, Hungarian, Croatian, and Bulgarian; also into Yiddish.

2. For general works in English on Key, her context, and her relation to later design theorists, see especially Clarence Burton Sheffield, Jr., "Social Needs and Aesthetic Demands: Ellen Key, Gregor Paulsson, and Swedish Design, 1899–1939," in *The Brilliance of Swedish Glass 1918–1939: An Alliance of Art and Industry*, eds. Derek E. Ostergard and Nina Stritzler-Levine (New Haven, CT: Yale University Press, 1997), pp. 34–51; and Kerstin Wickman, "Homes," in *20th Century Architecture: Sweden*, eds. Claes Caldenby, Jöran Lindvall, and Wilfried Wang (Munich: Prestel-Verlag, 1998), pp. 198–225. Still useful on a number of issues is Ronald De Angelis, "Ellen Key: A Biography of the Swedish Social Reformer" (dissertation, University of Connecticut, 1978).

3. See, for example, Key, *Folkbildningsarbetet: Särskildt med hänsyn till skönhetssinnets odling* (Uppsala: Appelbergs Boktryckeri, 1906); and Thorbjörn Lengborn, *Ellen Key och skönheten* (Stockholm: Gidlunds förlag, 2002).

4. "Skönhet," *Tankebilder*, vol. 1 (Stockholm: Albert Bonniers förlag, 1898), pp. 130–31. Key dated this essay 1897–98. Translated in its entirety in German as "Schönheit," in *Die Wenigen und die Vielen* (Berlin: Fischer, 1900), pp. 283–307.

5. According to Key her concept of a "Third Empire" came from Henrik Ibsen's 1873 play *Emperor and Galilean: A World-historic Drama*. See *The Torpedo under the Ark: "Ibsen and Women"*, trans. Mamah Bouton Borthwick (Chicago: Seymour, 1912), p. 28; and *The Century of the Child* (New York: Putnam, 1909), in which she relates the idea to the millenarian teachings of medieval mystic Joachim of Flora, p. 315, and to Nietzsche's idea of the age of the superman, pp. 105, 121.

6. "Skönhet," pp. 140, 146.

7. "Skönhet i hemmen," in *Skönhet för alla*, Studentföreningen Verdandis småskrifter no. 77 (Stockholm: Bonnier, 1913); facsimile edition (Stockholm: Rekolid, 1997), pp. 3–37. *Skönhet för alla* (Beauty for all) was first published in 1899, and in five further editions (another in 1899, an expanded version in 1904, again in 1908 and 1913, and finally in 1939, thirteen years after Key's death). By the start of the First World War it had sold twenty thousand copies in Sweden, a significant number in a country of about five million people. *Skönhet för alla* was never translated as a whole, but a version of "Skönhet i hemmen" appeared in German newspapers in 1910; see Reinhard Dräbing, *Der Traum vom "Jahrhundert des Kindes"* (Frankfurt am Main: Peter Lang, 1990), p. 516. An early, extremely short version of "Skönhet i hemmen" appeared in the magazine *Idun* in 1897 as part of a series on "the modern home." See Key, "Skönhet i hemmen: Små utläggningar af Ehrensvärds text," *Idun: praktisk veckotidning för kvinnan och hemmet*, julnummer (Christmas issue, 1897): p. 4.

8. See Ronny Ambjörnsson, ed., *Ellen Key: Hemmets århundrade* (Stockholm: Aldus, 1976), p. 54.

9. Key, in the present volume, p. 36.

10. *Barnets århundrade* (Stockholm: Bonnier, 1900); translated into English as *The Century of the Child*, 1909. On Key's educational ideals, a useful English source is Thorbjörn Lengborn, "Ellen Key," *Prospects: The Quarterly Review of Comparative Education*, vol. XXIII, no. 3/4 (1993): pp. 825–37. See also Lengborn, *En studie i Ellen Keys pedagogiska tänkande främst med utgångspunkt från 'Barnets århundrade'* (Stockholm: Ljungberg, 1977).

11. Ronny Ambjörnsson, *Samhällsmodern: Ellen Keys kvinnouppfattning till och med 1896* (Göteborg: Göteborg Universitet, 1974). See also Ambjörnsson, "Family Ideas in Sweden and the Tradition of Ellen Key" in *Traditional Thought and Ideological Change: Sweden and Japan in the Age of Industrialism*, eds. S. Cho and N. Runeby (Stockholm: University of Stockholm, 1988), pp. 49–56; and Ambjörnsson, "En skön ny värld—Om Ellen Keys visioner och en senare tids verkligheten," *Fataburen* (1991): pp. 260–78. Ambjörnsson is preparing a definitive biography of Key.

12. Key was one of the first Swedish women to call for female suffrage. She also consistently argued that women must and should have additional rights in society, a position that in the 1890s led her into conflict with the emerging Swedish suffragist movement. She scandalized many feminists of her time (and others ever since) by arguing (in *Missbrukad kvinnokraft*, 1896) that women, being biologically different from men, should remain at home in nurturing roles. This publication has been much misunderstood: it was an overstatement of her views, almost certainly intended to provoke controversy and also to protect working women and children from exploitation. Key never wavered from a commitment to women's political and economic rights; she simply wanted to add to them. She modified her statements on careers for women in *The Century of the Child* and her 1909 *Kvinnorörelsen*, published in English as *The Woman Movement*, trans. Mamah Bouton Borthwick (New York: Putnam, 1912), and certainly her own public life was not restricted by concerns for home and family. Key's personal life has been troublesome to those who have tried to understand her feminism: she carried on a long and ill-fated affair with Urban von Feilitzin, Norwegian landowner and intellectual, from 1875 to 1890, but she never married, bore children, or otherwise conformed to traditional women's roles. In *Om kärlek: Litteratur, sexualitet och politik hos Ellen Key* (Stockholm: Symposion, 2002), Claudia Lindén has argued persuasively against trying to understand Key's philosophy in terms of her personal life. On the same point, see Sabine Andresen and Meike Sophia Baader, *Wege aus dem Jahrhundert des Kindes: Tradition und Utopie bei Ellen Key* (Neuwied: Luchterhand, 1998), pp. 85–89.

13. *Individualism och socialism: Några tankar om de få och de många*, Studentföreningen Verdandis småskrifter, no. 55 (Stockholm: Bonnier, 1895).

14. Key carried on a lively correspondence with Prince Peter Kropotkin (1842–1921), a leading Russian anarchist, from 1900 on, and arranged to meet him during one of her European lecture tours (Ellen Key Archive, Manuscripts Division, Royal Library, National Library of Sweden, Stockholm; and De Angelis, p. 228). Key's library at Strand includes six of his books (in German, English, and Swedish); four contain inscriptions or dedications to Key.

15. Ambjörnsson, *Samhällsmodern*, p. 28.

16. A movement to promote schools for farmers that began in the 1860s in Denmark and spread to all the Scandinavian countries. Key founded a school of this type for women in her home district. See De Angelis; and Barbara Miller Lane, *National Romanticism and Modern Architecture in Germany and the Scandinavian Countries* (New York: Cambridge University Press, 2000).

17. Key grew up in an eighteenth-century manor house in Sundsholm, in the southeastern province of Småland (near Kalmar).

18. For Key's description of the Mora Cottage and Skansen, see Key, in the present volume, pp. 38–39. On Skansen, see Lane, *National Romanticism*, p. 40. On Key's work for Hazelius, see Louise Nyström-Hamilton, *Ellen Key: Her Life and Her Work* (New York: Putnam, 1913), p. 57.

19. For Key's views on the proper role of art in education, see especially her *Folkbildningsarbetet (Uppsala: K. W. Appelberg, 1906)*, which contains many references to Lichtwark. On Key and Lichtwark, see Lengborn, *Ellen Key och skönheten*, pp. 91–98.

20. In 1866 the Swedish Parliament democratized to some extent: a bicameral legislature replaced the four-part parliament of "estates" and the electorate was broadened. Emil Key, one of the founders of the large Lantmannapartiet (Ruralist party), represented his district in the lower house from 1867 to 1883. In 1869 Key and her parents moved to Stockholm during the winters. In 1875 the rest of the family moved back to Sundsholm for most of the year, while Ellen Key remained with her father as his housekeeper and secretary.

21. The Opponents (Ernst Josephson, Richard Bergh, Nils Kreuger, Karl Nordström, Anders Zorn, Carl Larsson, Georg Pauli, and other young artists and students) seceded from the Royal Academy in 1886 and founded the new and ultimately very successful Konstnärsförbundet (Artists federation). The Young Sweden movement, including Gustaf af Geijerstam, Victoria Benedictsson, and (for a time) August Strindberg, called for an emphasis on current social and political issues in literature and drama.

22. At the Stockholm Workers' Institute from 1883 to 1903, Key taught the history of Swedish civilization, with an emphasis on the history of literature and art. She also taught at Anna Whitlock's progressive new elementary school from about 1880 to 1899. During the same period she gathered together the daughters of Stockholm's intellectual elite for informal tutorials that later grew into large classes on literature and art. See Nyström-Hamilton, *Ellen Key*, p. 70; and Ambjörnsson, *Samhällsmodern*, p. 26.

23. Wickman, "Homes," p. 203.

24. See Gerd Örtegren, *Ellen Key och Tolfterna* (Väderstad: Ellen Key-sällskapet, 1982); and Svante Hedin, "Bildning och solidaritet: Ellen Key och Tolfterna," in *Ny syn på Ellen Key*, ed. Siv Hackzell (Stockholm: Bembo Bok, 2000), pp. 52–79.

25. Hedin, "Bildning," pp. 64–67. Idun was the Norse goddess of eternal youth; the name was adopted by the women's magazine for which Key often wrote, and by the Idun society for men; Nya Idun was founded as a rival to the latter.

26. Another friend was Anton Nyström (1842–1931), founder of the Workers' Institute and early social democratic leader. Nyström was married to Key's friend and disciple Louise Nyström-Hamilton, her earliest biographer. For her defense of Palm, Branting, and others, see *Några tankar om huru reaktioner uppstå jämte samt om yttrande–och tryckfrihet* (Stockholm: Bonnier, 1889); and De Angelis, p. 152. On Gustaf Steffen, see Benny Carlson, "Wagner's Swedish Students: Precursors of the Middle Way?" *Journal of the History of Economic Thought*, vol. 25, no. 4, pp. 437–59. See also *acceptera*, in this volume, p. 337 and n. 65. Key was also close to Georg von Vollmar (1850–1922), Bavarian aristocrat, chairman of the Socialist Party in Bavaria, journalist, member of the German parliament (1881–87, 1890–1918), and to his wife, the former Julia Kjellberg. Through the Vollmars, whom she often visited in Bavaria, she became acquainted with the ideas and politics of "revisionist" (non-revolutionary) socialism in Germany.

27. "When she enters a lecture room there is something of the priestess about her, and by the time she has reached her place on the platform, such absolute silence reigns that one would think oneself alone. . . . Her first words are uttered so low that one hears them with a slight effort, but the silence in the room sharpens the hearing, and without raising her voice, her words reach the farthest corners." Nyström-Hamilton, *Ellen Key*, p. 83.

28. This was the Juntan group, which included the painters Georg and Hanna Pauli, Eva Bonnier, and Richard and Gerda Bergh. Also often present were publisher Karl Otto Bonnier and his wife (Eva Bonnier's parents). Bonnier was the publisher of the Verdandi booklets and of Carl Larsson's books; he came to be Key's principal publisher.

29. Michelle Facos, *Nationalism and the Nordic Imagination* (Berkeley: University of California Press, 1998), pp. 110–11; and Lengborn, *Ellen Key och skönheten*, pp. 35–38.

30. "Skönhet," pp. 133–35, 140–41. Key argues that "the northern countries" (Norrland) will be the purveyor of English and Belgian arts and crafts ideas to Germany and elsewhere. But she also says that many people in these northern countries have had the same ideas "without reading Ruskin." In these northern countries, she believes, people have a special awareness of nature–of light, stillness, and solitude–and a special aptitude for bringing the experience of nature to everyone.

31. Föreningen Handarbetets Vänner, founded in 1874 by Sophie Adlersparre; Svenska Slöjdföreningen, founded in 1845. Key also knew, and mentioned in the 1899 text of "Skönhet i hemmen," the influential Austrian art historian Jacob von Falke, director of the Austrian Museum of Art and Industry, whose Swedish lectures and publications promoted a notion of "the home as a work of art." See especially Elisabet Stavenow-Hidemark, "Hemmet som konstverk. Heminredning i teori och praktik på 1870- och 80-talen," *Fataburen* 1 (1984): pp. 129–48; and Ingeborg Glambek, "Jacob Falke og Justus Brinkmann: rerpresentanter for to stadier av den kunstindustrielle bevegelse," *Om kunst-industry, Årbok for kunstindustrimuseene i Norge* (Trondheim, 1991), pp. 31–45. Erik Folcker was an officer in the Svenska Slöjdföreningen and proprietor of the shop Sub Rosa, which sold products of the English Arts and Crafts movement.

32. According to Lengborn, Key's first acquaintance with Ruskin's work dates to 1894 and with Morris's, probably to 1895; *Ellen Key och skönheten*, pp. 39–40. Key mentions both in *Individualism och socialism* (1895), and Ruskin makes frequent appearances in "Skönhet," 1897–98. A reference to Morris appears in the 1899 edition of "Beauty in the Home," but not in the 1897 version. She returns to Morris in "Folket och konsten," *Varia. Illustrerad månadstidskrift* vol. 1, no. 1 (January 1900): pp. 34–44. (My thanks to Eva Eriksson for obtaining this rare article for me.) As so often in her publications, Key reissued this text at a later date, after changing it substantially; see *Folkbildningsarbetet*, pp. 77–90, 139–45.

33. See Key, in the present volume, pp. 41–42 Key and Larsson had been friends since the mid-1880s. Larsson, *Ett hem: 24 målningar* (Stockholm: Bonnier, 1899); revised with the addition of one further image in 1904; further editions in 1910, 1912, 1913, and 1920. On Key and Larsson, see Wickman, "Homes"; Michael Snodin and Elisabet Stavenow-Hidemark, eds., *Carl and Karin Larsson: Creators of the Swedish Style* (Boston: Little, Brown, 1997); and Lane, *National Romanticism*.

34. Lengborn, *Ellen Key och skönheten*, pp. 69–75; Lengborn, *Ellen Key–Richard Bergh* (Linköping: Ellen Key-Sällskapets årsskrift, 1997); Wickman, "Homes"; and Key, "Folket och konsten," *Varia*. Carl G. Laurin was one of the founders of Föreningen för skolors prydande med konstverk (The association for the decoration of schools with works of art), which Key mentions in her essay in the present volume, n. 29. He was also the brother of prominent art collector Thorsten Laurin and a partner in the publishing firm P. A. Norstedt & Sons.

35. Key, "Folket och konsten," *Varia*, pp. 40–41.

36. Ibid., p. 42.

37. Ibid.

38. Verdandi was a Norse goddess. The Verdandi student organization was founded at Uppsala in 1882 as a political opposition group, liberal and increasingly tending toward socialism. It also favored temperance, pacifism, and efforts to retain closeness to nature. It sponsored lectures and arranged debates. See Facos, *Nationalism*, p. 13. The "Verdandi booklets" series, begun in 1888 and published by Bonnier, came to offer progressive intellectuals an important forum. In the early twentieth century, the series included, in addition to studies of the working classes and of a multitude of philosophical issues, important books on the artists Carl Larsson, Anders Zorn, and Bruno Liljefors, together with Ragnar Östberg's *Ett hem* (see n. 51 below).

39. Windows must admit light, especially in the northern countries, and, she says, only those countries that have a tradition of the hearth really have a tie to a notion of home or homeland. It was this conception of "home," reaching beyond the dwelling to include local traditions and homeland, that so appealed to Rilke, who corresponded with Key about "homelessness." See Lane, *National Romanticism*, pp. 132, 352, n. 169; and Facos, *Nationalism*, pp. 62–63. Key

does not differentiate here among the "northern" countries.

40. Key, in the present volume, p. 34.

41. Ibid.

42. Ibid., p. 43. The same phrase occurs in all editions. Key's preoccupation with light was shared by Swedish artists of the 1890s. Since the publication of Kirk Varnedoe's *Northern Light: Nordic Art at the Turn of the Century* (New Haven, CT: Yale University Press, 1988) art historians have paid increasing attention to the treatment of light in Scandinavian painting and to its influence on the development of modern painting elsewhere. As yet, there has been no comparable study of the role of light and sunshine in the development of modern architecture and interior design.

43. Key, in the present volume, p. 42. A short passage on the Larsson home appears in the 1899 edition.

44. The 1904 edition includes a new mention of Axel Lindegren. Minor variations over time included changing references to authorities she approved of and changing bits of advice about decoration. The list of buildings and works of art she liked includes Boberg, Östberg, and Wahlman by name in 1908, but omits the names in 1913. A line-by-line comparison of the five editions and the first publication of 1897 would show a good deal about Key's intellectual development, but is beyond the scope of our publication.

45. Rasmussen's work was not very well known in Sweden; perhaps she chose him because of the family connection and for financial reasons. He designed a number of railroad stations, in which Key was interested. See her essay, in the present volume, p. 34.

46. There were many other paintings, drawings, and reproductions at Strand. Reproductions of Renaissance masters vied for space with Larsson prints and original oils by Prince Eugen, Hanna Pauli, and Richard Bergh. Another of Key's favorite images was "Prayer to Light" (*Lichtgebet*, 1905) by the contemporary German artist Fidus, who was prominent in the German "Life Reform" movement; see Lane, *National Romanticism*, pp. 140–42.

47. It also resembled Heinrich Vogeler's Barkenhoff house at the Worpswede art colony in Germany; Key knew of this house through Rilke, who sent her his book on

Worpswede in 1903. She also kept in her workroom at Strand a picture of the Barkenhoff, with a note describing it as Rilke's house.

48. Strand was made a national monument in 1992; today it offers short-term accommodations to female scholars. Nearby is the Ellen Key institutet (www.eki.nu), which organizes exhibitions, publishes works on Key, and in 2006 issued a modernized and popularized Swedish version of *Skönhet för alla*. I am grateful to Helena Kåberg and Hedda Jansson, curator at Ellen Key's Strand, for much of my information on the contents and history of Key's home.

49. A few examples from the vast collection of letters to Key preserved in the Ellen Key Archive, Manuscripts Division, Royal Library, National Library of Sweden, Stockholm: Rainer Maria Rilke, Prince Peter Kropotkin, Lou Andreas-Salomé, Emile Jaques-Dalcroze, Mamah Bouton Borthwick, Stefan Zweig, Georg Brandes, Bjørnstjerne Bjørnson, Edmund William Gosse, Romain Rolland, Frank Lloyd Wright, Knut Hamsun, Juhani Aho, Isadora Duncan, Maurice Maeterlinck, Yrjö Hirn, Franziska Mann, Upton Sinclair, Bertha von Suttner, and Emile Verhaeren.

50. Borthwick signed the guestbook at Strand (which had opened for visitors at the end of December 1910) on June 9, 1911. (Our thanks to Hedda Jansson, curator at Ellen Key's Strand, for providing us with photocopies of the first pages of the guestbook.) Borthwick's translations of Key's works (from the German) included *The Morality of Woman and Other Essays* (Chicago: Seymour, 1911); *The Torpedo under the Ark: "Ibsen and Women"* (Chicago: Seymour, 1912); *Love and Ethics* (Chicago: Seymour, 1912); and *The Woman Movement* (New York: Putnam, 1912). *Love and Ethics* bore Frank Lloyd Wright's name as co-translator. The details of Borthwick's and Wright's contacts with Key remain unclear. They are explored in two excellent articles: Lena Johannesson, "Ellen Key, Mamah Bouton Borthwick and Frank Lloyd Wright: Notes on the Historiography of Non-existing History," *Nova: Nordic Journal of Women's Studies*, vol. 3, no. 2 (1995): pp. 126–36; and Alice T. Friedman, "Frank Lloyd Wright and Feminism: Mamah Borthwick Cheney's letters to Ellen Key," *JSAH*, vol. 61:2 (June 2002): pp. 140–51. Unfortunately the documentation accessible at the time of their research led both Johannesson and Friedman to date Borthwick's visit to Strand as June 9, 1910, and their

further deductions about dates of contact, based on the series of undated letters from Borthwick to Key in the Ellen Key Archive, Swedish Royal Library Manuscript Division, are colored to a certain extent by this misunderstanding. Friedman still believes, however, that internal evidence in these letters suggests a first personal contact between Borthwick and Key in the spring of 1910 (letter to the author, August 19, 2007). In any case, Borthwick's and Wright's later letters to Key from the United States display deep admiration and attachment. As a token of gratitude, at some point between 1912 and 1914 Wright sent Key a Hiroshige print, which now hangs in the upper hall at Strand (Johannesson).

51. Westman's work on the "Green Room" was significant for his future interior design. Westman and Östberg were active in the movement to help workers build their own small homes in new suburban settlements outside Stockholm; Key praised their work in the essays collected in *Folkbildnings-arbetet*, pp. 188–89; Östberg acknowledged her influence in his *Ett hem, dess byggnad och inredning*, Studentföreningen Verdandis småskrifter no. 131 (Stockholm: Bonnier, 1905). On Key's influence on Paulsson, see Kåberg, Introduction, p. 61. On the movement for "owner-occupied

homes" see especially Elisabet Stavenow-Hidemark, *Villabebyggelse i Sverige 1900–1925: Inflytande från utlandet, idéer, föverkligande* (Lund: Nordiska museets handlingar, 1971); Lane, *National Romanticism,* pp. 120–22; and *acceptera,* in the pressent volume, n. 51.

52. On the role of individualism in Swedish Social Democracy, see Henrik Berggren and Lars Trägårdh, *Är svensken människa? Gemenskap och oberoende i det moderna Sverige* (Stockholm: Norstedt, 2006).

STUDENTFÖRENINGEN

VERDANDIS
SMÅSKRIFTER·
77.

SKÖNHET FÖR ALLA

AV

ELLEN KEY

FEMTE UPPLAGAN

STOCKHOLM   25 ÖRE   ALBERT BONNIER

e·L

Beauty in the Home

Ellen Key

Some comments on Ehrensvärd's text [1]

I.

According to Ehrensvärd, *it is man's needs that set him in motion.*[2] After he has satisfied his needs for food and for protection against the elements—the latter through clothing and shelter—his thoughts soon turn to satisfying his *needs for joy*, those which in one way or another are awakened through his sense of beauty. Even primitive man seeks to express his sense of beauty. Every human being possesses some form of longing for beauty, although so far in most people it manifests itself only in a taste for finery with which to surround themselves or wear. But finery—especially the finery of today—is often the exact opposite of beauty. These days finery is factory made, usually of some imitation material seeking to mimic something precious. This circumstance goes against the first prerequisite of beauty, namely that it contain no ostentation or empty show. *Ostentation may come close to the thing itself, may give a dazzling illusion of it, but it is not the thing—Beauty—itself. It settles for dishonest expression, which substitutes for its own emptiness either ingratiating redundancy or a certain exaggeration.*

But, you may wonder, how can one tell whether something is empty show or genuine, ugly or beautiful? Ehrensvärd replies: *You discern the beautiful to the same degree that you yourself are well formed and well brought up.* And the very point of your upbringing should be *to find the fundamental law* for the thing in question. For once you have found this law, you easily develop your *faculty for choosing what is beautiful*, in other words, your taste.

Taste is the keen sense of nature's finest, most secret truths. And if we observe nature, we find one of its finest truths to be this: pure nature works in simple ways. Superior taste is therefore *the one that chooses what is perfect, namely fresh, unspoilt nature*. Thus one finds *Beauty, which is Perfection*.

When we apply these tenets to our homes, the first rule will be that for each thing we acquire we should always ask ourselves: Does it obey the *fundamental law*? And this law is that each thing must serve the purpose for which it was made! On a chair one ought to be able to sit comfortably, at a table one ought to be able to work or eat easily, in a bed one ought to be able to rest well. The uncomfortable chair, the rickety table, and the narrow bed are thus intrinsically ugly. On the other hand, it does not necessarily follow that the comfortable chair, the sturdy table, and the wide bed are beautiful. Be it ever so useful, each man-made thing must, like each beautiful thing in nature, serve its purpose with simplicity and ease, with delicacy and expressivity, or it will not have achieved beauty. Thus though utility is a prerequisite for beauty, beauty does not guarantee utility. A home must of course be arranged very differently depending on whether it is located in the north or the south, in town or in the country, and whether it is a winter residence or just a summer house. It must above all be different to the extent that it reflects the needs of the people who will live in that home. The greatest mistake with most buildings is that they do not express real needs or real purpose. This is the primary reason for their ugliness and lack of style, but also the reason why some useful new materials or techniques—for example, sheet metal roofing—have not yet been refined in either color or form by a sense of beauty. The old, plain, red-painted farmhouses have a certain style. But the new communities cropping up around railroad stations, in which a quantity of badly built, light-colored wooden houses are clustered around the station itself, are abhorrently ugly.[3] All it would take is beautiful station buildings along a railroad line for their beauty to gradually influence the other buildings springing up around them.

In the countryside one often builds and furnishes one's own home; in the city, on the other hand, one is dependent on building contractors. And among them the dominant taste in the years from 1870 to 1900 has been the most garishly cheap German taste, dictating not only exteriors but also interiors. Dark wallpapers with pointless ornamentation, ceilings painted in loud colors and decorated with plaster moldings, and gaudy, multicolored tiled stoves with mirrors and knickknacks have become the rule. The only way to introduce more taste into city apartments would be for everyone to begin demanding that the rooms be decked out not with this ugly and pointless finery but instead simplified in line with a wholesome and refined taste. And the only way for everyone to really be able to acquire beautiful things inexpensively would be for manufacturers—particularly makers of furniture, wallpaper, textiles, glassware, china, and hardware—to connect with the practitioners of the applied arts so that the latter could impart beautiful form and appropriate decor to all things, from the simplest and smallest object, for example a matchbox, to the largest. Only when there is nothing ugly available for sale, when beautiful things are as inexpensive as ugly ones are now, can beauty for everyone be fully realized. Until recently, swarthy upholstery and curtain materials, dark wallpapers with pointless patterns, furniture with glued-on excrescences, and unwieldy household utensils were often less expensive than objects of beauty and style, and articles created for the home by artists benefited only the rich.

The following discussion will concern only what can be done already now, under present conditions, in ordinary Swedish homes—homes with, say, one single room or at the most three or four—to avoid what is ugly and with easy, inexpensive means create a beautiful environment.

In all instances, personal taste must of course be the primary deciding factor. Nothing could be more unwise than to remodel my home according to any presumed "rules for beauty," if by so doing I had to sacrifice those things already part of my surroundings that I have found comfortable and serviceable, or things that are precious to me as mementos from my childhood home or people dear to me. What will be proposed here is not meant to condemn furniture or decorative items that custom or affection have endowed with special value. It merely offers advice for furnishing the *new* home, the new things purchased, and the new decorative items selected. As emphasized above, in the country you often have the opportunity to build and outfit your own home. In the city, on the other hand, you usually have to accept an apartment as laid out and equipped by the landlord, though sometimes you may be consulted in matters of ceilings, wallpapers, and paint. When it comes to furniture and decorative items you can of course always to some extent make your home express your personal taste. But unfortunately most people's taste is undeveloped. And that is why they satisfy their thirst for beauty—paradoxical though this may sound—in an ugly way.

Still others do it in a dreary way, for example, when they simply imitate what is beautiful in other people's homes. A room does not have a soul until someone's soul is revealed in it, until it shows us what that someone remembers and loves, and how this person lives and works every day. If a grandmother's room resembled that of her granddaughter, the painter; if the latter's room in turn resembled that of her father, the engineer; then these would lack style. For they would lack truth; they would give a false picture of the spirit of the personality, which ought to be expressed in the respective rooms. In each case there would be no *truthful raison d'être for it all*, and it is only in this way that a room acquires style, personality, and—in the presence of good taste—even beauty. One must, however, take care not to judge people too quickly on the basis of their home, for they are not always free to shape it according to their own wishes. A good example in this context is the Queen of Romania, the author Carmen Sylva.[4] She describes her "ideal home" thus:

"There would be no salon but rather a music room and a very big library. What would be the point of a salon without music or books? It would simply be the most boring place in the house, the 'best room,' from which all sense of true home would be banished.[5]

The rooms must not have too many pieces of furniture; the walls should be painted with oil-based paints; and the furniture should have the same colors as the walls. I would welcome a quantity of loose covers, which can be washed. I do not want any beds in the house. In their place I want divans. My bedroom would be green so that one had the impression of resting in a green arbor. My cabinet would be blue, and both floor and curtains would have the same fresh blue color as the furniture. In my boudoir all should be snow-white in color, with furniture in a clean, simple style.

In every room of the house there should be a desk and books. Books are the foremost ornament of a house. All the members of the family must feel that their home is always able to keep them entertained, and to this feeling books contribute most of all. People do not realize how much true education is imparted nearly without conscious effort in a home with good books!"[6]

We do know, though, that however much she may be Queen, Carmen Sylva has not been able to fully realize her ideal! And many are, like her, bound by circumstance. But the ideal, toward which all people under all circumstances ought to strive, is to have their personality reflected in their own home.

II.

That whatever is useful is worthy of respect, all women realize; that whatever is beautiful is worthy of being loved, many realize; but that the only thing worth striving for is harmony between the useful and the beautiful—how many realize that? And even the few who really do understand this rarely have a clear idea of how such harmony may be achieved. Even more rare is a firm commitment to the creation of beauty in their own surroundings, a commitment undeniably still very much needed in order to overcome existing practical obstacles.

Unfortunately even the aesthetically aware woman very often sees striving for beauty merely as a pleasurable pursuit and not as a duty. Beauty is considered a superfluity which some can afford, others not. But it is undeniable that every person who has a sense of beauty can achieve a certain harmony between the useful and the beautiful, as long as the beautiful is not confused with luxury—the latter often an obstacle to true beauty. Beauty can be achieved by simple means and without great expense. By striving for beauty at the same time as observing the need for utility, the woman not only satisfies a legitimate desire in her own nature but also exerts a profound influence on the other members in the home of which she is the soul. The children's senses are educated and refined through the beautiful impressions they receive; the adults experience a peace and a joy that cannot fail to make them more agreeable and often nobler; and the woman herself is made happier through that joy of creativity always accompanying the practice of an art.

A great step forward in taste has been taken in Sweden in the last thirty years. The movement begun by Mrs. Sofi [sic] Adlersparre has broadened and taken hold.[7] Even the countryside has been strongly influenced by the new direction in taste. Nowadays few people commit the major lapses of taste of times past, like inviting us to recline against or tread on horses, lions, and birds embroidered on cushions and stools; to wander around with Turk's heads on our slippers or step into pastoral scenes on our carpets. We no longer have to see floral still lifes on our carpetbags, landscapes on our fire screens, ruins on our desk pads, or any of Thorvaldsen's bas reliefs stitched in pearls on the decorative edging of a corner shelf![8] People no longer make clock stands out of slippers, or pen-wipers out of flowers! In other words, people have learned not to use as decorations items whose appearance has nothing whatsoever to do with the purpose in question, indeed, in which the particular decorative elaboration often even makes the object awkward to use. People have also begun to realize that knitted and crocheted objects are rarely beautiful, and above all that it is abhorrent to give our rooms the appearance of drying attics by filling them with dead white blotches in the form of dust covers, tablecloths, and antimacassars, the latter—since they are crocheted—also catching on everything, thereby doubly abhorrent. Less and less do you see those treasures made of hair, cork, wax, pearls, feathers, seashells, pine cones, and the like, materials whose nature and fragility made them into dust traps as useless as they were ugly! Unfortunately there is now another aberration, namely the desire to make "use" of anything and everything—from cake boxes to matchboxes, from old hats to bottles—to fashion "decorative" items from trash, while believing you are beautifying your home! A woman would benefit and gladden the world more if she slept away the hours she spends on this dreadful foolishness—not to mention how much better she would use them by taking a walk or reading a book! And the same is true for nine-tenths of all the little items of plush, wool, and cross-stitch worked in silk or gold thread, as well as most of the little wooden and leather objects that people now paint, cut out, press, or decorate with pokerwork. These objects may, it is true, turn out to be more beautiful than the old knickknacks, but they are not one iota more useful. Thus even these objects can only complicate our homes and fill them to overflowing but not beautify them, since they lack the *raison d'être* of both the true work of art and the true utilitarian tool.

But, as mentioned above, on the whole there has been an improvement. First came the discovery of vast treasures of beautiful decorative motifs and techniques in old peasant weavings, carvings, and fine needlework. With time the impressions these treasures made resulted in the present, advanced Swedish textile crafts.

Even in the countryside one can now see truly artistic examples of these crafts. Unfortunately, in many craft schools—as well as in schools and workshops offering needlecraft and woodworking lessons—a quantity of objects are produced that are as ugly as they are useless.[9] And even when this is not the case, the products of artistic textile crafts still rarely blend with the rest of a home's furnishings but instead often stick out against their generally tasteless surroundings. Most women do not yet understand how to treat a room—or an outfit—as a whole, where nothing should exist that is beautiful only by itself, but where colors and shapes should work well together; where the main thing should be emphasized and all secondary things, however beautiful, be subordinate; where all separate entities ought to work together harmoniously; where one should understand how to achieve an effect, one time by filling a void, another time by not filling it.

Among Ehrensvärd's words of wisdom: *In the North, pomp is used in situations where needs could be satisfied just as well without it.* The truth of this is borne out in public as well as private life. In the North, one seldom understands that true beauty exists only in that which is without ostentation, that which *is fashioned in accord with its purpose, thus satisfactorily lending itself to fill the true needs of man's unspoilt nature.* This is one of the reasons why—as discussed above—useless luxury gives an unpleasant feeling of vague unease: the aesthetic faculty takes *true pleasure only in moderation and restraint.* The works of art amassed in rooms filled from a love of ostentation have no way of being appreciated since they lack a dignified setting. And the objects intended to be useful are so needlessly complicated that they do not reveal the reason for their existence, thus becoming ugly while the simplest things are able to bear out the truth of Ehrensvärd's words:

It is unbelievable how beautiful a thing becomes when you discern its true purpose.[10]

It is bad taste to imagine that the useful becomes beautiful by concealing its purpose behind decoration. But no household implement can be beautiful which does not convince you, first, of its usefulness, and second, of a neatness that is in full agreement with its intended use. Thus the cottages at Skansen give impressions of beauty and style, since every implement there has received a fitting and restrained decorative treatment.[11] These everyday objects satisfy both the demand for utility and the *need for joy*, for they are connected to one another and to their common folk origin—in other words, they possess style and are thus, in their own category, beautiful. One can, for example, hardly find a simpler interior than that of Morastugan [Mora cottage], with its built-in bed, bench, table and shelf, its hanging bar on the ceiling, its simply ornamented wooden and pottery vessels, its show towels and wrought-iron candlesticks.[12] All fitting for their purpose, durable, and tasteful; nothing unnecessary and nothing wasted. The cottage gives a unified impression, since people here have satisfied their real needs in accordance with their own preferences, and these preferences have always been honest and beautiful.

Our times have of course brought many new needs and many new means to satisfy them. It would therefore be as tasteless as it would be foolish to imitate the old cottages at Skansen. But from them one can learn with what simple means beauty can be achieved. One can, by the way, learn this anywhere in the countryside, where the ugly city goods of our times have not yet been introduced. Every sensitive soul appreciates the mood of a room and is captivated by its charm when it is a faithful expression of a certain human being or a certain era or a certain class of society, of real needs and true spirit. How at ease one feels in a room where simple, light-polished furniture of elm or birch shows the beautiful wood grain itself, and where upholstery and curtain material signals joy with its red and white checks, as does the cow-hair rug in a couple of clear colors! All of them seem to say: "No empty show or falsehood tolerated here!" And how cozy and beautiful is an old parlor in a country parsonage, where the furnishings are pearl gray, the floor shines blinding white, and beautiful rag rugs create pathways on the floor; where white homemade curtains let in the sun on well-tended flowerpots, where there is a simple, handwoven tablecloth on the table and an old blue-and-white tiled stove in the corner—a parlor where no one cares to use the dreary white dust covers on chairs and sofas, allowing them to appear in all their handwoven glory! Likewise the simple peasant cottage with its homemade, red-painted furniture—bed sofa, drop-leaf table, chest, and chairs—and big grandfather clock ticking in the corner; the floor strewn with chopped juniper, and the whitewashed hearth with its big fire in winter and oak leaves in summer!

It is the whole, the agreement between the parts, which above all makes these rooms beautiful. Moreover, they seem so honest, clean, and sound. There are no dust traps, no cheap ornaments, no imitations, nothing false or dishonest. They are the complete opposite of the ugly rooms one now finds in hundreds of thousands of homes in our country, rooms in which you see a dusty Turkish divan covered in a motley upholstery fabric; a thin, flimsy, big-flowered, store-bought cloth on the table; curtains of ugly yellow-gray burlap printed in blue, red, and brown, with stiff, sharp pleats and rough fringe; where the chairs—with uncomfortable, curved, loop-shaped backrests and padded, lumpy seats—are made of imitation mahogany; the table of imitation walnut with silly curved feet, and the chest of drawers of imitation oak; where a gaudy lamp of bright-yellow bronze hangs from the ceiling; where chromolithographs of oil paintings in gilded frames and round, painted terracotta medallions with figures adorn the walls; where a red, plush photograph album and a sky-blue glass platter for visiting cards share the tabletop, and a couple of painted china vases with artificial flowers "decorate" the chest of drawers!

It is all these things, factory-cheap, dishonest, garish, disparate, that make most homes of our times so lacking in style.

The falsehood of the notion that beauty in the home is only gained through wealth can be seen in, among other things, the many homes crammed with meaningless luxury items and art objects, where no deep-seated thirst for beauty or personal taste has selected the objects or given them the space they require to have an impact; where the most unrelated things are brought together and arranged— by the upholsterer! In such rooms—full of drapes, fireplace cushions, screens and mats, painted china and pokerwork, statuettes and paintings—the lover of beauty is seized by a passionate longing for the direct opposite, the unity and simplicity of an old-fashioned country room with straight-backed furniture lining the walls, white, sheer nettle-cloth curtains, and empty walls! But he knows that such rooms are seldom found these days, that even in the most remote provinces he is destined to encounter the pointless in the form of Makart bouquets, Japanese fans, painted plates, pressed bronze or brass ornaments, pink or blue vases, and the like.[13] Add to this that the worktable is often too small or so situated that the light falls from the right instead of from the left; that the lamp is too high or too low; that the beds are too narrow; that the curtains shut out the daylight—in other words, that all this ugliness prevents both easy work and rejuvenating rest. Work is thus in the long run hampered through indifference to what is essential and in the short run increased through the amassing of things that must be kept clean and keep getting in the way! Someone has said—speaking of another country—that "those who have money have no taste and those who have taste have no money."[14]

[   ]But of Sweden at the end of the nineteenth century, it can be said that good taste shunned wealth and poverty in equal measure and thus was made utterly homeless. Most women who inherited an old-fashioned home did not even have enough good taste either to leave it intact or to rearrange it to meet modern demands without completely destroying its uniqueness. All of these now disfigured rooms could still have looked pleasing if these women had kept only the furniture that was really needed; if they had hung a few woodcuts or fine photographs on the walls and arranged a few branches in a simple yellow-brown or green-brown pottery bowl—the kind you can get for a pittance at the market; if all bric-a-brac had been thrown out and replaced with nothing but flowers in plain glass vases on the chest of drawers; if a few books had been placed on the table; if the colors of the room had been harmonized instead of screaming at each other; and if all the ugly hand-stitched needlework items had been exchanged for simple, homemade tablecloths, rugs, and curtains.

An American authoress relates how she once came to a log cabin out West and, upon entering the room, was immediately seized by the feeling, as unexpected as it was pleasant, that she was in a home arranged by a woman of taste.[15] The walls were plain logs, the tables were made of unpainted wood, the seats of packing crates. But these were covered with nankeen of a warm yellow-brown color, with a straight trim of blue ribbon, as were the curtains and tablecloth. A light straw mat lay on the floor; a vase of wildflowers and a few books were the only decorative items. But with these simple means, the room—far from the richer opportunities of civilization—nevertheless gave an impression of culture and harmony.

A young artist couple, who could not afford to order even the simplest furniture, made all the furniture for their drawing room and dining room themselves from packing crates—a solution that is of course not recommended as particularly practical, merely mentioned as an example of how one can manage when necessary. The dining table and the wife's sewing table were made of a larger and a smaller overturned packing crate with their bottoms intact but the sides sawed so that only four legs remained. Another crate became a serving table or "buffet," simply by being turned upside down. Wall shelves were obtained by keeping the bottom and one short side or long side of a couple of smaller boxes and cutting out the sides, leaving only a distinctive edge. Low stools were created out of square packing boxes, on which the lower parts of the sides touching the floor were cut out in the shape of semi-circles. All of this was then painted red or white, with decorative flowers here and there; table and "buffet" were covered with handwoven, white, fringed cloths, and old pottery and wooden bowls were put on the wall shelves. Two other packing crates were placed at right angles to each other in a corner, and peasant weavings and bench pads were spread on them, so that the most inviting little corner sofa was created. Through a few weeks' labor of their own this young couple thus created a homey, comfortable room with style, which cost them in öre what others pay in kronor, often without achieving the same pleasing effect.[16]

[   ]These days we have seen a revival of appliqué, with which a beautiful effect can be achieved with relatively little effort—if combined with tastefully chosen colors and patterns—in borders on tablecloths and draperies, on cushions and such. There are even simpler techniques for similar purposes. But as quality materials are costly, and time should not be wasted on inferior ones, such needlework items are never inexpensive. Handwoven curtains and tablecloths in simple patterns and beautiful color combinations will, in most cases, prove the most durable as well as the least expensive.

If one wants to see a home that makes the coziest and most personal impression, one should preferably visit Carl Larsson's home up at Sundborn in Dalarna—that is, study it in the four sets of color plates he has published about his home.[17] In the introduction to the first set, *Ett hem* [A home], he himself writes:

"Ours are difficult times for an artistically inclined person to live in. Either you find the application of the practical mind's lackluster motto 'no nonsense' or the luxury-lover's tasteless, machine-made glittering trash.

The factory, the army barracks, the hospital, the school, and the country estate—all are equally insufferably regimented and straight-lined, inside and out.

The farmer, too, does his best to achieve the same tedium, although, thanks to its red paint, his farmhouse nevertheless possesses what city folk with a nostalgic sigh call 'country charm.' And then we have the opposite of regimented, straight institutional lines: the ridiculously draped curtains above doors, in corners, and behind pictures in the home of the man of some social standing, his étagères and easels and stands for displaying cheap bazaar trinkets, as well as artificial flowers with ribbons, dust, and germs. Goodness, what lamps! And, dear me, what shades! And plush and cretonne! In the midst of this garish trash and brilliant misery sit 'lord' and 'lady' with a self-satisfied smirk, because they have to the utmost degree fulfilled the demands made by modernity upon the leaders of society.

'I'm just as good as they are,' figures the Swedish farmer.

From the furniture factory there's an 'invention sofa' of pine, stained to look like mahogany;[18] a chest of drawers with dreadful nickel hardware; a walnut commode; a rocking chair (in black and gold); and, in the middle of the floor, a round and rickety parody of an extension table, spread with a mud-colored floral tablecloth ('printed patterns'); and on top of this a kerosene lamp, much cheaper but just as hideous as the one found in the home of the just-mentioned gentry."[19]

Then Carl Larsson proceeds to tell how his own home was created: by inspired whim, in festive moments, through joyful efforts. And so it became a home, such as is created only by happy human beings and, in turn, is destined to create happy human beings! It is clear, for example, that the furniture in his home is only of the simplest kind: wooden beds, wooden chairs, and wooden tables. In one room they are painted green; then the ceiling in that room is also painted green; the walls are whitewashed with simple ornamentation of yellow, red, and green. In another room the walls are completely white and all of the furniture white. Only a touch of red here and there enlivens the whiteness: around the room runs a narrow, red-painted bookshelf supported by pillarlike, closely spaced brackets, and in each space between these red brackets there is a piece of paper of deep-blue color. By these means the most pleasing decorative effect is achieved and everyone who wakes in this room must be filled with joy! Even the very simplest of rooms, with nothing more than natural wooden walls, with green- or red-painted furniture or a little green or red stripe here and there, exudes sheer hominess, airy freshness, and joy of color. The arrangements mentioned here are so simple that anyone can create a similar impression with similar means, that is, anyone with an aesthetically keen eye and a practiced hand, for without these the result will of course not be beautiful.

An example of simple, tasteful interior decoration can be found in some new villas on the outskirts of Stockholm as well as in some of Stockholm's reading rooms. At the reading room in Kungsholmen, the inner room has walls of intense yellow, the outer one has walls painted with blue-green oil-based paint, and both rooms are furnished with simple, brown-stained pieces and yellow and white curtains. In

Katarina, the walls are gray-green and the furniture is varnished yellow; in Maria, on the other hand, the walls are yellow-white, the wainscoting and shelves blue-green, and the chairs red. In each place there are some works of art, whether originals, photogravures, or colored prints.

For the person whose taste is unsure and still developing, it is advisable to retain the natural form and color of the material itself as much as possible. The requirements for beautiful furniture are: utilitarian form, which firmly stresses the piece's purpose and is free from all ludicrous embellishments; and sound raw material, which in the case of precious woods ought to be kept in its natural distinctive state, but which in the case of ordinary wood ought to be heightened by color. Even an unpainted or stained chair is more beautiful than a curved and polished one of imitation material. But the chair glazed all red or all green or pearl white is more beautiful than the unpainted chair. On the other hand, the black-painted chair seat sometimes found in farmers' homes is not beautiful, for black seems cheerless, and moreover, a black seat gives the impression of a dark void instead of a safe place to sit.

Someone with good taste can achieve a very beautiful effect with straightforward, strong, clear, well-composed color combinations, for example, yellow and blue, green and red, red and deep blue. Also, certain—though far from all—nuances of yellow or green or red or blue together with white or in yet other combinations make a pleasing color scheme on walls as well as in upholstery materials and curtains. As is well known, when white sunlight passes through a prism you get a so-called spectrum of the colors red, orange, yellow, green, blue, indigo, and violet. White light is produced by combining red and blue-green, or orange and cyan blue, or yellow and indigo, or green-yellow and violet. Those colors which, when combined, produce white light, are called complementary colors, and by pairing such complementary colors a beautiful color effect is most easily achieved.

For those who do not themselves possess unerring taste the best advice is to avoid twisted and convoluted shapes or gaudy, boldly variegated, and loud colors and instead choose simple forms and single color schemes.

A certain way to make even the poorest attic room more beautiful is this: if those who live there are inclined toward books and flowers, a shelf with nicely cared-for books, a few well-tended plants, and a couple of good woodcuts and prints immediately gives an impression of comfort and refinement, be the furniture ever so plain and worn! If in addition they are fortunate enough to have a room facing the sun and let the sunshine come flooding in, then such a room can be more beautiful than many a rich person's magnificent chambers.

For those who themselves have the opportunity to decorate their own little apartment or room, in town or in the country, I would like to emphasize some helpful pointers.

There is hardly anything more tasteful than the Norwegian practice of making walls and ceilings of wood, which is either only lightly stained, allowing it to retain its natural color, or painted in some compatible tones. For example, in Norway you can see a pale-blue wall with red tulips as a running border at the top, a red wall with green and white lilies at the top, and so on. On the other hand, if you want wallpaper, you must—just as you guard against illness or debt—guard against the standard dark wallpapers with pointless ornamentation in the form of red-brown or black-green or brown-gray indistinct splotches, sometimes even "beautified" by embossing in gold. Such wallpaper alone—especially in a land like Sweden, with its long, dark winters—can make you almost sick with melancholy. Above all, truly important for your health is a light, calm wallpaper in some mild color in your bedroom. It is harmful to your nerves as well as your eyes to be repeatedly exposed to the ugly, the messy, and the pointless! It has been scientifically proven that calm, warm, cheerful colors not only increase the vital energy of healthy people, they also have a calming influence on nervous dispositions. Moreover, ugly wallpaper mercilessly kills all that is hung on it or placed against it!

Nowadays one can quite inexpensively obtain the beautiful, light-colored, cheerful English wallpapers with their stylized plant and animal motifs, but one ought to watch out for their big-flowered, tasteless imitations. The former are suitable in rooms where there are few things on the walls. For works of art, however, these wallpapers rarely provide a very good background. Such a background is best provided by a wallpaper whose pattern deviates only minutely from the ground, or, best of all, by a wall painted in one solid color. Monochrome wallpaper can now be found at little cost, namely so-called unprinted paper in golden brown, olive green, yellow, or other colors. In the past, people living in the countryside made their own plain-colored wallpapers by limewashing cardboard or heavy paper—pale red or pale blue or green. And painting on the wall itself, especially with oil-based paints, of course holds up best. For schools and other public spaces the colors gray-green or gray-blue, blue-green or yellow-green have the most calming effect in the long run and still give that delight in color that eye and mind crave in a winter land. In homes, on the other hand, the chalk-based limewash is preferable as it is less shiny and hard than oil-based paint. In Danish, German, French, and Italian country homes, as well as some English artists' homes, you find old-fashioned whitewashed walls or walls of some light color, and what is placed against these walls does, as a rule, show to advantage.

In monumental buildings—castles, museums, churches, assembly halls, and the like—wall and ceiling paintings are appropriate. But not in our homes, in rooms where people live. In our homes, all wallpapers and wall paintings that imitate buildings or landscapes are in poor taste. The purpose of the walls of our rooms is to enclose us, not to make us believe we are out in the open air. And it is just as tasteless to have the walls filled with figures. These become unceremoniously amputated by whatever is placed against them; they give a busy impression and provide a poor background for anything hung on them. Even if the wall paintings in and of themselves are excellent, a room thus decorated is therefore lacking in taste as a room to live in. For we do not wish to live *in* works of art, but in rooms we decorate with works of art! It is only on a gobelin tapestry with muted colors that human figures do not unduly clamor for attention.[20] And in a nursery—where figures entertain the children and where there are usually few pieces of furniture to compete with these figures—a figured wallpaper will do very well.

But the most beautiful wall in a room for living is always that wall which is no more than a simply decorated surface, which never seeks to hide its role of wall in a closed room, the wall which, according to Morris's rule, ought to "have color without colors" and which should get its division, its "rhythm," from the furniture placed against it.[21] This is the main requirement for the wall to be a good background for everything you wish to place against or hang on it.

The woodwork in the room—paneling, doors, and windows—is always tasteful if it is only lightly stained and allowed to keep its natural color. If you wish to paint it, you ought to choose the complementary color of the wall color or a darker or lighter nuance of the wall. Against blue, for example, yellow and yellow-brown tones are always beautiful; yellow-white and deep red go well together, as do white and green. Also beautiful is a green wall with red-painted woodwork, and the reverse, green-gray or green with red walls. The muddy yellow-gray or brown-gray, which is now so often used on woodwork, is in most cases objectionable. If the wallpaper is light and floral, the white-painted woodwork will as a rule look most beautiful if the sharp white is softened by a tone harmonizing with the wallpaper's dominant note. Simply matching this dominant note with the woodwork is probably the best assurance of success, unless you have a very sure color sense guiding your choice of complementary combinations.

Using progressively lighter colors as you move up the wall from floor to ceiling is more beautiful than the opposite, for the color scale lightening upward makes the room appear lighter and more cheerful. A beautiful border running along the top of the wall up against the ceiling—or at least a wide band marking the margin between wall and ceiling—gives the wall a finished look and conveys the transition to the ceiling well. If the rooms are not very high, the border should be narrow, or the rooms will appear lower. A border with stylized plant or animal motifs looks good at the top of a monochrome wall. The ceilings ought to be light-colored, light in feeling, and plain, or, if decorated, graced with only a few stylized, faintly discernible decorations. Although the greatest masters did ceiling paintings, such paintings are ultimately lacking in taste. If the paintings are masterpieces you are pained by not being able to see them fully and effortlessly. And to have animals and people above your head in the room where you live dispels all quiet ease and comfort! Ceiling moldings of plaster are often pointless. Most beautiful in a simple home is a moderately decorated or completely plain wooden ceiling and—barring that—an absolutely plain ceiling in a white tone slightly softened toward the color of the room.

Most newer city rooms are marred by garishly colored tiled stoves. Such stoves should preferably be light-colored in light rooms and dark in darker rooms. Now solid-colored, dark-green tiled stoves of an older model are again being made. And next to an open hearth a big tiled stove is the one item providing the most warmth and hominess. In a room with fine, subdued colors, however, a white tiled stove seems hard and cold. If a room has mostly subtle tones, the white tiles of the stove can be painted in some color blending with the tone of the entire room, but the paint must then be burned on at just the right temperature, or it will flake and give off fumes.

If the room is generally light-colored, the floor can also be white. In that case, you must as a rule use runners. For this purpose traditional "rag rugs" are the strongest and potentially also the most beautiful alternative, if the rags are dyed in two harmonizing colors and used to create a pattern. But in rooms with darker furniture and walls, white-colored floors seem hard and cold. It is true that the impact can be softened with small rugs. But a better solution is to varnish the floors. This is best done with new or relaid floors.[22] With old floors, cracks must be filled in order for the floors to be whole and neat. In such cases, solid-colored linoleum flooring—deep green, deep red, and so on—is therefore preferable. Linoleum floors, like varnished floors, can be washed each day. But linoleum flooring imitating stone mosaic looks cold and hard and is as dreary as stucco imitating marble, paper imitating gilt leather, and furniture with glued-on ornaments imitating solid carved wood! If one needs a simple word capturing the essence of good taste, one should use the word *honesty*. This word does not say it all, but it says at least half. Unfortunately a word of foreign origin, *rejäl*, is often used instead.[23] But the meaning is the same; whether used about a person or a thing, what is *real* is honestly what it appears to be; it does not deal in curlicues or roundabouts, evasions or contortions, either in action or behavior, people or things!

If you need woven rugs for the sake of warmth, these should never be nailed down—this is one of the most unhealthy practices of the past. They should be laid loose, or, if necessary, simply hooked by means of sewn-on rings onto big-headed tacks so that they can be easily slipped off to be beaten. Rugs should always be muted in color, preferably in the room's predominant hue or a complementary color. If plain, single-colored rugs seem to get soiled too easily or give a monotonous impression, one should in any event choose no bolder pattern than a small floral. The foremost examples of good taste in rugs are Oriental rugs, whose somewhat indistinct geometric patterns produce a meltingly rich color effect but include no human figures. Obviously it is just as unpleasant to be forced to tread on landscapes, people, and animals as it is to see them above your head. The floor, like the ceiling, must appear quite restful, and neither should in any respect draw attention to itself.

The same is true of upholstery fabrics. Plain fabrics, or striped or checked ones in two colors, or else very fine floral patterns, are the only upholstery fabrics one does not tire of, the only ones against which beautiful needlework and people appear to true advantage; just as the latter also "show" best—as artists put it—against a calm, monochrome wall.

The most difficult choice faces those who are inclined toward the beautiful but do not have the means to satisfy this inclination, that is, cannot afford to acquire reasonably tasteful furniture. Older tasteful and comfortable furniture is expensive. Older tasteless furniture, from the 1840s to the 1870s, with its silly curved shapes and its pointless, often added carvings, is sometimes comfortable but hideously ugly. Wholly modern, comparatively inexpensive furniture—the iron bed, the invention sofa, the washstand, the dining table—is comfortable, but often just as ugly. Especially loathsome is that invention sofa known as a Turkish divan, a dust trap in daytime, a mean bed at night; the ugliest lump imaginable—especially with the standard coverlet of poor, dark-patterned upholstery material—blighting a room!

But with a little thought, a little effort, you can nevertheless have quite beautiful furniture at a reasonable cost. Most homes have a couple of spare mattresses and pillows for guests. If you make a simple structure of wood as wide and high as you need, nail some jute webbing to the top and then place your surplus mattresses and pillows on it, spread it with a cover of baize, friezecloth, or handwoven cloth, and place it all with one side along a wall against which you pile some pillows—there you have a simple "divan," comfortable to sit on, delicious to rest on in the daytime, and at night instantly transformed into a bed for a family member or guest. Four legs supporting a bed frame or a mattress on a frame can replace the wooden structure. If the divan is intended as a permanent bed, a fixed support should be attached for the pillow. An open table—on which there are a *big* washbasin and matching jug—is the best and most hygienic washstand. If you have only one room, a curtain of washable fabric or a modesty screen, covered with the upholstery material of the room, combines neatness with utility.

If you buy simple, deep wicker armchairs in a soft gray-yellow tone, and sew a few cushions for them of a tasteful cretonne—or even better, a beautiful handwoven fabric—you have a couple of comfortable as well as fairly beautiful easy chairs.

If instead of the usual expensive dining tables with extension leaves—introduced to replace the round tables with their obstructive legs—you order a simple square table with sturdy legs, and do not weigh it down with a lot of things, then you have a table around which your family can comfortably gather and work, and which can easily be cleared for meals if you have a living and dining room in one.

But even with a separate dining room, you should never have a dining table seating more than twelve. For in order to promote really rich, valuable dinner conversation, the old rule of Lucullus holds true: at table one should not number fewer than the graces, that is, three, nor more than the muses, that is, nine. At the most, you may add the number of graces to the number of muses and thus seat twelve. But to exceed the number thirteen is unfortunate—not for the sake of superstition but for the sake of good company!

As far as the rest of the furniture is concerned, you can of course acquire truly beautiful furniture for a very low price when you furnish your first home if you are able to follow the example of a young female artist who—with a traditional spindle-back sofa and a spindle-back chair as points of departure—composed a complete, tasteful set of furniture, which she had a country carpenter make, then painted it herself and made cushions for it out of peasant weavings.

The best armchair is the one from the seventeenth century with the straight, wide, moderately high armrests and the square backrest, padded and upholstered like the seat. The model is very simple and easy to copy in inexpensive materials. This armchair is perfect, since in a beautiful, real, and lasting way it serves the purpose of a chair, in which one wants to be comfortably supported while working and which is easily moveable yet not rickety.

Another excellent model of a simple chair has a backrest consisting of an evenly wide (circa fifteen cm.), semicircular bentwood piece, attached by vertical slats to a wide and somewhat hollowed-out seat: this is the only chair that is completely comfortable and beautiful without a padded seat or cushion.

As a model for a sofa there is none better than the type often seen—painted pearl gray—in old homes. It consists of a wide, deep seat of slats and webbing, resting on four or six legs, with a backrest of slats. On the seat lies a loose, long pad and along the back there are matching long cushions. This is the only simple sofa that is beautiful and provides a good place to rest; you can sit and sleep on it with equal ease. In addition, you can keep the pad and cushions well beaten and—if they are covered with strong, washable fabric—very clean. A bookshelf with only two shelves, the color and length of the sofa, may be hung above the sofa in an arrangement both useful and beautiful.

The person without means is not running the same risk as the wealthy person, who, when he wishes to arrange his home tastefully, often gives it the appearance of an exhibition of industrial art, with rooms in Renaissance and Rococo, Gustavian and Empire styles.[24] Or else, as mentioned above, he fills his rooms to overflowing with furniture and decorative items. In such homes you get the impression that the people are there to serve the furniture and the rooms, not the reverse. Even such "tasteful" rooms lack true taste to the keener aesthetic eye. For, as has already been stressed, rooms must not appear as if they exist for their own sake. They should be an expression of the personal needs and taste of their inhabitants, their memories and feelings, their history. Grandmother's Gustavian bureau can very well be placed among newer furniture, if only its noble simplicity is not disturbed by modern knickknacks displayed on it. Grandfather's heavy armchair need not at all be banished to the attic, only pushed into a corner where it is not in the way or, better still, where it invites you to rest and contemplate a beautiful vista or picture. The small eighteenth-century taborets may be combined to advantage with modern furniture, as long as they are not upholstered in a fabric of a completely different style but in something with a small floral pattern or light-colored stripes. White-painted furniture mixes well with mahogany or walnut furniture; one should, on the other hand, avoid all imitation wood. A screen is useful in the bedroom but is often only in the way in the parlor. In the family's living room a large, sturdy table—preferably square and with only one leg at each corner—should afford space for all the various activities around it. It is not necessary for each bust to have its own pedestal, but it is of the utmost importance that no bust be placed on any object wrapped in plush, since the soft fabric gives an impression of no weight-bearing capability. This and a thousand other such things are what a woman learns when, in choosing each item, she asks herself whether it possesses style. In other words, whether the item not only serves its purpose, but also expresses this purpose clearly and perfectly by harmonizing purpose, form, and decoration. Why is a lamp on a plain, columnlike foot—preferably one that can be lowered and raised—more beautiful than one with excrescences? Partly because the former is easier to keep clean and is more easily moved, but also because the light source itself—the most important part of the lamp—should be held up by a support that neither clamors for attention nor obscures other objects. Why, for example, is the longer and slender-necked wine bottle more beautiful than the short and thick-necked one? Primarily because it is easier to pour from. Why is a plate beautiful when its rim is decorated with finely stylized flowers but on the other hand ugly when it features a *dalkulla*, a woman from Dalarna in folk costume, in the center? Because it is ridiculous to eat on a *dalkulla*! Why is the flower vase of plain, colored glass more beautiful than the one painted with flowers? Because the painted flowers confound the purpose of the flower vase, which is only to set off unassumingly—but not compete with—the live flowers. And the same holds true for painted fruit on fruit plates. Both painted fruits and flowers seem dead next to their living models. On the other hand, a fruit plate is beautifully enhanced by a floral border along the edge. All china dinnerware should preferably be decorated only on the rim or, at the most, enlivened by some discreet motif in the middle. Highly twisted glasses or overly ornate glasses of cut crystal are on one hand too fragile, on the other too heavy, to be truly beautiful. The plainer the shape of a glass, the more beautiful as a rule; the goblet shape probably remains the most beautiful.

Why do artificial flowers and colored grasses fail to please? Because they deceptively imitate that *bliss of vibrant life* that the flower itself communicates in real life.[25] Even if it is no more than a twig of autumn-red leaves, an asparagus stalk with berries, or a thistle put in a vase in wintertime, these are still more beautiful than artificial flowers. Why is the Japanese manner of arranging flowers—according to the flowers' own way of growing and using only one kind—in most cases more beautiful than any other manner? Because it gives an impression of that *bliss of vibrant life*, an impression that the flower is still growing. Why is it tasteless to hang beautiful plates on a wall but tasteful to display the same plates on the wall shelves in a dining room? Because in the latter case they not only decorate, they are also ready to serve their purpose. Why is a tablecloth covered with needlework less appealing than a plain tablecloth with only a border? Because the purpose of the cloth—to protect the table—should not conceal the table's purpose, which is to bear things. And the purpose of the table is seen more clearly through the surface of the smooth cloth than through a cloth filled with embroidered ornament, the lines of which moreover are interrupted by objects placed on the table. The same is true about mats under lamp feet or pedestals. Why is a light, airy drapery around a window more beautiful than a heavy and dark one? Because the latter is contrary to the principle of a window, which is to let in light. And in order to respect this principle and be able to dim, let in, and even temporarily shut out light or sound, curtains or drapes should not be fixed in place but run easily, on curtain rings or through wide hems threaded on round rods, whether more expensive ones of wood or less expensive ones of metal. The curtains can then be drawn and pulled like vertical shades when there is no roller blind, or if such a blind, when down, would give a forbidding impression. By means of a pleated straight valance at the top such a rod as well as a roller blind can be concealed. The straight lines of the curtains not only frame the window beautifully but also strengthen the impression of light given by the window. Curtains and drapes should also comply with the rule of small patterns; if they are striped, the stripes should be fairly narrow and vertical rather than horizontal. Draperies of one color with borders are the most beautiful. Large patterns or big florals are unsuitable, since their patterns are confused when they are disrupted by the unavoidable folds; moreover, big patterns look busy. Permanently attached drapes and weavings are pointless, unless they are intended to provide a background or frame of sorts.

If we continue our questions, we may, for example, wonder why a mirror goes well on a wall between two windows but not facing them? "Because one can see oneself better in the mirror in the first case," all women reply at once. Why is the white tablecloth the most beautiful? Because only the white tablecloth gives that dazzling impression of cleanliness, which is an important part of the pleasure of dining. It is, however, in good taste to enliven the white with colored borders in clear suitable colors or with a table runner and, above all, with flowers! Low bowls with flowers, as well as flowers placed on the tablecloth and a platter of fruit, are the most beautiful table decorations. All table centerpieces with rocks, palm trees, ostriches, deer, and such are ludicrous, for these things have no business on a table, and all tall table decorations—even those made of flowers—are also unsuitable since they screen the dinner guests from one another.

A thousand other such questions a woman learns to answer herself, insofar as she obtains or gives herself that education of eye and thought which results in discerning taste. The more this taste is exercised, the finer will be the choices made, the surer the judgment, and the greater the eagerness to combine the useful with the beautiful within the home, thus making her family happy by creating outer as well as inner harmony.

Architect A[xel] Lindegren has maintained that natural feeling or instinct nevertheless remains the essential requirement when it comes to aesthetic sensibility and that any attempt to draw up rules for good taste and true beauty must be undertaken with great care.[26] For everything that stirs our imagination, piques our curiosity, and appeals to our heart is beautiful to us. Above all, we should not believe that beauty is a joy reserved for the few. No, each and every one of us can pay homage to beauty through the care taken in our deportment, speech, person, and dress. In this way, a life filled with beauty is not the exceptional lot of artists and art connoisseurs. These days we are becoming more and more consciously aware of nature, and if we continue in this direction, good taste will eventually be nature's own: *clear and simple expression in every respect*. Nothing will be puffed up to appear to be what it is not, but neither will anything be diminished through lack of aesthetic responsibility. People have lost their feeling for measured moderation and simple, natural dignity in their own behavior and clothes, as well as their eye for form and color, rest and motion, in everything surrounding them. Those who possess such an eye dictate the taste ruling their era, a taste that is called "modern." No one can stay completely untouched by fashion, and—as soon as "modern" means in good taste and with artistic style—it is even fortunate if as many as possible "follow fashion; for then they achieve through mimicry that taste which only a few possess naturally."[27]

This summary gives a few main points for "the aesthetic of everyday life." While striving to live by this aesthetic, the more active and creative a woman can be when it comes to ways of making life pleasant, beautiful, and tasteful, the better. Especially the revived craft of weaving in the home using homespun and natural, dyed-wool yarn is a superb way for a woman to make her own clothes and decorate her home with a personal touch. In her own community, each woman should also work against the discounting or giving away of old tasteful furniture, wooden vessels, pewter tankards, pottery plates, and such, which have a much greater sentimental and decorative value in their original milieu than they would in a collector's possession. In addition, it would be a blessing if women would gradually lose their taste for the small, useless, hideous objects with which our homes are now overflowing. For the simple homes discussed here, the most treasured beauty is that which is achieved with the least expense and the least possible loss of time. If only this main rule is followed, personal taste can then express itself in many different ways, the more the better. It is the habit of *blindly* following fashion that has put a stamp of uniformity and tastelessness on today's homes. True taste is that which understands how to create an appealing overall impression out of the most disparate elements and with the most different means. True taste, in the final analysis, is the refined taste that knows moderation and unity are the conditions for beauty as much in the home as in other areas of artistic creativity.

During the sixteen years that have passed since this little pamphlet was first published, the clarion calls to a more refined taste have been manifold, and an increasing number of professional craftsmen have labored in the service of that taste. It will therefore be increasingly easy for people to make their home beautiful, and already there are more and more people who are indeed doing so. They are greatly helped by Svensk Hemslöjd [The society for Swedish home-crafts], where one can find all sorts of items for the home—weavings, furniture, pottery, wrought-iron work—often inexpensive, almost always beautiful, and always handcrafted in Sweden.[28]

Of great importance would be more taste and joyous use of color in the decoration and furnishing of schoolrooms, especially in the countryside. City children have other ways of developing their sense of beauty, but in the countryside it is of primary importance to use the school as a place to exhibit and demonstrate beautiful arrangements and objects of true art. These works of art should not be selected primarily for historical or religious reasons but on aesthetic grounds, and artists, not teachers, must make the selection. Above all, art must not be allowed to become a new subject of painful rote learning for the unfortunate children. It should simply surround them so that they, without effort and quite naturally, receive impressions of beautiful buildings, noble female and male beauty, and the ways in which great art portrays human beings and landscapes.[29] The fact that education and beauty now are closer to each other will surely contribute more than anything else to develop the children's desire to have some works of art—originals or at least reproductions—in their own homes as adults. And quality reproductions can now be had for a few kronor. Even people with very limited means could now afford to gladden their eyes and those of their guests with one or two quality reproductions of works of art if in their hospitality they took Ehrensvärd's tenet to heart:

If people in the North were not so strongly enticed by food, they would instead be able to gladden one another with the noble and lasting fruits of higher pleasures.[30]

If one has succeeded in obtaining some artistic reproductions, one must display them by carefully selecting both the placement and the background. For copperplate engravings, woodcuts, and photographs, plain dark frames and a fairly light wallpaper are appropriate; for example, blue-gray is an excellent background color for copperplate. For oil paintings, very simple gold frames or inexpensive, plain wooden frames are often preferable. Most oil paintings or colored lithographs look best against a deep red or—better yet—gray-green wall. Fine yellow, blue-gray, or white walls can also set off certain paintings well. Reproductions of sculptures—white, black, terracotta, or bronze—look good against the same backgrounds as oil paintings, with the exception that terracotta does not show to advantage against a red background, which conversely admirably sets off objects of green bronze.

It is, however, rare indeed that someone without means has the opportunity to acquire a good oil painting. He therefore preferably ought to stay with quality reproductions. But he must guard against the oleograph.[31] Why is the oleograph ugly while the well-taken photograph is beautiful? Because the latter modestly and honestly gives a truthful, though pale, idea of the work of art, while the oleograph in a cheap way strives to imitate it. If an oleograph is of high quality, then it is also expensive. On the other hand, there are now fine color prints resembling water colors, sometimes even included as supplements to some Christmas publications; there are excellent photogravures, woodcuts, and photographs at a low cost; indeed, even some copperplate engravings and etchings are inexpensive in relation to their artistic value. When selecting such art objects I must of course choose what I myself find beautiful, not what I know others find beautiful! For it is my own eyes, not the eyes of my friends, which I should please. Moreover, it is only by truly loving an art object that I possess it, not by buying it. The rich person, his walls full of paintings acquired because it is prestigious to own paintings, is much poorer than the laborer, who on Sundays visits the paintings he has learned to love in the museum, or in his own home every day enjoys one single really beautiful reproduction of a major work of art. Personal taste is best developed by seeing beautiful art around you and learning to appreciate it. Unfortunately, people who live in rural areas do not have much opportunity to develop their taste in this way. A beautiful cathedral, an old castle, the odd statue, one or two new houses—not counting Visby, the university cities, and Göteborg, that is all there is to see in ten or so of our provincial towns in the way of buildings and visual arts![32] In the rest of them there is almost nothing. As far as paintings are concerned, there is even less in the countryside. Stockholm has a couple of splendid old buildings, the royal palace and Riddarhuset [House of nobility], and a few recently erected public buildings. Among the city's temples of worship we may delight in the Jewish synagogue, the cupola of Katarina kyrka [Katarina church], and a few church spires. There are a few preserved older palaces and some more recent ones, which can give an idea of beautiful architectural style.

Of statues there are, for example, *Gustaf III* and *Karl XIV Johan*, *Olaus Petri* and *Axel Oxenstierna*, *Fosterbröderna* [The foster brothers], *Farfadern* [The grandfather], and *Snöklockan* [The snow bell], which make an artistic impression in public open spaces, in addition to some of the sculptures by Christian Eriksson, [Carl] Milles, and [Carl] Eld [*sic*, Eldh], which now adorn public buildings, open areas, and parks.[33] There are the several collections of applied arts at the Nationalmuseum [National museum of fine arts], Skansen, and Nordiska museet [Nordic museum],[34] in which one can get to know both simpler and more precious objects of applied art as well as various period styles. There are the departments of painting and sculpture at the Nationalmuseum and the magnificent Thielska gallerie [Thiel gallery] at Djurgården.[35] In certain elementary and secondary schools, as well as in public and private high schools, there are murals by prominent modern Swedish artists, for example, in the Norra latinläroverket [North Latin school], the elementary schools on Valhallavägen and Norrtullsgatan, and others.[36] They are also found in the new central post office building on Vasagatan, the national bank, and in the new Dramatiska Teater [Royal dramatic theater].[37] But it takes time and guidance to really learn to discern beauty in all this.

Through assiduous visits to museums and through an open eye for everything encountered, in the streets and squares, beautiful or ugly, Stockholmers learn easily enough to discover why one building pleases more than the buildings surrounding it: for example, Petersénska huset [Petersen house] at Munkbron or Hallwylska palatset [Hallwyl palace] at Berzelii Park or some other rich private residences; the electricity building at Regeringsgatan;[38] Nordiska museet; the new central post office building; or the country houses on Djurgården or in Stockholm's environs, built by older or younger architects. They learn why a banqueting hall like Höganloft [The high loft] at Skansen *immediately* puts us in a festive mood—while in most other such facilities we first have to overcome our irritation at its tastelessness before we can enjoy ourselves.[39] They learn why one statue gives an impression of life, another one of death, and therefore leaves us quite cold. Or why one painting gives us increased joy with each viewing, while we tire of another, the subject of which perhaps at first appealed to us so that we initially preferred it to other, actually more rewarding paintings.

The condition for finding beauty is to seek it; the condition for learning to understand it is to love it! Then we will with each passing day penetrate ever more deeply into its soul, learn to find what constitutes true beauty, and thus also understand that it is possible to set our personal stamp on our own single, small, poor room, such that whoever enters there shall feel that its walls enclose a person whose life has been made happier by the ability to enjoy and choose that which is beautiful.

In the countryside it is sometimes the manor and the church, but most of all nature itself, that support and develop the sense of beauty. There flowers and greenery offer the best possible decoration for homes; there it is the varying pictures of the seasons that people must learn to appreciate and love. From the twinkling light of spring above the still bare earth to the gray sky of autumn, against which the trees are so delicately or strongly silhouetted; from the hoarfrost-covered white birches of winter to the varicolored splendor of the summer meadow, the one with eyes to see will find ever new pictures to enjoy. And although in the country people have less opportunity than in town to acquire beautiful objects for the home inexpensively, on the other hand they have more time and means to decorate their homes with beautiful handcrafted items—weavings, carvings, and fine needlework. In other words, neither town nor country lacks opportunity when it comes to beauty. Beauty can everywhere exert its ennobling influence, if only people begin to open their eyes and hearts to all things beautiful. But above all they first have to learn to realize that the beautiful in life is not at all an extravagance; that you work better, feel better, become friendlier and more joyful if you surround yourself in your home with beautiful shapes and colors. If you understand how to seek out the beautiful in art and nature, then you soon realize from your own experience that beauty gives you comfort and lifts your spirits even in the midst of the heaviest drudgery.

No art, no luxury can render truly pleasing that wealthy home which lacks a deeply felt sense of beauty as well as joy in beauty. Efforts to replace them with ostentation are futile. These suggestions—about the means with which beauty can also be created in the simplest home—are therefore best concluded with Ehrensvärd's golden words:

Things increasingly lose their beauty as they become more complex and less useful to man's unspoilt nature.[40]

Translated from the Swedish by Anne-Charlotte Harvey.

Notes

"Skönhet i hemmen" ("Beauty in the Home") was initially published in 1897 in an extremely shorter form in the magazine *Idun*. Key reworked and expanded it for various editions of her collected essays, *Skönhet för alla* (Beauty for All) (Stockholm: Albert Bonniers förlag, 1899). This translation is from the fifth edition, published in 1913.

1. Key noted here: "Ehrensvärd's text, whether directly quoted or paraphrased, is given in italics." This convention has been preserved by the editors of this volume. (Key made just three notes to her essay; they are quoted and incorporated into the editors' annotations.) Carl August Ehrensvärd (1745–1800) was a count, naval officer, art theorist, artist, and architect. Key in fact draws on two of his texts, both first published in 1786 by Kungliga tryckeriet: *De fria konsternas philosophi* (The philosophy of the fine arts) (Stockholm: Sigma, 1974); and *Resa til Italien, 1780, 1781, 1782* (Journey to Italy, 1780, 1781, 1782) (Stockholm: Bokförlaget Rediviva, 1978). In each, Ehrensvärd considers the relationship between cultural differences and artistic expression. Key owned a copy of Ehrensvärd's collected writings, which can still be found in the library at her lake-side home, Strand. Page references for direct quotations from the facsimile editions of these two texts are noted. While acknowledging Ehrensvärd as a source of inspiration, Key expands well beyond the substance of Ehrensvärd's writings in this essay.

2. Ehrensvärd, *De fria konsternas philosophi*, p. 68.

3. In the late 1800s many small communities sprang up around junctions or stops (Sw. *stationssamhälle*) on Sweden's rapidly expanding railroads.

4. Elisabeth af Wied (1843–1916), queen of Romania, writing under the pen name Carmen Sylva, was a prolific author of poetry, novels, essays, and maxims often published in Swedish magazines.

5. Sw. *det fina rummet*: lit. "fine room," the "best room" reserved for special occasions and receiving visitors. See also Paulsson, in the present volume, n. 5.

6. The editors attempted to determine the source of this quote, without success.

7. Sophie Adlersparre (1823–1895) was the founder in 1874 of Föreningen Handarbetets Vänner (The association of friends of textile art).

8. Bertel Thorvaldsen (1770–1844) was a Danish sculptor famous for his neoclassical bas reliefs and sculpture. His art inspired both handcrafted and industrially produced objects in the late nineteenth and early twentieth centuries.

9. Beginning in the mid-nineteenth century many craft schools were established throughout Sweden to counteract a gradual disappearance of traditional craft skills and a flow of inferior quality goods from abroad, as well as to train farmers to make products that would supplement their incomes.

10. Ehrensvärd, *Resa til Italien*, p. 20.

11. Skansen, one of the world's oldest open-air museums, was founded by Artur Hazelius (1833–1901) in Stockholm in 1890 to preserve and exhibit folk culture from all parts of Sweden.

12. Morastugan, an eighteenth-century log house from Mora, Dalarna, was the first building moved to Skansen in 1891. The hanging "crown pole," with its decoratively carved ends, served many functions, from hanging clothes and food to demarcating areas of the room. A show towel is a purely decorative, long towel, often embroidered, hung over ordinary kitchen or hand towels. See Lane, Introduction, fig. 5

13. Makart bouquets were a popular late nineteenth-century parlor and atelier decoration of dried flowers, straw, and palm branches, named after the Austrian painter Hans Makart (1840–1884). Here and elsewhere Key shows her awareness of Alfred Lichtwark's *Makartbouquet und Blumenstrauss* (Leipzig: Hesse & Becker, 1892), a widely read and reprinted fable that compares the dry, dusty, and contrived "Makart bouquet" to the "old art," and the vase of fresh flowers, reflecting nature, to the "new art."

14. Key did not indicate her source for this quote; the editors' attempts to identify its author were unsuccessful.

15. The editors have attempted to determine the identity of this "American authoress" without success.

16. In other words, which cost them one hundredth of what others pay.

17. Carl Larsson (1854–1919), leading painter and book illustrator, was a close friend of Key. The four volumes referred to are *Ett hem* (A home) (Stockholm: Bonnier, 1899; enlarged edition 1904); *Larssons* (Stockholm: Bonnier, 1902); *Spadarfvet, mitt lilla landtbruk* (Spadarfvet: my little farm) (Stockholm: Bonnier, 1906); and *Åt solsidan* (On the sunny side) (Stockholm: Bonnier, 1910).

18. The invention sofa (Sw. *inventionssoffa*) was a high-backed sofa bed popular in Sweden and often a showpiece in country homes at the end of the nineteenth century. Distinguished by a mechanism that allowed both its arms and seat to be maneuvered to form a single bed, it was usually manufactured in dark wood with plush, patterned upholstery.

19. Larsson, *Ett hem* (1904), p. 3.

20. Key uses the term *gobelin* to refer not to French Gobelin tapestries specifically but to large pictorial tapestries in general.

21. It is unclear to which of William Morris's axioms Key is referring. She may be paraphrasing an article by Erik Folcker (1858–1926), who in addressing the characteristics of contemporary English wallpapers refers to Morris's "slogan" that "a room should give the impression of color, not colors." See Folcker, "Engelska papperstapeter," *Meddelanden från Svenska Slöjdföreningen* (1892): p. 90.

22. In unnumbered notes at the end of the 1913 volume in which this essay appeared, Key directed readers to this point in her essay and wrote: "The varnished floors . . . are easily prepared as follows. At the paint store, buy boiled linseed oil, a stiff brush, and a can of matte varnish. Give the floors two to three thin coats of linseed oil and allow to dry well between coats. Repeat this exact process with the varnish. All this should be done preferably in the summertime when things dry most rapidly. In this way the floors of one very large room or a couple of smaller rooms can be given a beautiful yellow-brown tone for only five to six kronor. In addition, there is no need for the unhealthy scrubbing of floors—they need only be wet mopped. Unfortunately this varnish is not especially durable. If you want the floors to look fresh and neat they must be touched up every three years wherever exposed to constant wear."

23. Sw. *rejäl*: from French, *réel*; or real.

24. Gustavian, or Swedish neoclassical style, developed during the reign of King Gustav III (1771–1792).

25. Ehrensvärd, *De fria konsternas philosophi*, p. 19.

26. Axel Lindegren (1860–1933), architect, artist, and writer, frequently published essays on aesthetics, some of which are collected in *Konsten och samhället: vardagslivets estetik med flera uppsatser* (Stockholm: Lagerström, 1913).

27. Key did not indicate the source of this quote, nor of the phrase "the aesthetic of everyday life" that follows. The editors have been unable to determine a precise source in Lindegren, whose book cited in n. 26 above includes the phrase, as Key added these phrases to the 1904 edition of her essay, and it is unclear whether the architect's title essay was published by 1904.

28. Svensk Hemslöjd was founded in 1899 by reformer Lilli Zickerman (1858–1949) with the aim of preserving and promoting traditional Swedish handicrafts; elsewhere in this volume "hemslöjd" is translated as "home-crafts." See Barbro Klein, "The Moral Content of Tradition: Homecraft, Ethnology, and Swedish Life in the Twentieth Century," *Western Folklore*, vol. 59, no. 2 (Spring 2000): pp. 171–95.

29. In notes at the end of the 1913 edition, Key directed readers to this point in her essay and wrote: "The above-mentioned closer relations between art and the school system is made possible by the Föreningen för skolors prydande, which has its board in Stockholm. Membership is ten kronor per year and entitles members to take turns sharing in the association's distribution of works of art." Föreningen för skolors prydande med konstverk (The association for the decoration of schools with works of art) was founded in 1897 by Carl G. Laurin (1868–1940), and renamed Konsten i skolan (Art in schools) in 1903.

30. Ehrensvärd, *Resa til Italien*, p. 63.

31. Oleographs are chromolithographs printed on canvas in imitation of an oil painting.

32. The university cities Key refers to are Uppsala, Lund, and Stockholm—the only cities in Sweden with universities when this essay was written.

33. *Gustaf III* (1808), by Johan Tobias Sergel; *Karl XIV Johan* (1854), by Bengt Erland Fogelberg; *Olaus Petri* (1897), by Theodor Lundberg; *Axel Oxenstierna* (1890), by Johan Börjesson; *Fosterbröderna* (1888), by Theodor Lundberg; *Farfadern* (1886) and *Snöklockan* (1881), by Per Hasselberg.

34. Nationalmuseum, by Friedrich August Stüler, 1846–66, murals by Carl Larsson, 1896. Nordiska museet, by I. G. Clason, 1889–1907, founded in 1880 by Artur Hazelius for the collection, preservation, and exhibition of historic material culture from the Nordic countries, primarily Sweden.

35. Thielska galleriet, by Ferdinand Boberg, 1904–05, permanent exhibition of the Nordic turn-of-the-century art collection of financier Ernest Thiel (1859–1947), housed in his Djurgården residence.

36. Norra latinläroverket, by Helgo Zettervall, 1876, site of important mural series by Carl Larsson, Prince Eugen, and Bruno Liljefors, ca. 1898–1901. Engelbrektsskolan, by Ernst Haegglund and Konrad Elméus, 1899–1900, murals by Nils Kreuger, 1904. Key is probably also thinking of the Östra Real (Eastern senior high school), by Ragnar Östberg, 1906–11, with murals by Prince Eugen, Georg Pauli, and Axel Törneman.

37. Centralposten, by Ferdinand Boberg, 1898–1904, mural by Carl Wilhelmsson, 1907. Riksbanken (Bank of Sweden), by Aron Johansson, 1892–1905, murals by Georg Pauli, 1906. Kungliga Dramatiska teatern, by F. Lilljekvist, 1901–08, murals by artists including Julius Kronberg, Carl Larsson, and Georg Pauli, all executed in 1908.

38. Petersénska huset, built in 1647 and notable for its well-preserved double portals and sandstone ornamentation. Hallwylska palatset, by I. G. Clason, 1893–98, Spanish-inspired private palace built for Count Hallwyl to display works by contemporary artists. Brunkebergsverket, by Ferdinand Boberg, 1892, Stockholm's first electricity works.

39. Höganloft restaurant, by Norwegian Karl Güettler, 1904–05, a great hall in revival "Viking" style.

40. Ehrensvärd, *De fria konsternas philosophi*, p. 14.

HVAR ~ 8 ~ DAG

ILLUSTR. ... MAGASIN

28:DE ÅRG.
N:o 26

DEN 27 MARS
1927

PARTI FRÅN JÄMTLAND.   Amatörfoto. O. ÅHLÉN, Göteborg.

Hovfoto. JAEGER, Sthlm.
Nytaget för Hv. 8. D.

Kliché: Sjöberg, Gbg.

1. Gregor Paulsson. Photographed by Hovfotograf Jaeger
for the cover of *Hvar 8 Dag*, March 27, 1927

An Introduction to Gregor Paulsson's *Better Things for Everyday Life*

Helena Kåberg

Gregor Paulsson (1889–1977; fig. 1), Swedish art historian, educator, and interdisciplinary theorist, was a pioneering advocate for modern architecture, design, and town planning and for the scientific study and interpretation of art-historical artifacts. An outspoken idealist and social reformer, he saw aesthetics as an important socio-political tool. Paulsson's polemic pamphlet *Better Things for Everyday Life*—translated into English for the first time in this volume—was published in 1919 by Svenska Slöjdföreningen (The Swedish arts and crafts society).[1] Founded in 1845, the society strove to safeguard traditional handicrafts, promote higher manufacturing and aesthetic standards, and help Swedish products compete with cheap, industrially manufactured imports.[2] Paulsson's text expresses similar aims, with the added notion that modern—which is to say industrial and rational versus handmade—production methods, if artfully exploited to their fullest capacity, would benefit not only aesthetic and economic development but social progress.

Published in connection with Svenska Mässan (The Swedish trade fair) in Göteborg, the text unfolds in nine chapters, speaking to such subjects as taste, industry, beauty, the artist, the salesman, and society.[3] Within this broad scope, it primarily addresses manufacturers and retailers, introducing them to new business practices. Paulsson and Svenska Slöjdföreningen encouraged artists and industry to voluntarily enter into creative joint ventures. In his essay, Paulsson rejects the old-fashioned notion that art and industry, or beauty and technology, are opposed; in fact they are perfectly attuned: "Technology, condemned by nineteenth-century beauty zealots as the enemy of beauty, is for us that which creates beauty," he writes. He then stresses that beauty is a rational concern. Incorporating beautiful form into manufactured goods would "lead to the elimination of the ugliness that prevails in modern society and liberate us from the historical styles that bedevil contemporary architecture and decorative art."[4] Having established the aesthetic impetus, Paulsson then moves on to the economic benefits of merging technology and beauty. Cooperation would result in more beautiful quality goods, fit for everyday use, available and desirable to everyone.

The new modern beauty was not to be seen as an aesthetic or economic end in itself. Again, social progress was Paulsson's greater goal. While art has a social function, he argued, it is often isolated to a select audience, and this need not be. Paulsson believed that art was deeply relevant and could have wide social impact.[5] To him art was "the expression of its age," "a movement of a social nature," and "intimately linked to the overall changes in economic and cultural life." He predicted that the new era, in contrast to the old, would not permit any "display of such a pointless waste of people, time, and raw materials, nor such a restriction of culture to a few individuals."[6] To stimulate change on a grand scale, Paulsson recommends in his final chapter, influential officials should serve as models by commissioning post offices, telegraph offices, and railroad, customs, and school buildings. Public architecture plays a significant role in people's everyday lives: it determines their daily comfort and whether they will take pleasure in their work; it is also edifying and influences the development of taste. The greater goal is nothing less than a better life for all, a life in which art generates economic, social, and cultural well-being.

Better Things for Everyday Life was an early yet telling step in Paulsson's long intellectual career. After receiving his Ph.D. in 1915 Paulsson accepted a curatorial position at the National Museum of Fine Arts, where he became head of the department of prints and drawings.[7] In 1920 Paulsson was appointed director of Svenska Slöjdföreningen and editor in chief of its journal, Svenska Slöjdföreningens Tidskrift. After 1924, upon leaving the museum, he dedicated himself entirely to the society and to promoting the ideals of Better Things for Everyday Life in exhibitions, publications, and collaborations with pioneering artists and architects such as his acceptera co-authors. He acted as Commissioner-General of the Swedish Exhibition at the Paris 1925 Exposition internationale des arts décoratifs et industriels modernes, the 1927 and 1928 Swedish Contemporary Decorative Arts Exhibitions in New York, Chicago, and Detroit, and the 1930 Stockholm Exhibition.[8] At the end of 1934 Paulsson left Svenska Slöjdföreningen. Appointed professor at Uppsala University and chair of the art history department from 1934 to 1956, he continued to focus on the interplay between art and society and on problems of art-historical interpretation. Persistently he explored how artistic expressions could be studied systematically and objectively and how art history as an academic discipline could contribute unique and important knowledge about humanity and society. Already in the late 1910s he had begun to incorporate psychology and sociology into his work.[9] In 1943 he expanded this interdisciplinary approach and introduced what he called the "art-historical field," in which he gave the social sciences important support roles in the study of interaction between works of art, individuals, and society. His wide definition of art-historically interesting artifacts is exemplified in his book Svensk stad (The Swedish town).[10] In addition to his many professional accomplishments, Paulsson was part of an influential network of Swedish social democratic politicians and people active in the national cultural arena. These connections paved the way for him to inspire the grand-scale implementation of modern ideals.

The roots of Paulsson's progress run deep in his history. In his memoirs Paulsson recalls a decisive moment in his early education: reading Ellen Key's Folkbildningsarbetet (Adult education) as a teenager.[11] Published in 1906, Key's book expands on a central idea in her Beauty for All and "Beauty in the Home," namely that beauty in the individual home would lead to a better society. Key expressed the far-reaching nature and promise of beauty as an essential human need and an urgent sociopolitical matter. In Folkbildningsarbetet she further argues that adult education is necessary for social progress, and that aesthetics, in particular, can contribute to enlightenment. Beautiful surroundings and intellectual stimulation, she proposes, can foster harmony and human dignity, along with optimism, perseverance, and integrity. In other words, beauty and education produce a state of mind that encourages people both to create a better life for themselves and to make valuable contributions to society. Key describes the contemporary educational situation in Sweden as dire, especially in the countryside. While agricultural, political, religious, and temperance associations play important social roles in communities all over Sweden and contribute greatly to adult education via lectures, reading circles, and courses, they could do much better, she argues. Educated young people must offer their help. Efforts in England, Germany, France, Japan, Denmark, Norway, and Finland should be emulated, along with a few inspirational Swedish organizations and initiatives.[12]

Key's text had a significant impact on the young Paulsson, strengthening his beliefs and commitment to participate in various clubs and organizations, to lead a study group for the children of members of Nykterhetsorganisationen Verdandi (The temperance society Verdandi), the labor movement's organization for community and solidarity, and ultimately to search for an occupation that would involve both aesthetics and social reform.[13] Paulsson grew up in Helsingborg, an emerging, class-segregated industrial and commercial center in which officials in select areas were hard at work developing a bourgeois townscape boasting monumental facades in symbolic and eclectic styles.[14] Paulsson lived in the more affluent part of town, but those he met and talked politics with while tutoring children in the working-class district made him acutely aware of inequalities. Paulsson later wrote that this experience drove him to dedicate himself to social democratic causes.[15] An ambivalent science major in high school, Paulsson also found himself increasingly interested in the arts, and seriously considered becoming a painter or theatrical director.[16] Key opened up the prospect of combining his interests. In 1907 Paulsson enrolled at Lund University, switching after one month from studies in law to the seminar for aesthetics and the history of literature and art.[17] He also became a member of the radical, party-independent student political association and debate club Den Yngre Gubben (The younger old man), also known as D. Y. G., which Key acclaims in *Folkbildningsarbetet* for its lecture series, classes for workers, confession-less Sunday school, and evening soirées.[18] Friendships forged during his university years, in D. Y. G. and other groups of the ideologically likeminded, would later prove productive.[19]

Paulsson attended university at a time when the purpose and merits of art history as an independent academic subject were matters of lively international scholarly debate.[20] The will to turn art history into a discipline—ruled by laws, with systematic methods and theoretical ideals similar to those governing the social and natural sciences—drove the debate. A related important aim was to dispense with subjective aestheticism and aesthetic-philosophic idealist speculations.[21] Crucial to Paulsson's understanding of these issues were the writings of the Viennese art historian Alois Riegl, who argued that art is always a manifestation of its age. Paulsson later wrote that when he understood the implications of Riegl's theories he felt as if freed of "the positivistic straightjacket."[22] He was convinced that historical facts could only become science if studied in relation to the circumstances that brought them about.

Riegl's influence is evident in Paulsson's 1915 doctoral thesis, *Skånes dekorativa konst* (Decorative arts in Skåne), in which he strives to place sixteenth- and seventeenth-century church interiors and religious sculpture in the province of Skåne into a local Swedish context.[23] The topic was typical of its time; many scholars undertook similar studies in defense of national heritage, good taste, and quality, which were widely perceived as threatened by industrialization, historicism, and eclecticism. Paulsson's aim was to investigate how "imported Renaissance style" evolved into regional form.[24] Opposed to art-historical research that sought to place Swedish artistic expression into a schematic international history of style, he opted rather to consider local form in its own right. To Paulsson this meant showing how specific circumstances, local people, history, and traditions generated something unique. He argued that even when foreign patterns were literally at hand or when immigrant craftsmen and artists were employed in the production of Swedish goods, their products were never blind copies of imported models. At first there might be a clear external influence, but eventually an indigenous style, even one deriving from an imported style, would evolve as a domestic form dependent on and reflecting immediate local circumstances. In Paulsson's study, for instance, a distinctively Nordic Baroque style emerged.[25]

Paulsson could have continued his academic career in stride, approaching other art-historical topics similarly. He chose, however, to apply his methods and insights to his own time, and to a vision of the future, convinced that social context was essential and that evolution was an ongoing process dependent on changing circumstances. With this realization Paulsson's social and aesthetic goals and his art-historical ambitions merged. Social and cultural factors could not, in his view, be described as making up some sort of vague and general zeitgeist. They must be understood as part of complex and changing relationships comprising specific and various interacting or counteracting factors. Thus, Paulsson concluded, one can and must constantly work toward realizing the style of one's own period.

Paulsson's most important contemporary influence was the German arts and industry organization Deutscher Werkbund, which he praises in *Better Things for Everyday Life*.[26] Indeed, the Werkbund influence is suggested on the very cover of the pamphlet: the society's "SSF" logo closely resembles the Deutscher Werkbund's "DWB" emblem.[27] The Deutscher Werkbund was founded in 1907 in Munich as a cooperative organization of applied artists, architects, politicians, and manufacturers.[28] Paulsson describes its mission as one of promoting "the concept of quality, advocating it to the state and to public opinion and encouraging it through the fruitful cooperation of art, industry, handicraft, and trade."[29] Increased German exports and socioeconomic well-being were its further concerns. The organization's headquarters moved to Berlin in 1912, the year in which Paulsson lived there briefly and discovered in a university bookshop the Werkbund's first annual publication.[30] Still a student at Lund University, Paulsson moved to Berlin in part to take advantage of the libraries and museums, but also because it was cheaper to keep house abroad.[31] For students from Lund, Berlin was a cultural metropolis. Here, Paulsson came into contact with radical and socialist thinking and emerging modern movements in art, architecture, and town planning. His ideas about art matured among the creative avant-garde circles surrounding the German art periodical *Der Sturm* and its founder, Herwarth Walden.[32] Just as Key and Riegl had opened up new perspectives, Berlin's avant-garde and the Werkbund reformers inspired Paulsson to add another social-aesthetic dimension to his thinking.

Paulsson was not the first Swede to take an interest in Werkbund ideas. In 1909 Svenska Slöjdföreningen invited the influential co-founder of the Deutscher Werkbund Hermann Muthesius to the opening of an exhibition in Stockholm called *Den vita staden* (The white city) and named him an honorary member of the Swedish society.[33] Raising the quality of both handmade and manufactured goods had been a priority ever since the foundation of the Swedish society in 1845. How to accomplish this, however, and what should motivate higher quality, were now matters of intense debate. In the early 1910s a new generation of Svenska Slöjdföreningen members sought to focus more on modern manufacturing methods and everyday objects for all than on handicraft and luxury objects for the few. Change would eventually come with Erik Wettergren (1883–1961), the industry-minded art historian and actor who in 1913 became secretary of Svenska Slöjdföreningen.[34] That same year textile artist Elsa Gullberg (1886–1984) lectured at a society meeting on her recent study tour to Germany.[35] The event was a milestone in the history of Svenska Slöjdföreningen and of Swedish design. A pressing question in both Germany and Sweden at the time was why manufacturers would make investments in new designs and hire artists as designers when they already made good money copying and employing untrained factory foremen. Citing Werkbund examples, Gullberg acknowledged that industry would only change their practices given economic incentives.[36] It was not enough to argue aesthetic and social benefits: reform had to be promoted in economic terms. Industry had to be convinced that the specialist skills of trained artists could elevate the value of manufactured goods and make their products more profitable and competitive. Change was a matter of national interest too: it would sustain economic growth, create jobs, and stimulate social development.

Paulsson first affiliated with Svenska Slöjdföreningen in 1915. Drawn by his progressive art and architectural freelance criticism for Swedish newspapers, including an enthusiastic report on Muthesius's support of rationalization and standardization in the industrial production of consumer goods, and of the creation of types (*Typisierung*) for such goods by artists and craftsmen, the society invited him to give a lecture.[37] Yet to present his dissertation on Nordic Baroque, he now offered his convictions to contemporary Sweden. In his lecture, "Anarki eller tidsstil" (Anarchy or a style of the times), he criticized the "anarchy" of historicism and eclecticism and the ignorance of arts and crafts–inspired practices that did not attend to the needs of contemporary society nor make the most of industrial manufacturing.[38] He proposed the development of a new style appropriate to the modern period—not a formal style or an aesthetic end in itself, but an artistic style that truly reflected a wide range of modern circumstances, from the technical to the economic to the social.

Paulsson argued that such a development would depend on cooperation and education. Engineers understood modern construction techniques, while artists had aesthetic training. The ideal would be to merge the two into one creator who could fuse practical skills and aesthetic values, without one overwhelming the other. Artists, for example, should not practice complete artistic freedom; they should focus on usefulness, not decoration.[39] Paulsson believed that the applied arts were intimately linked to use, and only in "exceptional cases could a vase or some other applied art object serve the same purpose as a painting"—to be a work of art.[40] And where would this cooperative education take place? Not, Paulsson insisted, in the intimate medieval-style workshop between master and apprentice. Rather, the factory should be the new workshop, the place where modern machine tools would be mastered and from which, through collective effort, a modern style would emerge.[41]

In 1916 Paulsson published *Den nya arkitekturen* (The new architecture), in which he argues for the importance and benefits of standardization and types for society.[42] He now expanded his scope beyond architecture and the applied arts to include town planning. For example, Paulsson criticizes the grandiose town planning approach of Haussmannization for ignoring the existing fabric of the city and the actual needs of its inhabitants. The Austrian architect Camillo Sitte, on the other hand, is beset by "medieval unconstraint."[43] Paulsson preferred the English garden city movement model, but of course a Swedish garden city would have to be responsive to local conditions.[44] When it comes to individual buildings Paulsson describes the architecture of the last decades as marked by a "strange reluctance to reveal its purpose," as magnificent shells disguising their insides.[45] He argues instead for a "new monumentality" in which exterior and interior correlate and matter-of-factness is elevated to form and beauty. Just as Walter Gropius had imagined "Monumental Art and Industrial Building" in his well-known 1911 lecture, Paulsson envisioned a new architecture suited to modern needs that honestly recognized and proudly revealed modern life. Gropius and Paulsson would return to these values when they participated in the 1948 *Architectural*

2. Ceramic industry display in the 1917 Home Exhibition, Liljevalchs konsthall, Stockholm. Photograph: collection Svensk Forms arkiv, Stockholm

3. Carl Bergsten. Liljevalchs konsthall, Stockholm. 1913–16. Photograph: collection Arkitekturmuseet, Stockholm

Review symposium "In Search of a New Monumentality."[46] In the final chapter of *Den nya arkitekturen*, Paulsson turns to the applied arts, expressing hope that in twenty years or so production in Sweden would be more robust. "Beauty is a precious thing," he writes, but in the future beauty will not be "lonesome, carefully nursed plants that one single night of frost can destroy, but a large mighty forest that can withstand the ravages of vandals."[47]

Paulsson's wish for a healthier production climate quickly came true—at least in the case of one critical event. In 1917 Svenska Slöjdföreningen organized *Hemutställningen* (The home exhibition) (fig. 2) to publicly display its ambitions. The exhibition of model homes and products was held at Liljevalchs konsthall (Liljevalch art gallery), which had just opened in 1916 (fig. 3). Designed by architect Carl Bergsten (1879–1935), an active member of Svenska Slöjdföreningen, the building boasted a large exhibition hall with generous overhead light emanating from a band of windows made possible by modern skeleton construction. Located on the picturesque island of Djurgården, it was considered a radical addition to Stockholm. Indeed, in *Den nya arkitekturen* Paulsson hailed it as an example of "new monumentality."[48] The progressive character of the venue suited the ambitious aim of the exhibition, though the intended low-income target group was not impressed. The rather radical products presented at the exhibition were in many cases commercial failures, apparently of no interest to the working class. Nonetheless, forty thousand people visited the exhibition, which prompted a national debate on housing issues that would persist for years to come.[49]

A milestone in the development of socially engaged modern Swedish architecture and design, the Home Exhibition sought to alleviate the severe housing crisis that followed the rapid industrialization and urbanization of the 1890s. Svenska Slöjdföreningen invited architects and manufacturers to show well-designed small model homes and everyday goods affordable for low-income families.[50] Those who contributed to the exhibition, including Gunnar Asplund and Uno Åhrén, became some of Sweden's leading modern architects. Products were required to be manufactured in Sweden using rational mass-production methods. Visitors were shown how with very limited means they could create beautiful and comfortable surroundings. The smallest apartments shown comprised just a room with a stove (fig. 4). The purpose of the exhibition was thus manifold, addressing aesthetic, social, and economic concerns. There was also a section of the exhibition documenting promising new low-income housing projects throughout Sweden.[51]

4. Gunnar Asplund. Stove. 1917. Displayed in the 1917 Home Exhibition, Liljevalchs konsthall, Stockholm. Photograph: collection Arkitekturmuseet, Stockholm

5. Simon Gate, Knut Bergqvist, and Heinrich Wollman. Goblet (once owned by Gregor Paulsson). 1918. Graal glass, 8 ¼" (21 cm) high. Mfr.: Orrefors glasbruk. Photograph: collection Bukowskis Auctioners, Stockholm

6. Edward Hald. Assorted glass for everyday use. Mfr.: Sandvik glasbruk, Hovmantorp. Photograph: collection Bukowskis Auctioners, Stockholm

Many of the products shown in the model homes and in the product displays of participating manufacturers were the direct result of creative alliances forged between artists and industry by Svenska Slöjdföreningen's referral agency, founded the previous year.[52] Some of these joint ventures were short-lived, some long-lasting. One especially successful collaboration, between Orrefors glasbruk (Orrefors glassworks) and the artists Simon Gate and Edward Hald, lasted for decades. Gate and Hald developed advanced techniques such as *graal* glass and unique showpieces that brought the company international fame.[53] The expertise behind such techniques was later adapted to the production of everyday glassware (figs. 5 and 6). A similar synergy took hold at the porcelain maker Gustavsberg, where artist Wilhelm Kåge was hired in 1917 and stayed on as artistic director until 1949, creating both ornamental objects and everyday wares (fig. 7).

Many of the images in *Better Things for Everyday Life*, published two years after the Home Exhibition, picture objects and interiors shown there. This, Svenska Slöjdföreningen's first promotional publication, was rife with illustrative and explanatory photographs. As an educator, Paulsson sought ways to explain complicated issues simply and directly. True to late nineteenth-century educational practice, he often illustrated his texts with contrasting images in pairs to stimulate comprehension through comparative analysis. In *Better Things for Everyday Life*, for instance, a French 1880s interior and a room by Uno Åhrén shown at the 1917 Home Exhibition are juxtaposed (see Paulsson, pp. 76 and 77). Similar strategies were used in the manifesto *acceptera*, as well as in Paulsson's 1934 *Hur bo* (How to live), a consumer advice booklet published by Kooperativa Förbundet (The Swedish cooperative wholesale society), which contrasts a contemporary and a turn-of-the-century salon, and "ugly" and "beautiful" fruit plates (figs. 8 and 9).[54]

Paulsson clearly believed in the possibility of absolute distinctions and in his own objectivity. But he also understood that the relationships between society and style, and beauty and utility, are complex. In *Better Things for Everyday Life* Paulsson argues that

7. Wilhelm Kåge. Workers' service with printed Lily Blue pattern. 1917. Mfr: Gustavsberg. Photograph: collection Bukowskis Auctioners, Stockholm

8. "Salon c. 1900" and "Living room 1934." Seen here as published in Gregor Paulsson, *Hur bo* (How to live) (Stockholm: Kooperativa Förbundets bokförlag, 1934)

9. "Ugly and beautiful fruit plate." Seen here as published in Gregor Paulsson, *Hur bo* (How to live) (Stockholm: Kooperativa Förbundets bokförlag, 1934)

10. Edvin Ollers. Vine glass and lidded bowl. 1917. Mfr.: Kosta glasbruk. Nationalmuseum, Stockholm

"determining beauty is an extremely precarious task, but one condition would be fulfilled if uniformity and simplicity of form could be found in every product, especially if this uniformity were also that which was best suited to its purpose."[55] Simplicity and purpose are key virtues. Practicality does not require them—Paulsson notes that "when making glass it makes no difference if you blow a bottle with straight sides or with the most exuberantly varied profile"[56]—but still they are virtues. Take Edward Hald's clear glassware, for instance (fig. 6). As Paulsson in 1934 preferred the unadorned glass fruit plate to the putto-decorated one, we might easily surmise that he would find the perfect machine-made look of Hald's glassware far more appealing than Edvin Ollers's air bubble–filled, preindustrial-looking glassware (fig. 10). Not only is Hald's glassware more purposeful, it is more beautiful for reflecting modern versus outdated times.

Given Paulsson's affinity for the contemporary, it is not surprising that in the 1950s he declined an offer to reissue *Better Things for Everyday Life*, convinced that he would have to rewrite it and expand its scope to lend it currency.[57] The clever pamphlet title *Vackrare vardagsvara* had become a familiar catchphrase in Sweden, so interest in the text remained high: after Paulsson's death the original was published as a facsimile edition twice.[58] Reading *Better Things for Everyday Life* as a valid style guide today clearly neglects Paulsson's central tenet: to place art and design values in the context of contemporary society. But even if the text is primarily appreciated as a historically important design document, Paulsson's progressive and pioneering attitude remains inspirational. The will to continuously move ahead, using all modern means available to improve everyday life for all, will always be an essential ambition. The question is what such an ambition entails today. What would it mean today to use aesthetics as a progressive sociopolitical tool that would pave the way for a sustainable society and a better life for everyone?

Notes

1. The original Swedish title of the pamphlet, *Vackrare vardagsvara*, is an eloquent and descriptive alliteration phrased by someone Paulsson calls a "press officer" in his memoirs. Paulsson, *Upplevt* (Stockholm: Natur och Kultur, 1974), p. 100. In a 1927 address before the Advisory Committee on American Industrial Art in New York, Paulsson noted that the title is difficult to translate. Paulsson, *Swedish Contemporary Decorative Arts* (New York: The Metropolitan Museum of Art, 1927), p. 4. In a 1931 lecture in London in connection with the Swedish Applied Arts exhibition held at Dorland House, he suggested an option which the editors of this volume have adopted: "We . . . invented a slogan which, unfortunately, cannot be literally translated without losing most of its force, but which means something like: 'Better things for everyday life.'" He also noted the salience of the original Swedish title: "This slogan has been a very important instrument in our movement. . . . The slogan was a good headline for the newspapers, firms adopted it, it was on everyone's lips." Paulsson, "The Alliance Between Designers and Manufacturer," unpublished manuscript, Uppsala University Library, Gregor Paulsson Papers, 501 K:1 (Föredrag), ca. 1931. Published as *Design and Mass Production* (London: Design and Industries Association, ca. 1931); quotes on p. 5. Scholars have alternately rendered the title in English as *More Beautiful Things for Everyday Use* and *More Beautiful Everyday Things.* Earlier in 1919, on April 12, during Industriveckan (Industry week), Paulsson delivered a lecture, "Konst och industri" (Art and industry) (Stockholm: Svenska Slöjdföreningen, 1919), that presaged much of *Vackrare vardagsvara.*

2. See for example Gunilla Frick, *Svenska Slöjdföreningen och konstindustrin före 1905*, dissertation, Department of Art History, Uppsala University (Stockholm: Nordiska museet, 1978), with summary in German, pp. 247–72.

3. Svenska Mässan Stiftelse (The Swedish trade fair foundation), founded in 1918 and now called The Swedish Exhibition Center, continues to organize trade fairs to this day.

4. Paulsson, in the present volume, p. 86.

5. See Paulsson, "Konst och Industri," 1919, p. 17.

6. Paulsson, in the present volume, pp. 121 and 122.

7. Some in his immediate circle criticized Paulsson's dissertation for being one-sided and overly influenced by modern German theory, prompting him to seek employment outside of academia. Hans Pettersson, *Gregor Paulsson och den konsthistoriska tolkningens problem*, dissertation, Department of Art History, Uppsala University (Stockholm: Brutus Östlings Bokförlag, 1997), with summary in English, pp. 34–40.

8. Swedish applied arts gained international fame at the 1925 Paris exhibition. It was not everyday objects that drew attention, however, but unique pieces, especially engraved art glass from Orrefors glasbruk. The attention paved the way for exhibitions and press coverage in the United States and elsewhere. See Joseph Beck, *Exhibition of Swedish Contemporary Decorative Arts*, exh. cat. (New York: The Metropolitan Museum of Art, 1927), pp. ix–xii; and Derek E. Ostergard, "Modern Swedish Glass in America, 1924–1939," in *The Brilliance of Swedish Glass 1918–1939: An Alliance of Art and Industry*, eds. Derek Ostergard and Nina Stritzler-Levine (New York: The Bard Graduate Center for Studies in the Decorative Arts, Design, and Culture, and New Haven, CT: Yale University Press, 1996), pp. 137–55.

9. After finishing his Ph.D. Paulsson took an interest in psychology. Alois Riegl's *Das holländische Gruppenporträt* (Leipzig: G. Freytag, 1902) convinced him that psychological perspectives were fundamental for art-historical interpretation. While working for Svenska Slöjdföreningen and the Nationalmuseum he enrolled in psychology studies and in 1923 he received a Ph.Lic. from Institutionen för psykologi och pedagogik, Göteborgs högskola. His thesis was published as "The Creative Element in Art: An Investigation of the Postulates of Individual Style," *Scandinavian Scientific Review*, vol. 2 (1923). See Paulsson, *Upplevt*, p. 81; and Pettersson, *Gregor Paulsson*, pp. 52–53, 220.

10. Published in 1950–53, the two-volume exploration was the outcome of a research project, realized in cooperation with doctoral candidates at Uppsala University, designed to go beyond illustrating the social history of art to encompass a social analysis of culture as a whole.

11. Paulsson, *Upplevt*, p. 14. Ellen Key, *Folkbildningsarbetet. Särskilt med hänsyn till skönhetssinnets odling* (Uppsala: K. W. Appelberg, 1906).

12. In an appendix Key offers a bibliography and lists Swedish associations she finds exemplary. Key, *Folkbildningsarbetet*, pp. 207–37.

13. Nykterhetsorganisationen Verdandi is not to be mistaken for the student organization Verdandi found in Lane, Introduction, p. 25.

14. For more on Helsingborg and the history of architecture, town planning, and public art as a means to build urban identity, see Henrik Widmark, *Föreställningar om den urbana världen. Identitetsaspekter i svensk stadsbild med exemplet Helsingborg 1903–1955*, dissertation, Department of Art History, Uppsala University (Uppsala: Fronton förlag, 2007), with summary in English, pp. 324–27.

15. Paulsson, *Upplevt*, pp. 12–14.

16. Living in Berlin in 1912, Paulsson studied with the expressionist painter Ernst Ludwig Kirchner (1880–1938), one of the founders of Die Brücke. Paulsson, *Upplevt*, pp. 15–17.

17. Pettersson, *Gregor Paulsson*, pp. 21, 26.

18. Key, *Folkbildningsarbetet*, pp. 226–27.

19. Paulsson *Upplevt*, pp. 27, 31–35. Pettersson, *Gregor Paulsson*, p. 27. D. Y. G. was active at Lund University from 1896 through the 1930s. Several prominent Social Democrats were members during their formative university years. In D. Y. G. Paulsson met Ernst Wigforss (1881–1977), for instance: Social Democrat, member of parliament 1919–53, minister of finance 1925–26, 1932–49, and promoter of J. M. Keynes's ideas.

20. Art history evolved internationally as an academic discipline in the late nineteenth century. A chair was established at Stockholm University in 1889. At Lund University the topic was studied under aesthetics until 1917 and in 1919, Professor Ewert Wrangel's chair in aesthetics was transformed into a chair in art history. The art history chair at Uppsala University, which Paulsson occupied from 1934 to 1956, was established in 1917. Hans Pettersson, "Konsthistoria som universitetsdisciplin," in *8 kapitel om konsthistoriens historia i Sverige*, eds. Britt-Inger Johansson and Hans Pettersson (Stockholm: Raster förlag, 1999), pp. 64–70.

21. Pettersson, "Konsthistoria," p. 66. Paulsson, *Konsthistoriens föremål* (Uppsala: Lundequistska bokhandeln, and Leipzig: Otto Harrassowitz, 1943), p. 27. Swedish scholars, influenced by German discourse, had adopted style-critical methods, designed to bring systematic order to the history of art based on what was perceived as objective identification and description of unique stylistic criteria. While this approach may qualify as a factual and rational method, critics argued that it was superficial, an end in itself only when creating catalogues and inventory lists. The advocates of these methods were accused of ignoring the problems of art-historical interpretation.

22. Alois Riegl's (1858–1905) concept of *Kunstwollen*, presented in his *Die spätrömische Kunstindustrie* (Vienna: Österr. archäologisches Institut, 1901), argued that art, in every era, is always a manifestation of a contemporary will to create an artistic expression. Art can be described as classical or anticlassical in nature, but never judged as if on its way toward or away from a culminating point. Another important influence on Paulsson was Franz Wickhoff (1853–1909), who in *Die Wiener Genesis* (Wien: F. Tempsky, 1895) argued for the existence of an art-historical continuum. Rejecting the established idea that art evolved in cycles of rise, culmination, and decline, he claimed that every epoch must be studied in its original context, not judged on comparisons with artistic expressions created under other conditions. See Paulsson, *Konsthistoriens föremål*, pp. 27–33, 45; Paulsson, "Konstens sociala dimension," in *Konstsociologi*, ed. Sven Sandström (Lund: Glerup, 1970), p. 23; Paulsson *Upplevt*, pp. 39, 49–50; and Pettersson, *Gregor Paulsson*, pp. 43–45.

23. At the 1658 Peace of Roskilde the Danish province Skåne became part of Sweden. Among efforts at integration were the founding of Lund University in 1666–1668, posting Swedish priests in Skåne's churches, and giving Swedish nobility the opportunity to acquire land.

24. Paulsson, *Skånes dekorativa konst under tiden för den importerade renässansens utveckling till inhemsk form* (Decorative arts in Skåne during the period when imported Renaissance style developed into domestic form), dissertation, Lund University (Stockholm: P. A. Norstedt & Söner, 1915).

25. Ibid., pp. 5–6.

26. See Paulsson, in the present volume, pp. 92–95.

27. See Gunnela Ivanov, "Den besjälade industrivaran," in *Formens rörelse: Svensk form genom 150 år*, ed. Kerstin Wickman (Stockholm: Carlssons, 1995), p. 44.

28. The leading figures among Deutscher Werkbund architects were Hermann Muthesius, Richard Riemerschmid, Theodor Fischer, Josef Hoffmann, Heinrich Tessenow, Henry van de Velde, Peter Behrens, Fritz Schumacher, and Walter Gropius. On the Werkbund, see Frederic J. Schwartz, *The Werkbund: Design Theory and Mass Culture before the First World War* (New Haven, CT: Yale University Press, 1996); and John V. Maciuika, *Before the Bauhaus: Architecture, Politics, and the German State, 1890–1920* (New York: Cambridge University Press, 2005).

29. Paulsson, in the present volume, p. 93.

30. Paulsson, *Upplevt*, pp. 73–76. Paulsson married Ester Wägner (1883–1985), the daughter of his Helsingborg headmaster, in January 1912 and the couple settled in Berlin. They had already spent long periods of time in Germany as Wägner worked as a physical therapist in Heidelberg. In the autumn of 1912 Paulsson returned to Sweden and a temporary position at the Nationalmuseum in Stockholm. He returned to Berlin for short periods, but in the spring of 1914 settled permanently in Sweden to work at the Nationalmuseum. Ester's sister was the feminist author and journalist Elin Wägner (1882–1949), who was married to Johan Landqvist (1881–1974), professor of education at Lund University, translator of Sigmund Freud, and an important influence on Paulsson. Paulsson, *Upplevt*, p. 23, 48, 56. On Paulsson and Germany, see Pettersson, *Gregor Paulsson*; and Gunnela Ivanov, *Vackrare vardagsvara–design för alla. Gregor Paulsson och Svenska Slöjdföreningen 1915–1925*, dissertation, Department of Historical Studies, Umeå Universitet (Umeå: Umeå universitet, 2004), with summary in English, pp. 86–93.

31. Pettersson, *Gregor Paulsson*, p. 21.

32. Paulsson's introduction to *Der Sturm* was facilitated by the fact that Herwarth Walden's wife, Nell Roslund, was Paulsson's cousin's sister-in-law. Paulsson, *Upplevt*, p. 61. Pettersson, *Gregor Paulsson*, pp. 25, 29.

33. Pettersson, *Gregor Paulsson*, p. 30. Muthesius's *Stilarchitektur und Baukunst: Wandlungen der Architektur im XIX Jahrhundert und ihr heutiger Standpunkt*

(Mühlheim-Ruhr: K. Schimmelpfeng, 1902) was translated into Swedish as *Stilarkitektur och byggnadskonst* (Stockholm: Norstedt, 1910) by Axel Lindegren (see Key, in the present volume, n. 26). Hermann Muthesius (1861–1927) was a German architect, publicist, and theoretical writer on arts and crafts and industrial design; also co-founder of the Deutscher Werkbund in 1907 and chairman, 1910–16.

34. See Paulsson, in the present volume, p. 106; the 1915 reorganization of Svenska Slöjdföreningen to which he refers began with Wettergren's appointment.

35. See *Elsa Gullberg: Textil pionjär*, Nationalmusei utställningskatalog nr 523 (Stockholm: Nationalmuseum, 1989).

36. See Erik Wettergren, "Meddelanden," in *Svenska Slöjdföreningens Tidskrift* (Stockholm: Svenska Slöjdföreningen, 1913), pp. 111–12.

37. Sw. *typisering*: derived from Ger. *Typisierung*, the creation of types. See also Paulsson, in the present volume, n. 11.

38. Paulsson, "Anarki eller tidsstil. Reflexioner öfver våra dagars arkitektur och konsthandtverk," lecture held on February 11, 1915, published in *Svenska Slöjdföreningens Tidskrift*, häfte 1 (1915).

39. Paulsson saw new industrial conditions as new tools offering new possibilities for painters and sculptors to work skillfully and creatively. In a 1914 article inspired by Muthesius's ideas presented in the 1912 Werkbund yearbook on standardization and types, Paulsson argued that if artists adjusted to essentials and true needs, it would strengthen the reliability of the artistic creation, separating "metal from slag." As an artist adapted to industry, artistic expression would be pared down and the benefits for society as a whole would surpass individual needs. Further, new rational production methods gave artists and architects the same opportunity as authors to reach a wide audience. See Paulsson, "Typisering af konsthantverk och arkitektur," *Stockholms Dagblad*, February 11, 1914. Uppsala University Library, Gregor Paulsson Papers, Box: 501 H:1, Binder: untitled. Pettersson, *Gregor Paulsson*, pp. 30, 213–14.

40. Paulsson, "Anarki," p. 9.

41. Ibid.

42. Gregor Paulsson, *Den nya arkitekturen* (Stockholm: Norstedt & Söners förlag, 1916); rev. ed. published in Danish as *Den ny arkitektur* (Copenhagen: H. Aschehoug & Co., 1920).

43. Ibid., pp. 53–54f.

44. Here Paulsson's ideas are reminiscent of the German art critic Karl Scheffler's in *Moderne Baukunst* (Berlin: Julius Bard, 1907). Widmark, p. 53.

45. Paulsson, *Den nya arkitekturen*, p. 86.

46. "Gropius' Vortrag 'Monumentale Kunst und Industriebau,'" April 10, 1911, in *Walter Gropius*, eds. Hartmut Probst and Christian Schädlich (Berlin: Ernst & Sohn, 1986–88), vol. 3, p. 28–51. Paulsson with Henry-Russell Hitchcock, William Holford, Sigfried Giedion, Walter Gropius, Lucio Costa, and Alfred Roth, "In Search of a New Monumentality, A Symposium," *Architectural Review*, September 1948, pp. 117–28. See also Barbara Miller Lane, *National Romanticism and Modern Architecture in Germany and the Scandinavian Countries* (New York: Cambridge University Press, 2000), pp. 247–48; and Helena Kåberg, *Rationell arkitektur*, dissertation, Uppsala University (Uppsala: Acta Universitatis Upsaliensis, 2003), with summary in English, pp. 131–37.

47. Paulsson, *Den nya arkitekturen*, p. 159.

48. Along with Liljevalchs, two other buildings in Stockholm fulfilled Paulsson's standards of the "new monumentality": Rådhuset (The law courts), Carl Westman, 1908–15, and Enskilda Banken, Ivar Tengbom, 1912–15. All three buildings, according to Paulsson, displayed a tendency to elevate matter-of-factness to form and bring quality of life to architecture. Paulsson, *Den nya arkitekturen*, p. 105.

49. See Kerstin Wickman, "Homes," in *Sweden: 20th Century Architecture*, eds. Claes Caldenby, Jöran Lindvall, and Wilfried Wang (Munich: Prestel Verlag, 1998), p. 207; and Ivanov, *Vackrare vardagsvara*, p. 198.

50. Sweden's Nationalmuseum aquired some of the now-iconic objects from the exhibition beginning only in the 1960s, just as the history of the modern movement was first being written.

51. See Eva Ericsson, *Mellan tradition och modernitet. Arkitektur och arkitekturdebatt 1900–1930*, dissertation, Department of Art History, Stockholm University (Stockholm: Ordfront, 2000), p. 369.

52. Elsa Gullberg directed the agency, which was modeled on VAG, the Vermittlungsstelle für angewandte Kunst in Munich (Mediating agency for applied arts in Munich). See Arthur Hald, "Elsa Gullberg—Chef för Svenska Slöjdföreningens förmedlingsbyrå," in *Elsa Gullberg: Textil pionjär*, p. 15. The exhibition was also shown in Göteborg and Malmö. For texts in English on the 1917 Home Exhibition see Kerstin Wickman, "Homes," pp. 204–07; and Anne-Marie Ericsson, "The Emergence of Swedish Modern Design, 1917–1939," in *The Brilliance of Swedish Glass 1918–1939*, pp. 55–56.

53. Developed in 1916 by artist Simon Gate and master blower Knut Bergqvist (and furthered by Edward Hald and other artists), *graal* glass is made by layering variously colored glass and etching or engraving a decorative design into the surface. This cut piece is then reheated, blown, and worked to achieve a final form. Sw. *graal*: grail (*graal* glass was often used for making decorative cups, vases, and bowls).

54. Paulsson, *Hur bo. Några ord om den moderna smakriktningen*, (Stockholm: Kooperativa förbundets bokförlag, 1934). For an analysis see Helena Kåberg, "Ful och vacker frukttallrik: om 1900-talets moderna formsyn och nutida krav på en rik formvärld" (Ugly and beautiful fruit plate: on the twentieth century's modern approach to design and today's demands for greater variation), in *Förfärligt härligt / Dreadful Delight*, ed. Kåberg, Nationalmusei utställningskatalog nr 651, with summary in English (Stockholm: Nationalmuseum, 2007), pp. 216–29, 236.

55. Paulsson, in the present volume, p. 86.

56. Ibid., p. 84.

57. The offer came from Hjalmar Olson, director of the porcelain maker Gustavsberg, bought in 1937 by Kooperativa Förbundet (The Swedish cooperative wholesale society). Paulsson instead cowrote, with his son, Nils, an interdisciplinary, in-depth exploration of how society values things and gives them form, *Tingens bruk och prägel* (Things for everyday use and life form) (Stockholm: Kooperativa Förbundets bokförlag, 1956). While this text shares themes with *Better Things for Everyday Life*, it focuses on psychological and sociological approaches to reform and introduces the terms "practical use," "social use," and "aesthetic use."

58. Paulsson, *Vackrare vardagsvara* (Stockholm: Rekolid, 1986 and 1995).

VACKRARE
VARDAGSVARA

SVENSKA SLÖJDFÖRENINGENS
FÖRSTA
PROPAGANDAPUBLIKATION
UTGIVEN TILL SVENSKA MÄSSAN I GÖTEBORG
1919

GREGOR PAULSSON

BETTER THINGS FOR
EVERYDAY LIFE

STOCKHOLM
SVENSKA SLÖJDFÖRENINGEN
1919

For us Beauty is no longer mere enjoyment. Much less is it the enjoyment of a privileged class. For us Beauty is a spiritual force pervading all things, a heritage into which everyone is born, a state to which every one can attain—more or less, according to his power or sympathy.
    [Charles Robert] Ashbee, Where the Great City Stands [1]

In the end, there are only two things that are required in this world: distinctiveness and excellence. If a little country is to endure struggle in the world, it must insist on these things. It must distinguish itself from others in special qualities, it must surpass the others in its field to produce what is excellent. Where mass production is completely excluded, quality must be asserted.
    Edv[ard] Lehmann, The Land of Equality [2]

Silver sugar bowl and cream jug. Guldsmedsbolaget, Stockholm.

I.
DO TASTES DIFFER?

Tastes differ, people say, wanting to stifle any discussion about questions of taste before they begin. Do they? Is there anything that is beautiful for everyone or is that which one person finds beautiful ugly to someone else?

That tastes change hardly requires any proof at all, as this is made clear by historical developments, which have allowed one style to succeed another in popular affection. But some line could conceivably be drawn that would enable the various historical styles to be divided into the beautiful and the ugly. There is a lot to suggest this. If we consider cultured people today, or at least those with aesthetic interests, we discover that they hardly have words strong enough to condemn applied arts and architecture from the 1850s up until the end of the last century. On the minus side, they also condemn much of the furniture and painting of the sixteenth and seventeenth centuries and are indifferent to high antiquity. On the plus side, on the other hand, they strongly favor the furniture and decorative arts of the period from 1780 to 1830, the Gustavian, Empire, and bourgeois Empire styles, the sculpture

French interior from the 1880s.

of the Middle Ages and early antiquity, as well as that of primitive non-European cultures, indeed anything that can be labeled primitive, including folk art.[3] Opinions of taste are remarkably categorical and absolute, and it is easy to gain the impression that what is now being disparaged is something that is absolutely ugly. Twenty years ago circumstances were entirely the reverse: what is now despised was then esteemed. The same reversal can occur today. Two individuals faced with the same object may have entirely opposing opinions; a vase of cut crystal may be enormously beautiful for one, for the other loathsome. Who is right? The answer: to some extent both. And how can this come about? This is something that is never resolved in discussions on questions of taste: the fact that beautiful need not mean the same in every situation. Saying something is beautiful is the same as saying that it has qualities that please us, satisfy us, grant us peace of mind, and the like. It has been said of [August] Strindberg that when he once moved into a rented room somewhere in Östermalm

Room by Uno Åhrén at Svenska Slöjdföreningen's Home Exhibition.

in Stockholm, he walked into the room, caught sight of the tablecloth, a very simple Turkish imitation that his companion considered dreadful, and exclaimed, "No, how beautiful, indeed it is the entire Orient!" This impression was so strong that it prompted his fairytale play *Abu Casems tofflor* [*Abu Casem's Slippers*].[4]

There must be something unclear in our assessment of what is beautiful or ugly. We always mean something else, which is that the beautiful object possesses certain features that we value that the ugly one lacks. One person likes the impressive, the expensive, mastery of difficult materials, glistening luster, vivid colors. For him, a cut-crystal bowl is beautiful. Another will instead want simplicity, practicality, materials that are genuine and whose intrinsic qualities are enhanced; then the crystal bowl will seem ugly and a simple blown glass or one worked only slightly with large smooth surfaces is the ideal.

If we were to try to stock a shop that would satisfy all aesthetic inclinations and beliefs, we would need to produce magnificent and ornamental cut-crystal for the first person and simple blown glass for the second. That one of these is wrong would not bother anyone in the slightest. After all, tastes differ. . . . This conclusion, often reached, is however somewhat too hasty. We need to think the idea through to its end. *Why* does the one want magnificence but the other simplicity? And what kind of magnificence is desired by the first, what kind of simplicity by the second? That is the question. The forms are not absolute, nor are they the result of chance. There exists an essential link between them and the social and political character of the period in which they come into being. The magnificence of the crystal bowl beloved by some is an offshoot of the magnificence once created to exalt the absolute monarchies of the seventeenth century; the simplicity of 1830s furniture beloved by others and which they want to reproduce today is the expression of bourgeois taste at a time when the bourgeoisie began to take the lead in society instead of kings and the nobility. The style of the 1830s has become the symbol of the middle class, and when bourgeois furniture is referred to today this is what is mainly envisaged. An absolute monarch and a powerful nobility could afford extravagant magnificence; it goes without saying that the middle classes, when they were able to set the social tone, did not imitate the taste of the oligarchy they had recently overcome but created a style and taste based on their own circumstances, intended to give visible expression to the conditions in which they lived.

This is the way it has been through all the ages. Changes from era to era consist of alterations in political, economic, and social conditions; they find expression, as in everything else, in changing tastes as well. Thus *the tastes of different periods* differ. But within the same period *on the whole*, as anyone can see from a visit to an applied arts or cultural museum, one and the same taste prevails. Albeit with some differences between social classes, the style of the rural folk was always somewhat distinct from that of the upper classes, was always somewhat behindhand, surviving on leftovers. Aristocratic taste probably came to a standstill in the eighteenth century; as the middle classes gained control of society and of taste, naturally the nobility were not inclined to follow their lead.

But now this rule has been broken. Now imitations of every possible style contend with each other; what is new and original can hardly be noticed except by those who are especially interested. Only a small minority have a taste for what is new.

How did this happen?

Quite simply because social development has eliminated class differences so that the bourgeoisie have both the moral right and financial means to acquire the same ornamental objects as the nobility. Machine production has made this possible even for those in poor financial circumstances by enabling the manufacture of cheap imitations of the kind of goods that once required months of labor to afford. This fact—that we have overcome class differences, that our machines can imitate the handmade, can produce here in Sweden what had to be imported from China by the East India Company, that we are able to supply all our needs, crystal chandeliers for merchants, plaster dogs for smallholders, Oriental carpets for the "best rooms" of the workers,[5] Turkish divans for bachelors, battle-axes for Bantus, and dance masks for Australian aborigines—this must of course give rise to general pride over this new immense capacity to imitate and level everything, and at the beginning of the 1890s elevate imitation of the Baroque, the Renaissance, Chinese porcelain, and Oriental carpets above the manufacture of Swedish goods for everyday use by Swedish citizens. So during the period that has just elapsed and still, to a large extent, today, the "beautiful" has been equated with the imitated.

If we take this concept in its widest sense, it means not merely that Swedish carpet manufacturers imitate Turkey; that enamel imitates porcelain; iron, wood; electroplated nickel, silver, etc., etc.; but also that one object imitates another: a sideboard, the facade of a building; an inkwell, a seashell; a cast-iron stove, a tiled stove; an iron park bench, one made of wood; a ball and claw, a handle; wallpaper, a tapestry; with more examples *ad infinitum*.

It is obvious that there is something degenerate about this. It is obvious that individuals who in the things they use every day prefer reliability and truth above everything else must find these kinds of imitation repellent, and consider the industry that has occasioned such misdirection of public taste incompatible with beauty.

In other words, tastes differ today because the principles of design are not uniform, because individuals have totally different demands of beauty. If it were once again possible to bring about consistency of production, then taste would certainly become more uniform.

But with uniformity of taste there would also arise consistency of forms throughout society. This is the deeper significance of the proposition

BETTER THINGS FOR EVERYDAY LIFE.

Glazed earthenware by Emil [*sic*, Edvin] Olsson-Ollers, Uppsala-Ekeby.

2.
INDUSTRY AND BEAUTY

We established that it was the burgeoning of mechanical production in the nineteenth century that endowed that period and our own with its characteristic rootlessness of taste and general disinterest in the beautiful, but with an interest in other qualities such as imitation, technical perfection, and the like. One could say that during the nineteenth century interest in art on the whole waned, i.e., for art viewed as a social concern. For lovers of beauty of the old school, it is therefore quite clear that it was the growing manufacturing capacity and the new production methods, industry and machines, that made life ugly. Consequently, in order to obtain more beautiful objects we have to preach war against the machines and revive defunct handicrafts. Industry and beauty cannot be combined.

Is this really the case? Let us study the issue.

The difference between our age, the age of machines, and the past is from our point of view threefold. First, the new offended against nature: it sited large factories with smoking chimneys in smiling meadows, straight railroad lines replaced the delightful twists and turns of country highways, tall and utilitarian but

Stoneware from Höganäs-Billesholms aktiebolag.

prosaic railroad bridges spanned tranquil and beautiful valleys. It allowed electrical power lines, telephone poles, motorboats, in brief a multitude of factors to conspire to destroy the countryside. Secondly, this new age offended against the very nature of labor, the condition of the working classes. It is of course no coincidence that the trade union movement arose at the same time as industrialism, for even if workers previously had low wages, they did derive some ounce of pleasure from their tasks. This pleasure was totally destroyed by the machines, because in their wake came the division of labor. The old ways of working by hand in small workshops mainly disappeared; instead there came large factories in which the workers stood, day in and day out, at machines that perpetually produced the same detail. The machines' lifeless skill could never, of course, achieve the touch of beauty found in the work of an attentive craftsman, where the beauty lies in the work of the hands. Finally, our age offended in many ways against reason. The experience acquired by a craftsman set certain limits to changes in taste in his craft; if he permitted a specific detail to become too elaborate, if he altered a construction too radically, or used material that was too different, his efforts encountered technical obstacles. The resources of his workshop and his manual dexterity did not allow him to go as far as he may have wanted to. Then machines resorted to steam and electric power. These are capable of everything. They are able to make the most remarkable constructions, they are able to produce cheap imitations of costly materials, they are able to combine things that the hand cannot, etc. But when they do so, their products lose the logic, the self-evident character of style, technique, and material that they once possessed. This is where the fussiness, variability, and falsity of many modern goods comes from. They have the air of being old, but they are not.[6]

From this it might seem to follow that beauty and modern production cannot be combined.

It is true that as long as it was a question of good taste in its *old* sense, this could not be done. But this old taste can of course never be totally revived, partly because machines generally produce goods more cheaply than hands can. And after all, economics govern production.

But a modern beauty [will be] the taste of our era.

As we now have machines, instead of imitating the products and techniques of earlier ages, let us seek to achieve products with the characteristic form of the machine-made. This would then become the taste of this new era, which would certainly be embraced by all. Let us not imitate past forms, but let us instead use our new technical resources to create a new one.

But what will this new form look like, one may ask. So that I can give a completely frank response to that question, the central question that everyone wants answered, and not rest content with a few programmatic phrases but try to answer sensibly, I must, for a while, deal with the somewhat abstract issue of the relationship of form to technology.

Machine technology and form are hostile to each other insofar as technology endeavors to overcome the obstacles posed by form. A technical improvement, at least in mechanical terms, consists of conquering some material obstacle. A clumsy detail will then become more elegant and better suited to its purpose. Let us consider the attainment of greater speed. When the construction of the internal combustion engine had advanced to the point where it could be used to drive vehicles, the current ideal form had not yet been reached. It is a long way from a horse carriage equipped with a motor to a 1919 model. In fact it has taken longer to adapt form to technical function and to greater speeds than it has taken technology to master them. Another example: How long did it take before airships were given rounded noses and pointed tails even though it was understood in theory that this would overcome air resistance?

Thus traditional form—here as in many other of life's circumstances—is something *conventional* that has to be overcome. This is what makes the problem of the relationship of art to industry so difficult to solve—but also explains it. A multitude of people adhere to the old forms and consider what is new ugly. In our case: machine-made products should be given the old forms of the handicrafts. This is how it used to be. Therefore endeavors to make industrial products beautiful are bound to fail.

But the modern advocates of cooperation between industry and art fundamentally *do not* want to endow the products of machines with the kinds of beauty found in ages past or obsolete techniques.

For once in art the issue of taste is one of understanding. What matters now is to furnish industry with modern form. The demands we make of form are demands of truth, because we want to prevent the kind of forms that belonged to handicraft and were often linked to techniques that are alien to machines. Instead we want to create a form that better agrees with the machines' technical capacities. Just as the appearance of a handmade object is highly dependent on the tools used, so there are in most cases certain forms that are more suitable for machines than others. It is a question of trying to determine these forms, trying to refine them, freeing them from inessentials and in this way arriving at the modern form. But what then are these modern forms? The answer is that modern form is indirectly the fruit of today's technology. Modern technology is at its most obvious in engineering products, in the new design values created through the new construction materials of iron and concrete. Our finest artists and architects want, to the best of their abilities, to liberate machine-made products from the kind of forms that do not belong to them and instead provide them with designs that suit modern technology.

[   ]When one views the problem as a duel between old and new, one can, as it were, divide industry into two camps, the conservative and the radical.[7] The radical camp includes areas where technology has prevailed to such an extent that it can determine its own forms itself. The center of this camp can be found in buildings of iron and concrete, where form is determined exclusively by calculating tolerances and deducing measurements, where, in other words, the products have been manufactured for the exclusive purpose of adapting swiftly and well to the demands made of them. In such cases conservative design is totally eliminated.

In this world of technical inventions, machines, and objects of use that are produced rationally with no consideration of form, nothing, as [Henry] van de Velde says, is ugly. Technology, condemned by nineteenth-century beauty zealots as the enemy of beauty, is for us that which creates beauty. It would be ridiculous to deny, for instance, that the objects manufactured by the optical and electrical industries, hygienic apparatus, surgical instruments, and a large number of metal tools offer the most consistent expression of modern beauty.

[   ]It is generally recognized today that the buildings of iron and concrete that offer the most elegant solutions from the point of view of statics in most cases also offer the most elegant solutions from the point of view of form. What is the consequence? Precisely this: that modern technology has acquired its own form, a modern form that earlier ages could not achieve because they lacked our technological resources. This was the radical camp in industry, where theoretical calculation determines the general direction that manufacturing is to take, if not perhaps in every detail. In this artists want no say, or if they do they are wrong. On the contrary they want to learn from these technologies and use their forms to prompt their own imaginations, to derive from them their own designs. Their desire is to transfer the forms discovered there, with the differences prompted by individual imaginations, to other industrial areas as well, where modern form is not obviously imposed through technology. These are for instance the glass, porcelain, and weaving industries, piano manufacture, picture-frame production, the textile industry, wallpaper industry, metal manufacturing, furniture production, and, by and large, all woodworking and linoleum manufacture and the like. These kinds of manufacturing industries belong to what I would call the conservative camp, where backward-looking forms exert a powerful influence. When it comes to the mechanical production of jacquard weave or linoleum, for instance, it is completely irrelevant whether one chooses a pattern of geometrical right angles or naturalistic floral motifs. To the best of my knowledge it is just as easy whichever one is chosen. In the same way, when making glass it makes no difference if you blow a bottle with straight sides or with the most exuberantly varied profile.

As has been pointed out above, during the nineteenth century it was quite obvious that mechanically produced articles endeavored to imitate the handmade. This was because the machine-made was considered ugly and needed the embellishment of borrowed forms that the machine, of course, *was capable* of producing because it can do everything, even if to do so would be alien to the nature of the machine. This is what was false. Today no perceptive constructor of a concrete bridge would dream of giving it the appearance of a Baroque structure in granite. The requirement of remaining true to his construction prevents him from doing so. It is this *demand for truth* that we would like to see maintained in industrial production as well, where forms do not have any necessary relationship to the technology.

But is artistic assistance required for this reason? The advocates of beauty were those who exercised restraint in the emergence of modern form. Instead this modern form is the creation of engineers and constructors. Maybe so, but engineers and constructors did not create modern form as form but as technology. The form was something secondary. For this reason the *technician* who produces a ceramic object, linoleum, or a glass bottle has no immediate interest in the form of his manufactured products but only in the materials of which they are made and their cost. Other than in relationship to the practical applications of the object, form is for him scarcely more than a question of novelty value, in other words an economic concern. For the public this is not at all the case. The public has no interest in the producer's profit or his technical problems, but the public wants a durable and beautiful product at a reasonable price. This is when the artist has to step in and provide the objects with a form that suits the method of manufacture, is up to date, and finally, is beautiful by virtue of these other characteristics. On behalf of the producers, as the representative of a direct interest in form, the artist wants to intervene and introduce modern beauty for those industries in which form is not intrinsic.

Truth also means fitness for purpose. The purpose of an object must find clear expression in its form. There are many earlier luxury objects for which this is far from the case, but which are nevertheless copied zealously. But a seventeenth-century tureen, whose beauty and magnificence we now admire, was perhaps intended to grace the table at some festive banquet and cannot have the same form as one that is taken out and used every day. We have neither the wealth nor the servants this would require. Yet no logical objection can be made to the copying of *simple*, older everyday objects provided that there is agreement between the manufacturing process and their use.

Our hygienic requirements are also more stringent. This means that we feel very comfortable with the modern, somewhat more austere forms that appear to offer greater cleanliness than all the old showpieces of the past.

With this I have tried to say that our endeavor to introduce beauty of form in industry is currently not merely an emotional matter but also a rational concern. If a demand for truth is introduced for all manufacture in order to attain a simple, beautiful form that is consistent with the method of production and takes advantage of what it offers, this will, I believe, lead to the elimination of the ugliness that prevails in modern society and liberate us from the historical styles that bedevil contemporary architecture and decorative art. Determining beauty is an extremely precarious task, but one condition would be fulfilled if uniformity and simplicity of form could be found in every product, especially if this uniformity were also that which was best suited to its purpose. Then, at some future date when we sit more firmly in the saddle and have regained our cultivated feeling for form, the time would be ripe to make once again both magnificent and technically complicated objects.

In this way industry and art could assist each other. Art assisting industry to attain beauty of form; industry assisting art to make closer contact with modern technology, and through this acquire new impulses and a wider sphere of action. Art and industry would be able to be natural allies rather than enemies.

Garden urn by Ivar Johnsson, Näfveqvarn.

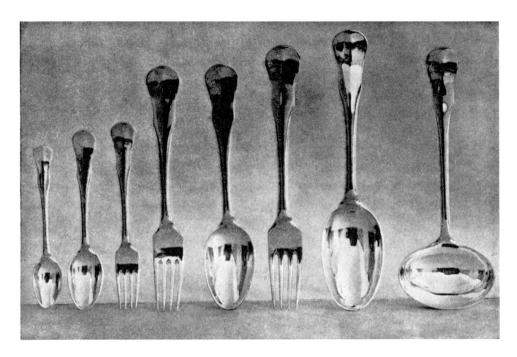

Cutlery from Guldsmedsbolaget.

3.

BEAUTY AND QUALITY

The discussions above can hardly have been of any great interest to manufacturers or retailers. They have been general, theoretical, and have focused on society as a whole, of which manufacturers and retailers only form parts. No individual parts of society consciously allow themselves to be governed by general motives, but obey in their actions only their own laws, that is, economic ones. Only if we demonstrate the economic importance of efforts to give their products good form can we count on any interest from manufacturers and retailers. It will now be proved that this is the case.

First, good form has value as a means of competition. Of two technically equivalent products, the one that also has good form should create greater demand. Particularly as the educated public in all sectors of society in our country are not generally content to accept inferior values in terms of form but look for the best available in this respect, it is obvious that they are likely to seek out improved industrial products avidly. A very large number of Swedish homes are set up from home-crafts shops.[8] People value the carefully crafted form and sound quality of home-crafted products and, when they are able to, avoid industrial products in their favor. But on the whole, because of the way in which they are made, home-crafted products are expensive, so it could be expected that if machine-made objects were to be given forms that were as good (and here I am in no way suggesting that they should imitate the home-crafted products, may fortune protect us from any more such attempts) because production is cheaper they would win over some buyers who do not value home-crafted products solely because they are handmade. I believe that one could very reliably conduct a survey of the Swedish businesses that sell well-formed products (for instance, the advertisers in this publication) and receive the response that they have only positive experiences of the importance of form as a means of competition.[9]

We must also consider our relationship to other countries where export and import are concerned. In the next section I shall refer to some major events abroad that show that in other countries this is a particularly current concern. For our exports, therefore, our products are required to be as good as, or rather better than, the foreign ones and by the same means we can prevent the excessive import of goods which for reasons of taste alone, but not their technical qualities or their cheapness, are superior to ours. Judging from the attitude of Swedish industrialists toward legislation on protection of design, it is more than likely that they are fully aware of the significance of design as a competitive factor but place little faith in being able to create this themselves, as their opposition to design protection is mainly that it would make it difficult for Swedish manufacturers to copy foreign designs with impunity. No importance seems to be attached to the protection that it would at the same time afford their own. This hardly indicates any self-esteem.

Now, the rallying cry in industry is the appeal for quality. The question of price, at least at the moment, does not have the overwhelming significance it once possessed. Now quality has taken its place. In one of his latest publications (*Die neue Wirtschaft*) [The new economy], [Walther] Rathenau refers to the national economic necessity of ceasing to manufacture goods that can only exist in the market because of their cheapness.[10] This leads to the waste of raw materials and labor. Only quality goods should be produced. His words can probably be applied with no amendment to circumstances in Sweden, given our scarcity of raw materials and our high wages. If quality goods are manufactured that can be used for longer periods than shoddy ones, there will be no need to reduce wages to make the cost of living cheaper.

It is in this context that the demand for *standardization* is made. Standardization is after all a creation of types by industry that reduces the production of surplus goods and organizes the production of useful ones so rationally that every working hour can be used to full advantage.[11]

Demands for quality and for standardization have arisen as a result of the war, but are in no way new. These demands are already found in the writings of most social reformers, comprising, for instance, part of the doctrine of theoretical anarchism formulated by [Peter] Kropotkin.[12] Economic conditions in society cannot be permanently improved through wage raises, but only by perfecting labor and working methods so that the amount of work required for existence can be reduced.

But in what way do these demands relate to the demand for good form? Well, good form can provide one means of enabling or facilitating the implementation of standardization and quality. Let us assume that at the moment we have one thousand types of a certain product. There would be economic advantages in reducing them to ten. But on what basis do we eliminate types when nine hundred and ninety versions have been produced to satisfy the specific desires of some individuals? Would not standardization when applied to haberdashery and other things for everyday use be regarded as *rationing*?! Then it would become impossible to implement because of its unpopularity. If standardization is to be possible for everyday goods where form is significant, this cannot be as the result of a simple process of elimination but through the creation of *new types*, which because of their form have novelty value and can therefore supersede the old ones in public taste! These new forms, both rational and of new types, will certainly be created most easily through the cooperation of forward-looking and perceptive industrialists and good artists.

In what way do form and quality belong to each other?

For quality, not only are good materials and production methods required. An object must also possess good form, which enables the other qualities to find expression. If a tailor sews a suit of handwoven cloth using the design a village tailor would employ for a jacket of homespun, he would be called a bungler, as in no way would he do the fine fabric justice. If a modern leather suitcase were to be designed like a carpetbag, its owner would be a laughingstock. But why does nobody laugh when a garden bench with armrests of first-class cast iron is designed to imitate artfully woven branches? This is difficult to understand. It can only be explained by considering the peculiar convention described earlier (page [82]) whereby for some products that are new in purely technological terms and have been allowed to acquire their form, good form is taken for granted, but for others all feeling has been lost for the connections that exist between form and certain techniques and materials. We do not notice the falsity in borrowing a tapestry design for wallpaper. But wallpaper is produced on a printing press and its decoration should appear to be printed and not woven. Graphic artists, not textile designers, should create these patterns. Let us now compare three such cases with each other. This involves choosing between 1) a wallpaper of excellent paper with long-lasting colors but an ugly pattern, for instance extremely loud colors: yellow, orange, green, or a confused, badly composed design; 2) a wallpaper of inexpensive but long-lasting paper printed with a simple but tasteful pattern; and 3) a wallpaper of inferior paper with a pattern that is neither beautiful nor ugly. The first costs five kronor a meter, the second one krona fifty öre, and the third seventy-five öre. Which should I choose? Naturally the second, even if I can well afford the first, because the good material in the first has been destroyed by bad form. There should never be any question of the last, as buying it would be a waste of the country's raw materials as well as of my own money.

A formal requirement for quality is also *originality* in the best meaning of the term. No object can ever have the best form if it is a copy. An original design made for a specific manufacturing process is better than a copy of what was originally a better product. Unfortunately, when a beautiful and striking new model appears on the market it is extremely common for Swedish manufacturers to leap at it immediately so that it can be copied and then in time marketed in garbled form. Here they never take into account the fact that in many cases it is the specific nature of the object, its novelty value, that makes it so attractive, and that when the copies reach the market they lack the charm of originality and therefore acquire no economic value. It is self-evident that a different value is placed on something made by an artist than on a copy, but this seems impossible for an industrialist to understand. This is not plucked out of the air: genuine instances can be cited. What I have in mind is a case in which someone intended to copy a design by an artist for a porcelain factory that was successful at Svenska Mässan [The Swedish trade fair] in 1918 in the belief that the copy would yield the same financial profit as the original.[13] Naturally this was a miscalculation.

Wall clock by Oscar Brandtberg.

Glasses by E. J. Margold, produced by L. Noack, Darmstadt.

4.

ABROAD

I have thus far attempted to give a presentation of what characterizes modern taste, its origins, its characteristic features, its conditions, its position in society, its links to industry and to commerce. Now it is appropriate to demonstrate these ideas in the *international* context of which they form a part.

In 1907 in Germany, artists, manufacturers, retailers, and art lovers founded the Deutscher Werkbund.[14] They wanted their members to comprise a selection of what was best in industry, handicraft, commerce, and art, to provide a meeting place for those who strove for quality in their work, and so foster "the ennoblement of work through the collaboration of art, industry, and handicraft, through education, publicity, and by adopting firm standpoints on related issues."[15] Decisive in this work is the concept of quality, advocating it to the state and to public opinion and encouraging it through the fruitful cooperation of art, industry, handicraft, and trade. "The former unity between the design of a work and its production can no longer be found in one and the same person; therefore fusing these different forces in mutually reliant collaboration is necessary for development."[16] The Deutscher Werkbund is intended to provide the forum required for cooperation of this kind. Ultimately, it was concern about German exports that the founders had in mind. The German art industry did not have the same long-standing reputation as its English and French counterparts; it had to earn its reputation, and therefore it was important to produce goods that from the point of view of taste surpassed their competitors. The founders came to believe that on the whole German products were rejected even though they were cheaper (*billig und schlecht*) than those from other countries, so that it was necessary to create products that were superior to those of the foreign competitors, irrespective of price.[17] As these competitors now had raw materials as good as Germany's and could therefore produce goods of equally high material quality, the only recourse for the Germans was to outdo the competition with higher formal quality; and as those who could best of all create formal quality were artists, artists were employed to serve in industry. Today German goods have, on the whole, good form. Of course we encounter national idiosyncrasies that are difficult for other tastes to accept, but I believe that we have a preference for many German products just because of their better formal qualities. The movement in Germany grew immensely, and in 1914 it had 1,870 members, most of them businesses. The state, which immediately recognized the national importance of this movement, soon began to cooperate loyally. The Werkbund concept was to be a guiding principle for all the forces that sought to unite culture, economics, and production in this modern, fragmented society. Almost all industries experienced a new revival as a result of this cooperation. And now, when the fate of Germany is really in the balance, people are once again turning to the Werkbund concept, which before the war opened up new world markets for German industry, in order to consolidate the country's domestic industrial situation. This trend is suggested by the following extract of a missive from the government to the Werkbund endorsing the organization's work:

"What utilitarian goods lack in the variety and richness of their materials must be compensated for by their sturdiness and artistic design, if their simplicity is not to be impoverished and cultural requirements stifled. Work on quality will therefore be the battle cry for German handicraft and industry. Only through this will we be able to develop the powers that reside within us and that nobody can deprive us of: ideas and diligence."[18]

In addition, this basic Werkbund philosophy is assured influence in the reconstruction of German economic life.

As a result of the work of the Werkbund in Germany, before the war German goods displaced those of other countries in many areas and created new markets for German exports. Competitors have paid careful attention to this, particularly since the outbreak of the war, and it is rather significant that in England and France movements developed during the war with the direct aim of transplanting German conditions to English and French industries. There, as in Germany, it has been found that in the long run the sole effective means of competition lies in the development of the quality of the form of products. In March 1915 an exhibition was arranged in England of all the wholly German-made products that had been imported to England before the war, and there was a great deal of amazement when it was discovered that German manufacturers dominated the English market to a far greater extent than had been considered.[19] As a result of this exhibition, one economist, Sir Leo Chiozza Money, wrote that the only way in which the United Kingdom could maintain its exports to the extent that had previously prevailed was to link artistic and scientific work with industry. Sir Leo added in this context that he had seen with gratification how those who had arranged this British exhibition of German goods had acknowledged this fact, and that hitherto in several industrial sectors, such as glass, porcelain, earthenware, paint, and linoleum manufacture, scientific production methods had been combined with artistic considerations.[20] Other eminent Englishmen, architects, art critics, and economists, are ardent advocates of the German movement and are attempting to persuade their fellow countrymen to imitate it.

This is not going to happen through imitation of their forms. It is not a question of getting hold of the German forms. Distinctive national features may still be retained as before. Indeed, it is by retaining them and by endowing products with appropriate but still completely distinctive forms that one can really follow this German movement. In England, laboring under the yoke of war, it has been possible to issue a categorical imperative to manufacturers that it is their duty to their trade to raise the quality of their production and every worker's duty to raise the quality of his own individual work. On the German model a "Design and Industries Association" has been established in which specialist groups have been set up, composed of manufacturers, artists, and retailers, with each group endeavoring within its area to reorganize production completely, attempting to eliminate customary routines and introduce modern artistic and scientific methods.[21] The charter of the English association contains the following statement: "Every manufacturer owes a duty to his trade: to improve the quality of the work under his control."[22] A statement about which the English writer A[rthur] Clutton Brock has made the following comment in an article entitled "Art and Trade": "Unless the manufacturers and the craftsmen of a nation are aware of this duty and perform it; unless they make an effort beyond the effort necessary to get money, they will in time cease even to get money."[23] In other words, it is clear that *between the possibility of selling an object and its autonomous and well-formed appearance there is a definite dependency relationship*. On this subject another Englishman, A[lfred] Lys Baldry, expressed his opinion in his article "A New Body with New Aims": "It must be frankly admitted that in many branches of industrial art we have been fairly beaten by Germany and Austria, because the relation of art to commerce has been more shrewdly studied and better understood in those countries than it has been here. [...] Fundamentally there is this difference between us and these, our most dangerous competitors; we do not properly appreciate the enormous commercial value of art and its earning power in home and foreign markets."[24]

Endeavors are being made in France to follow the example of England. In his book *Le guerre artistique avec l'Allemagne* [The artistic war with Germany], Marius Vachon deals with the Deutscher Werkbund.[25] In an issue of *Le Gaulois*, a General Cherfils describes the German organization for the artistic enhancement of industrial production. The general notes in particular the German organization of building operations. "Companies have been founded that take over the complete erection and furnishing of hotels down to the most insignificant trifles; others install gas, water, and electrical fixtures in the buildings, and there are yet others on whose plans the construction of the marshalling yards at Darmstadt and Aachen have been based."[26]

A "Werkbund" or associations with similar ambitions can also be found in Austria, Hungary, Switzerland, and Holland.[27]

Flower stand by Wilhelm Kåge. Gustavsberg.

5.
SVENSKA SLÖJDFÖRENINGEN
[THE SWEDISH ARTS AND CRAFTS SOCIETY]

The spokesman in Sweden for endeavors to introduce good form to industry is Svenska Slöjdföreningen [The Swedish arts and crafts society], which was reorganized in 1915 for this purpose. To the general public, the first visible result of this new association was the exhibition of furniture for small apartments arranged in 1917 at Liljevalchs konsthall [Liljevalch art gallery], and then in Göteborg and Malmö.[28]

Tea caddy by Wilhelm Kåge. Gustavsberg.

The idea of the exhibition was in principle to attempt to achieve for modern Swedish decorative art *a definitive shift from the isolated production of individuals to the purposeful collective endeavors of a whole generation for a culture of form founded on a broad social basis.*

Svenska Slöjdföreningen wanted to introduce Werkbund concepts in Sweden. While it was seeking ways to do so, the idea arose of an exhibition of the furnishing and equipment of simple apartments. As the proposed household objects (though not the furniture) had to be factory-produced for the first time, the exhibition could only be made possible by gaining the interest of manufacturers. For this purpose the society established its referral agency, whose work made it possible to display the first samples of collaboration between art and industry.[29] The companies exhibiting were Gustavsberg

Tableware by Edward Hald. Rörstrand.

and Rörstrand; Andersson & Johansson, Höganäs; Höganäs-Billeholms a.-b.; S:t Eriks lervarufabriker [St. Erik's earthenware factories], Uppsala; Uppsala-Ekeby a.-b.; Orrefors glasbruk [Orrefors glassworks]; A.-B. Svenska Kristallglasbruken [Swedish crystal glassworks]; Guldsmedsaktiebolaget [Goldsmith's corporation]; C. G. Hallberg, jeweler to the Swedish Court; K. A. Andersson, jeweler to the Swedish Court; A.-B. Wilhelm Becker; Petrus Forssberg; Elektriska industri a.-b. [Electric industry]; Böhlmarks lampfabrik [Böhlmark lamp factory]; A. S. E. A.; J. E. Sundquist, Kinna; Göteborgs nya matt- och möbeltygsaffär [Göteborg new carpet and furnishing fabric store]; Bolinders mek[aniska] verkstads a.-b. [Bolinder mechanical workshop], Husqvarna; Svenska velociped- och motorverken [Swedish bicycle and motor works], Ängelholm; Kockums järnverk [Kockum ironworks]; Näfveqvarns bruk [Näfveqvarn works]; Skoglund & Olsson, a.-b.; Järnverksmagasin [Ironworks store], Malmö; Elektriska a.-b. Volta; K. G. Berggren, Stocksund; Handöls nya täljstens a.-b. [Handöl new soapstone]; Svenska Metallverken [Swedish metalworks], Västerås;

Crystal vase by Edward Hald. Orrefors.

Stockholms nya tapetsfabriks a.-b. [Stockholm new wallpaper factory]; Kåbergs tapetaffär [Kåberg wallpaper store]; Norrby nya a.-b. [Norrby new]; Linderoths and Tornbergs urfabriker [Linderoth and Tornberg clock factories]; P. A. Norstedt & Söner förlag [P. A. Norstedt & Sons publishers]; Föreningen Originalträsnitt [Society for original woodcuts].

 The exhibition included furniture, stoves for cooking and heating, as well as articles of everyday use such as glass, crockery, kitchen utensils, light fixtures, together with wallpaper and textiles and, last but far from least, a specially arranged section for drawings and models of small apartments and cottages for allotment gardens.[30]

 The leading artists taking part were Hakon Ahlberg, E[rik] G[unnar] Asplund, Folke Bensow, Harald Bergsten, Oscar Brandtberg, S[ten] Branzell, D[avid] Dahl, Johannes Dahl, Petrus Forssberg, Einar Forseth, John Färngren, Simon Gate, Sidney Gibson, Elsa Gullberg, Edw[ard] Hald, Ragnar Hjorth, Eva Jahnke-Björk, Akke Kumlien, Wilh[elm] Kåge, Carl Malmsten, Carl Nilsson,

Bottle by Edward Hald. Orrefors.

David Nilsson, K[arl] Norberg, Ruben Nordström, E[dvin] Olsson-Ollers, Ture Ryberg, Ernst Spolén, U[no] Åhrén, J[acob] Ängman, Agda Österberg.

The exhibition was a major and justified public success. Its practical purpose was naturally not that easy to achieve, but some of the furniture, as well as many of the other objects created for the exhibition, are now on sale at Nordiska kompaniet [The Nordic company].[31]

On the other hand, it has not been possible to start factory production of most of the furniture. We must hope that this can be attributed to the current economic crisis.

Clock case by Harald Bergstens A. B. Industri- och
hantverksalster, Falun.

This exhibition—which, of course, if we look closely at details, displayed work
that did not fully live up to its aims but which, on the whole, was more than likely a
major and significant step in the establishment of a democratic culture of taste—was
also the first visible outcome of the general endeavors of Svenska Slöjdföreningen to
draw artists and industry together through its referral agency. As a result, a number of
artists were employed after the exhibition by several industrial companies.

The cases in which such cooperation has been arranged are the following:
Simon Gate and Edward Hald at Orrefors glasbruk, Edvin O[ls]son-Ollers at

Cretonne pattern by Greta Sellberg-
Welamson. Norrby nya a.-b.

Wallpaper by Uno Åhrén.
Kåbergs tapetaffär.

Förenade Kristallglasbruken [United crystal glassworks], Edward Hald at Rörstrand,
Wilh[elm] Kåge at Gustavsberg, Ivar Johnsson at Näfveqvarns bruk, Johannes Dahl
at Elektriska industri a.-b., Einar Forseth at Lidköpings porslinsfabrik [Lidköping
porcelain factory]. In addition cooperation has been initiated between the
following: a totally new series of sixteen tiled stoves for Oskarshamns kakelfabriks
a.-b. [Oskarshamn tile factory], the architect Nils Blanck has designed electric
heating stoves for A.-B. Elektraverken, some supplementary work has been carried
out for Uppsala-Ekeby kakelfabriks a.-b. [Uppsala-Ekeby tile factory] on the tiled
stoves displayed at the exhibition. Carl Malmsten, Einar Forseth, and Uno Åhrén
have created a number of popular wallpapers for Kåbergs tapetaffär. Forseth has
continued his work for Wilh[elm] Becker, etc. That these artists have not devoted
their attention to luxury products is shown by the fact that for at least one of
the above companies their payment consists in part of a bonus based on the *total*
production of the factory.

Wallpaper by Einar Forseth. Kåbergs tapetaffär.

Wallpaper by Carl Malmsten.
Kåbergs tapetaffär.

In addition to the more permanent relationships, a number of temporary commissions have also been arranged, in some cases through Svenska Slöjdföreningen. Cretonnes have been created for Norrby nya a.-b. by Carl Malmsten and Greta Sellberg-Welamson, Sven Jonsson has created electric light fixtures for Nordiska kompaniet, Böhlmarks lampfabrik, and Herman Bergmans konstgjuteri a.-b. [Herman Bergman art foundry]. A number of new commissions for wallpaper, tiled stoves, etc., have been completed for Bergslagets byggnadsbolag [Bergslaget building company], the most recent a new type of heating stove according to a design by Carl Malmsten. The same artist has provided the interior decor of the reading room at Uddeholms bruk [Uddeholm works]. Paper-yarn carpets have been produced on behalf of Nya Svenska möbeltygs- och mattfabriks a.-b. [New Swedish furnishing fabric and carpet factory] and Nordiska kompaniet using designs by Elsa Gullberg.

There is no room here to list the work undertaken for private individuals.

Soapstone stove by Ture Ryberg. Handöl.

Garden urn by Edward Hald. Rörstrand.

Moreover, it would not be too bold to suggest that the endeavors launched by Nordiska kompaniet through Carl G. Bergsten to produce furniture for bourgeois homes—the handsome results of which were exhibited at the recently opened display on the premises of its new furniture department—are an indirect outcome of the ideas of Svenska Slöjdföreningen, as Bergsten has been an active member of the society's executive committee since its reorganization. A similar position is held by the director of one of our leading quality publishers, the master printer Hugo Lagerström. In the same way it could well be claimed that Akke Kumlien's permanent position as adviser on design at P. A. Norstedt & Söner, with the ensuing rise in quality of this company's publications, is probably the outcome of the initiatives of some of the individual members of the committee.

There are of course considerably more industries as well as artists working in the spirit of our ideas than those listed here. Those named here merely serve to prove the possibility of raising the standards of the form of products with the help of artists.

It must be pointed out, however, that the cases in which cooperation with industry of this kind has been initiated are too few in number. Nevertheless, one would like to hope that the hesitation, indifference, indeed disinclination that has hitherto been shown in many cases by industrialists will be banished by insight into the importance of cooperation.

Svenska Slöjdföreningen is not acting on its own behalf; quite the opposite, it has been said that its referral agency is working "to ensure its own extinction." When its assistance in establishing cooperation between industry and art is no longer required, when this commonly exists, it will have attained its ends, and its current publicity activities will then be redundant.

Admittedly, this goal is a good way off. If the goal is to be reached at all, it will be paramount for the larger industries to realize the importance of the issue. Their greater capacity to deliver will rapidly enable them to influence the market and distribute their products so that they will gain the upper hand over old-fashioned ones and set the tone for the entire stock of the retailers. Until this has happened, there can be no talk of a general culture of taste.

Crystal bowl by Simon Gate. Orrefors.

6.
THE ARTIST

Theoretically it should therefore be clear that design, even of objects of everyday use, should be entrusted to society's specialists in form, the artists. Allowing applied artists, as is mainly the case today, to sit making trinkets for an interested and affluent few while the form of industrial products is determined by purely technical draftsmen can scarcely be considered right. Surely the special talents of the former group should be used to the benefit of as large a section of society as possible, in other words through uniting the labor of industry and art.

But it would be wrong not to reveal that this endeavor encounters practical obstacles not only in trade and industry but also among the artists. In all honesty this should be made clear right from the beginning. The public and the producers are often confused by the talk about the role of art in the business world when after all artists—admittedly to an extremely restricted extent—have previously been employed without attaining the results intended here. The current endeavors of the artists also in fact involve a struggle between one generation of artists and another. The younger artists—in years or at heart—are in more or less direct conflict with the older architects and applied artists, who are often hostile to cooperation with industry. The reason for this is that their hearts are set on unique works, and they consider industrial reproduction a form of profanation. Here, from their point of view, they are right, as a piece produced as a handmade original cannot be reproduced without being debased. Nor do they want to comply with the demands that industry makes of them. They want total freedom in all they do. We can well allow them to remain totally at odds with public needs. The artistic movement whose slogan was "art for art's sake" cannot, of course, develop a sudden interest in the socialization of art.

Finally the *style* of the work of the older generations is out of date. They employ illogical ornamentation and decorative motifs that are inappropriate to the materials used; this is exactly what the younger generation of artists wants to replace with ornament and decoration that is more appropriate to purpose and materials.

We therefore have every reason to make certain demands of the artists who would like to enter into cooperation with industry. Once done, many misunderstandings and shattered illusions may be avoided.

Only those artists who are prepared to subordinate themselves to certain production requirements may be considered for this collaboration. This expression is not of course to be taken literally, so that the managers of factories and workshops may treat artists as day laborers, but so that in his work the artist pays continual attention to ensuring that what he does is compatible with manufacturing methods. As his work is to be reproduced in many copies and has to be manufactured without his direct firsthand involvement, he may not base his artistic effects on what can only be produced once or by his hand alone. The form and decoration must be one that a machine can execute, and the composition one whose beauty is not dependent on temporary effects but on controllable assembly. He may not walk into the factory and tinker with his own projects and cause confusion, but must comply with the factory regulations. For certain artists, this can be difficult.

A dreary position some may say, but in error. Because it is conceivable—and indeed it has happened—that *mechanical techniques can be developed by the artist*. When cooperation has advanced to the point that the technological and the artistic have a mutual influence on each other, then the goal has been attained, then new and original styles will arise, and I believe neither the artist nor the technician will regret their mutual adaptation to each other.

That this is possible has already been demonstrated by many examples during the few years that such cooperation has existed in Sweden and abroad: when the three-color printing machine at Gustavsberg was used to print three shades of the same blue pigment instead of parading the full extent of the spectrum, or when at the same factory the artist drove technicians to invent "square" turning. When at Orrefors glasbruk experiments led to the development of *graal* glass.[32] None of these would have seen the light of day if the artist had not inspired the technician to new efforts, while on the other hand the technicians showed the artist what path to take.

Today, from the artist's point of view, is a very suitable moment for this kind of cooperation, partly because art now has a palpably decorative quality and also because it is seeking new forms of expression. On the whole, the goals that younger artists seek to attain differ from those of their predecessors: they want to cast a great deal overboard to enable instead a much surer mastery of the aesthetic entities, the decorative, the ornamental, and in architecture the purely cubic. They are not encumbered by the inherited prejudices of the previous generation of easel painters against the utilitarian applications of art, and in their forms they seek simple but powerful effects. This makes them ready to deal with technical processes. The demands now made of technology not to imitate handicrafts, whose beauty lies after all in the craftsmanship, fit well with the artistic inclination for simple effects.

The younger artists are, therefore, *on the whole*, well suited to serve the needs of industry.

But with applied artists of the old school, who do not have the adaptability required, industry should, however unjust it may seem to say to these apparently deserving men, proceed with caution. In nine cases out of ten they are the victims of prejudices which have arisen because the entire arts and crafts movement of the previous era came into being as a *reaction against* industry, to produce beautiful, unique pieces in contrast to the many ugly machine-made ones.

After what has been said here, it is clear that cooperation between individual artists and individual industrialists cannot be established immediately without mutual concessions. They are both bound—however honorable their desires—by the differences in their approach. But since knowledge of the causes of an evil also tells us a great deal about how to eliminate it, what has been said here provides no reason to shrink from the brief time it may take for both to become inseparable friends.

Stove by Ruben Nordström. Skoglund & Olsson.

Blown glasses by Emil [*sic*, Edvin] Olsson-Ollers. Pukebergs glasbruk.

7.
THE PRODUCER

The German architect Heinrich Tessenow says at one point in his book *Vom Hausbau und dergleichen* [House-building and such things]: "When I see the beautiful works that are at times produced in certain small workshops I always have an unconditional desire to pity them, just as I feel each autumn about the tiny dwarf apple trees: 'Poor little tree with such large, beautiful apples.' We do not want this kind of pity for our work, however; we want to be a large and sturdy tree that of course yields large, beautiful fruit."[33]

There is something mannered and alien to our big world in much of the applied art that is produced. We give it our respect, even our admiration, but at the

Room by Carl Malmsten. Nordiska kompaniet.

same time we feel sorry for the producer, who like a monk in his cloister, innocent of the condition of the world, creates these mannered works, airy as bubbles on the broad current of life. For the producer and the art lover, there is something sentimental in their affection for products of this kind, in valuing the solitary work of the hand over the work of the machine. In many cases, in fact, they object not to what the work produces but the *way in which the work is done*. The master's exultation in his beautiful and varied handwork is compared to the laborer's indifference to inferior goods made by the dozen. Yet it is obvious that work should be judged on the basis of what it produces: twenty beautiful machine-made products are of greater value than one made by hand.

But small workshops play an important role as examples, and in some respects as pioneers, where quality is concerned. In our day we have now found

Room from Nordiska kompaniet.

it necessary to produce beautiful goods mechanically, but if this is to be possible, factories are required to set the same lofty targets as the workshops. In other words, the demand for quality should come first.

Similarly it ought to be important to introduce job satisfaction in the factories. It was mainly because of the tedium of working at the machines that William Morris considered industry to be the enemy of art. Rodin says: "If the joy of the artist in his creation can infect the carpenter, bricklayers when they mix their cement, coachmen when they harness their horses, this would lead to a marvelous improvement of society."[34] The statement is paradoxical but well worth considering. Does the work in a modern factory have to be so taxing? Of course not. Pleasure can be found in most forms of work, and a good way of introducing it—apart of course from perfecting its organization—is to make the products of labor and the working environment beautiful. Almost everywhere we can see how bad conditions are in our factories: plaster that has fallen, paint that has disappeared, filthy walls and the like. But in the Deutsche Werkstätten in Hellerau the factory building is beautiful and flowers adorn the stairways![35] Nothing is ruined! The respect of the worker is aroused by this orderliness and beauty; he takes care of his place of work and finds pleasure in being there.

It is sheer necessity for society to make work more pleasant. Beauty is admittedly only a minor part of what is needed, but it is an important one that can support the others.

The aim should of course be to ensure that work is carried out with interest. Much of the intellectual, advanced commercial, industrial, and administrative work undertaken in our sordid times is *motivated by interest in the work*, and financial recompense takes only second place. Why should it be impossible to organize factory work so that it is also the case there?

When artists and industrialists cooperate, some adjustment in the organization of the work is required. Here we are bound by customs as everywhere else. The work of the artists may mean that some old stereotypes will have to be rejected, that some small details in the production process will have to be altered. This may arouse the anger of a conservative overseer. In the past the overseer had undisputed power over the organization of the work. It is therefore necessary to ensure that cooperation between him and the artist is arranged not on the basis of rivalry but in mutual trust. Some audacity and adaptability will be required of the overseer in adapting to what is new.

In factories we often find that the overseer or the superintendent adheres to the old models out of pure sloth and indifference. There, of course, the work of the artist will be difficult. But when, as is often the case, the managers of a factory have a genuine interest in form it should be easy for him to direct this interest away from the old, out-of-date routines to those that are in tune with the modern age. Nor should it be difficult to foster the interest of the workers, as they will gladly accept changes that will make their work more pleasant. In certain cases the interests of the artist may clash with those of the workers, which is when the former wants to eliminate an entire technique and render the skills that have been acquired redundant. Here, of course, for practical reasons the path of compromise must be adopted. If, rather than declaring outright that cut-crystal should be done away with, which would lead to conflict with an entire group of workers, attempts are made to see that cut-crystal becomes more beautiful, then one such compromise has been found, a compromise which should not be despised but can lead to new and unexpected ideas.

The references above to small workshops mean workshops that produce high-quality goods. But there are also small workshops that produce second-class work, owned by craftsmen with no real professional ambition, who because of their lack of enterprise and talent have not been able to endow their products with exemplary quality, but whose occupational pride will not permit them to work in a factory. These workshops are often strongly opposed to innovation. From our point of view, these workshops have no right to exist but are a burden on our shoulders. They are also certainly a hindrance from an economic standpoint. Small workshops only have the right to exist insofar as they produce the quality work that factories cannot manage.

The goods produced in the past were often made of better materials than those of today. Many things that will only last a short time are now being produced with poor materials. In the next section I shall return to this point, and here I merely want to state that it should be the goal of every ambitious manufacturer to refrain from such production.

However cheap a thing of this kind may be, its production is, from the point of view of the material, a waste. The world's supply of raw materials is not so large that in the long run we can exploit it as we have during recent decades. As the cooperation of art with industry will lead to quality products, this will lead to *economies with materials*.

In recent years attempts have been made to stimulate public demand for goods by labeling them "Made in Sweden." But it is self-evident that public demand cannot in the long term be stimulated if the quality of the products is not superior to those from abroad. A national effort such as the Göteborg trade fair must of course, if it is to bear fruit completely, be backed up by goods that are of better quality than foreign ones.[36] Only those Swedish goods that are superior to foreign ones should replace them. Swedishness is not in itself an objective reason in this context but merely a romantic justification.

Service by Wilhelm Kåge. Gustavsberg.

8.
THE SALESMAN

An effective form of sabotage recommended to shop assistants by syndicalists is to tell the truth about the goods they sell. This advice reveals with appalling cynicism the moral condition of the world of commerce. Businessmen base their actions on deceiving the public! It is not possible to object that the danger is not so great, as if poor and dishonest products form an exception. They do not form an exception, because they can be found in virtually every shop: a quantity of rubbish that looks good and of course appeals to the poorest purses. Anyone at all can go anywhere and will find that goods are on offer that are mere rubbish, shirts that are worn out when first used, leather bags that are not made of leather, shoes that cannot withstand water, etc. It all looks fine in the shop windows. This is the reverse face of the imitative skills of the nineteenth century.

If a retailer had but one ounce of feeling for quality, his conscience would forbid the sale of goods like this.

Pots and pans from Skultuna.

But now he defends himself by claiming to be a mere intermediary between the manufacturer and the public. What manufacturers want to produce and the public is prepared to buy—*à la bonheur*—he sells at a profit. But if one speaks to a manufacturer to reproach him, he complains in his turn about the retailer. The retailer would rather have poor and cheap products than good ones that are expensive. The manufacturer is probably correct. For in many cases the retailer wants to lower the quality of the goods against the manufacturer's will. The retailer considers quality to be of no account; his concern is to make the greatest profit as best he can.

The merchant blames the public: "This is what it wants." No, that is not the case. The merchant panders to the public's worst desires. In his display windows he spreads out a wealth of products with conspicuous price tags and the public is informed that here are the cheapest and most elegant scarves, handkerchiefs, hats, clothes, picture frames, etc. If you enter the shop and touch them with your hands, you will, if you are discerning, soon decline the goods, but how many can resist the low price? The merchant exploits cheapness, the greater inclination of the public to spend small amounts more often and large ones rarely. As the wages of the lower classes are usually paid each week, they become unwilling, not to say unable, to pay a large amount. They would rather spend ten kronor ten times over fifty kronor at once. This is presumably what the merchant has exploited. It may well be impossible to change this general tendency completely until another system of paying wages has been introduced, but one could nevertheless require an ambition among retailers not to sell pure rubbish in their shops. Because the rubbish can actually lead to the extinction of good products. When one fine piece of work stands out alone or together with others equally as fine it retains its beauty,

Tea caddy by
Edward Hald. Rörstrand.

but when placed among ugly ones its isolation makes it ugly too. The new tinted glasses manufactured by Kosta seem quite different when seen among others of their like in a quality shop rather than in the midst of the rubbishy offerings of an inferior furniture store.[37]

This question deserves more thorough study, as this is probably where the nub of the retailer's indifference to what is beautiful and new may be found.

In addition, the taste of the salesman's underlings and assistants needs to be trained, as does the taste of the traveling salesmen who link the manufacturer and the retailer. How does it help if a manufacturer produces a beautiful product when his traveling salesmen will make no effort to sell it? In Germany courses arranged to acquaint shop assistants and traveling salesmen with the new movement have turned out to have excellent results. The same thing should be organized in Sweden. Perhaps this would enable some moderation of the balderdash spoken by assistants about the spurious goods, and be the first step toward the abolition of these products. There is, moreover, something characteristic about the way in which more is said on behalf of a poor product than of a quality item. Is bad conscience at work? A quality item will always last, can always be sold, but it is best to make a profit from an inferior one as soon as possible.

It is not fitting for society to allow itself to be directed by profit motives whatever the outcome. But it must be conceded that bringing about any change in this respect will be extremely difficult, because of the nature of commerce as a whole. It can only be achieved if the best of our merchants set a good example and show that selling quality goods can be just as profitable. Here the small, specialized shops that have been able to survive in competition with the large department stores solely because of the quality of the goods they sell demonstrate the truth of this statement.

Department stores are based on the principle of mass sales, and the quality aspect has had to give way. This is not, however, a necessary consequence. Sweden's largest department store, Nordiska kompaniet, which differs significantly in principle from continental department stores, can thus be described as a quality shop. It has always shown itself willing to adopt new ideas concerning cooperation between artists and industry, and artists have often found valuable support there.

This may demonstrate that there is no risk involved for large stores in placing quality before quantity.

The principle of raising turnover by increasing the *number* of goods produced is erroneous from an economic point of view because of the waste of raw materials and labor. There can be just as much profit for the manufacturer, worker, and retailer, if not more, from the sale of quality products alone.

And last and finally, the finances of their customers will benefit as well.

This and the previous chapter have indicated that circumstances that are almost social in character give rise to the production and sale of a mass of goods of poor quality. Any change in these circumstances is therefore in some respect dependent on social initiatives.

Jam jar by Edward Hald.
Rörstrand.

Naturally, development toward the creation of better things for everyday use *in general* is only possible through the total elimination by the small specialist shops and the large quality department stores of the five-and-dime type of stores as well as small second- and third-class shops in the suburbs and the countryside. How this is to be achieved I cannot undertake to describe, but there are signs that suggest that current developments tend toward the elimination of the pure profiteers among retailers and manufacturers.

It is admittedly bold of a layman to venture any opinion on economic issues, but in certain cases they are so clear-cut that it is possible to do so.

One of the more recent American social theorists, Walter Lippmann, says in fact: "In science, art, politics, religion, the home, love, education—the pure economic motive, profiteering, the incentive of business enterprise is treated as a public peril," and "the real news about business, it seems to me, is that it is being administered by men who are not profiteers. The managers are on salary, divorced from ownership and from bargaining. They represent the revolution in business incentives at its very heart. For they conduct gigantic enterprises and they stand outside the haggling of the market, outside the shrewdness and strategy of competition."[38]

The new world of business has given rise to a new type of businessman. The life of a new industrialist or business manager is full of problems that lie well outside the spheres of interest to the old breed of merchant.

In the end, profit still dominates commerce as it once did, but as the units of economic action have now become so immensely larger, as trade has become a science in which earlier forms of "practical" experience play the least significant role but theoretical knowledge is decisive, the *interest* I referred to earlier as the prime incentive for working has become more important than the desire for gain. The new type of businessmen now emerging, with higher education and the theoretical interest this engenders, will I believe, when they eventually form the majority in their group, elevate the mercantile world. These men must, however, abstain from exploiting bad taste. Assuredly their homes, their offices, their clothes are seemly; would they then sell fairground baubles?

But of course they must be introduced to the problem. They must be aware of the forces that have made the production of beautiful goods their immediate goal, the ways that should therefore be adopted to do so, and the results that have been achieved. For this reason instruction is required in the schools of economics and colleges. Exhibitions should also be arranged to compare different goods that exemplify declines in taste and artistic design.

But despite the possibility of the improvements in commerce indicated here, there still remains in the public the desires once aroused to buy cheap frippery. Yet this may to a great extent be a transient illness resulting from development. In its most extreme form, in the shops in the countryside, delight in gaudy products may be a form of cultural disease. The curiosity and veneration for the village store's harmonicas and neckties and garish shawls resemble that of the savage for pearls of glass. With civilization the affliction abates. Many writers have described this: Knut Hamsun in *Segelfoss by* [Segelfoss town], Felix Moeschlin in *Der Amerika-Johann* [America-Johan], writing about a village in Dalarna.[39] They might have taken too pessimistic a view of the situation, because in this mortal world even decadence of taste must come to an end. When cultural circumstances stabilize, taste probably does as well. It is worse when the public *must*, for economic reasons, buy inferior goods. To a very substantial extent this is due to the short periods between the payment of wages. Farmers who receive their income annually each autumn plan their purchases for the entire year. They are therefore more prudent than the workers, who, even when they earn a great deal, live hand to mouth as their wages are paid at the end of every week.

Earthenware from Höganäs–Billesholms a.-b.

9.
SOCIETY

As I hope I have been able to prove with what I have presented here, the endeavor to unite art and industry is not a special affair restricted to two partners. It is a movement of a social nature whose success is not merely dependent on the goodwill of the two camps most closely concerned. On the contrary, it is intimately linked to the overall changes in economic and cultural life that at least in major respects it has been possible to trace with some clarity. All over the world one social group after another is liberating itself from dependence on such factors as economic individualism, free competition, pointless exploitation—factors that characterized society in the nineteenth century. They are all striving for—if one may venture to group them under a couple of slogans—improved organization and enhancement of working methods and the quality of the products of their work. As natural consequences there ensue changes in individuals themselves and the social and cultural structure of society. The twentieth century will certainly not permit the nineteenth century's display of such a pointless waste of people, time, and raw materials, nor its restriction of culture to a few individuals.

Art organized in a new way will form part of this new society. Art, however isolated it may appear to be, is in its essence the expression of its age. That it now deliberately wants to acquire a more extensive sphere for its activities than before can only be to the benefit of society. This does not imply any aestheticism—only an adjustment toward greater balance between the intellectual and the visible. The new use of art, as it is perceived by the younger generations, has every chance of being able to serve to cement society. There should, however, be no doubt now about the desire of art to undertake tasks that are at least considerably more important for society than hitherto.

The official stance of society toward this development is admittedly of no importance, because developments emerge from within social forms to finally disrupt them. But society can encourage the new in an active manner. Immediately, in the guise of the consumer. In all official undertakings there should be an unwritten rule that buildings and furnishing details should meet the most stringent demands in terms of taste. This is far from the case: as examples one could cite any institution at all, the post offices, railroads, customs, telegraph offices. And what a significant role they play. Partly for the well-being of officials and the pleasure they take in their work, partly for the edification of the general public. Particularly in the countryside, where the stations are, as it were, the visible outposts of the state and civilization, the nature of the architecture and the furnishings mean a great deal for public taste. If people in the towns and countryside were consistently exposed to good form in social institutions, their taste would undoubtedly improve considerably.

The other way in which society can intervene is through education. At the moment drawing instruction and vocational training in Sweden are poor in this respect. Drawing lessons should of course involve imparting the ability to make tasteful use of the artistic forms of expression and remold observed reality in a personal way. The way handicrafts are taught in Sweden, using the Nääs method, quite simply has a deadening effect, not only on conceptions of beauty but also on the ability of pupils to create their own independent forms.[40] This precision craftsmanship must ruin any natural inclination for design. Instead the examples that should be used to teach handicrafts are those that have been collected, for instance, in our museums of cultural history. This would enable these objects to serve a productive purpose, and the reproduction of their forms in a natural way to enhance the development of coming generations. Directly as handicraft, not through artistic reformulation.

It is also necessary for more advanced teaching of art and industrial art to be reformed with methods that are closer to reality and allow greater contact with everyday practices. It is no longer enough for a student to be taught according to principles that applied yesterday, so that, in other words, he must then teach himself when, awkwardly and spiritually bereft, he enters into real life. As a first requirement in this respect the demand can be made for teaching to be organized with greater contact with factories, workshops, and museums and for students to be allowed to work for their teacher's building companies or on more extensive decorative commissions.

The next generation should then be better prepared to undertake the task of making

ALL THINGS MORE BEAUTIFUL.

Translated from the Swedish by David Jones.

Garden urn by Edward Hald. Rörstrand.

Notes

Better Things for Everyday Life was first published as a pamphlet in 1919 by Svenska Slöjdföreningen (The Swedish arts and crafts society) and distributed at Svenska Mässan (The Swedish trade fair) at Göteborg. The original Swedish title, *Vackrare vardagsvara*, translates literally to "more beautiful everyday goods." While delivering a lecture in London in 1931, Paulsson himself suggested "better things for everyday life" as an alternative that captured the broad intention of the phrase and his text. The translator and editors have followed suit. For more on the publication's history and title translation, see Kåberg, Introduction, n. 1.

1. Charles Robert Ashbee, *Where the Great City Stands: A Study in the New Civics* (London: Essex House Press, 1917), p. 6.

2. Edvard Lehmann, *Lighedens land; en bog om Danmark* (Copenhagen: G.E.C. Forlag, 1917), p. 95.

3. The Gustavian, or Swedish neoclassical style, developed during the reign of King Gustav III (1771–1792). The Swedish Empire style was strongly influenced by the French Empire style, but adapted to incorporate Swedish symbols and insignia. The bourgeois Empire style, also known as Carl Johan style after the French-born Swedish King Carl XIV Johan (1818–1844), was a simpler version of the Swedish Empire style, also somewhat reminiscent of German Biedermeier.

4. August Strindberg (1849–1912), Swedish playwright, in reference to his rooms at Drottninggatan 85, Stockholm. *Abu Casems tofflor: Sagospel för gamla och unga barn på oräknade jamber i fem akter* (Stockholm: Albert Bonniers förlag, 1908).

5. Sw. *bästa rum*: the "best room" in a worker's house, in imitation of a middle-class parlor. In Swedish workers' housing of this period, the "best room" was strictly reserved for special occasions, even if there were only one additional room in which the entire family would live, eat, and sleep. See also Key, n. 5, and *acceptera*, p. 201, each in the present volume.

6. Paulsson noted here: "Compare H[enry] van de Velde, *Die drei Sünden wider die Schönheit*." (Zurich: Max Rascher Verlag, 1919); translated into French as *La triple offense à la beauté*, published and bound with the German edition. Henry van de Velde (1863–1957) was a Belgian architect, painter, and interior designer important to Art Nouveau in Belgium. A leading figure in the Deutscher Werkbund, from 1905 to 1914 he headed the Grand-Ducal School of Arts and Crafts in Weimar, Germany (which preceded the Bauhaus). According to van de Velde, the "three sins against beauty" were: "the sin against nature" identified by Ruskin; "the sin against the human dignity of the worker and craftsman" identified by Morris; and "the sin against human reason" that had become apparent in the unwillingness of artists to respond to the new forms required by machine production. These "sins" had led to "ugliness in all things": all buildings and objects of use hid their real purposes in an effort to look like something else (pp. 26–38).

7. The editors have inserted paragraph breaks at the start of this and the following paragraph to distinguish new lines of thought.

8. Sw. *hemslöjdsmagasin*: a shop selling traditional Swedish handmade household goods, for example, the shops of the organization Svensk Hemslöjd (The association of Swedish home-crafts). See Key, in the present volume, n. 28.

9. Seven full-page advertisements were published at the end of the *Vackrare vardagsvara* pamphlet for companies that Svenska Slöjdföreningen considered exemplary of the message of Paulsson's text. Drawn by Simon Gate, Akke Kumlien, and Eigil Schwab, the advertisements emphasized the beauty and quality of goods produced through the collaboration of artists and industry. Representing a broad range of manufacturers, they suggested that all types of industries should collaborate with the artist. The featured advertisements were for glassware from Orrefors glasbruk; heating stoves produced by Oskarshamns kakelfabrik; light fixtures and furniture available at Nordiska kompaniet; cooking utensils manufactured by Skultuna; cast iron products from Näfveqvarns bruk; and the printing services of Bröderna Lagerström.

10. Walther Rathenau, *Die neue Wirtschaft* (Berlin: Fischer, 1918). Rathenau (1867–1922), an economist, politician, and proponent of industrial rationalization, occupied a leading position in organizing the German economy for war. His father, Emil Rathenau, was a cofounder of the Deutscher Werkbund and as head of the German General Electric Company (AEG), employed architect and designer Peter Behrens to design buildings, products, and advertising, thus setting an example for other firms participating in the Werkbund. Walther Rathenau followed his father as head of AEG in 1915 and was also active in the Werkbund.

11. Sw. *typisering*: the development, creation, or formation of types, from the Ger. *Typisierung*. This concept is particularly associated with German architect Hermann Muthesius, who from 1911 onward proposed that a program of *Typisierung* should guide the various activities of the Deutsche Werkbund (architecture, industrial art, and craft), reorganizing disparate contemporary production according to a reduced number of types or norms that would be further refined through use and the process of production itself. The implications of *Typisierung* were famously debated at the Deutscher Werkbund Congress of 1914, where it was opposed by Henry van de Velde as a threat to individual artistic expression.

12. Prince Peter Kropotkin (1842–1921) was a leading Russian anarchist. See Lane, Introduction, n. 14.

13. Svenska Mässan (The Swedish trade fair), held annually in Göteborg beginning in 1918, is the same event for which this publication was produced in 1919.

14. The Deutscher Werkbund was founded in 1907 in Munich as a cooperative organization of applied artists, architects, politicians, and manufacturers. See Kåberg, Introduction, p. 62 and n. 28.

15. Alfons Paquet, Vorwort, *Die Durchgeistigung der Deutschen Arbeit: Wege und Ziele in Zusammenhang von Industrie/Handwerk und Kunst* (Jena: Eugen Diederichs, 1912), p. III. The German reads: "[Der Deutsche Werkbund erstrebt] die Durchgeistigung der Arbeit im Zusammenwirken von Kunst, Industrie und Handel durch Erziehung, werbende Tätigkeit und geschlossene Stellungnahme zu einschlägigen Fragen." Paulsson translated "Handel" (trade) as "handicraft," either a slip of the pen or an intentional change. *Die Durchgeistigung der Deutschen Arbeit* was the first of the Werkbund *Jahrbücher*; Paulsson recorded his purchase of the volume in his memoirs. See Paulsson, *Upplevt* (Stockholm: Natur och Kultur, 1974), pp. 73–74.

16. The editors attempted to determine the source of this quote, without success.

17. Ger. *billig und schlecht*: "cheap and nasty," a phrase coined by Franz Reuleaux, a German correspondent to the 1876 Philadelphia World Exhibition. In a scathing report on the German goods on display, which were of poor quality and in a variety of historical styles, Reuleaux proposed that "cheap and nasty" had become the guiding principle for industrial production in Germany. See Paulsson, *Upplevt*, p. 74; and John V. Maciuika, "Art in the Age of Government Intervention: Hermann Muthesius, Sachlichkeit, and the State, 1897–1907," *German Studies Review*, vol. 21, no. 2 (May 1998): pp. 290, 304, n. 29.

18. The editors' efforts to determine the source of this quote were unsuccessful.

19. Paulsson is referring to an exhibition of German and Austrian industrial art held at London's Goldsmith's Hall under the auspices of the Board of Trade and described in *A New Body with New Aims* (London: Design & Industries Association, July 1915). Paulsson could also have seen the description in *Englands Kunstindustrie und der Deutsche Werkbund: Übersetzungen von Begründungs und Werbeschriften der englischen Gesellschaft "Design and Industries Association"* (Munich: F. Bruckmann, 1916). A copy of the latter is in Paulsson's papers, now at Uppsala University Library.

20. Sir Leo Chiozza Money, "The War and British Enterprise," in *A New Body with New Aims,* pp. 32–39, and in *Englands Kunstindustrie*, pp. 9–12.

21. The Design and Industries Association, established in London in 1915, distributed its first manifesto at the exhibition of German and Austrian industrial art mentioned in n. 19 above.

22. Quoted by Arthur Clutton Brock, "Art and Trade," in *A New Body with New Aims*, p. 23.

23. Ibid.

24. Alfred Lys Baldry, "The Organization of British Art," in *A New Body with New Aims*, pp. 7–8; see also Lys Baldry, "Ein neuer Verband mit neuen Zielen. Die Organisation der Britischen Kunst," in *Englands kunstindustrie*, p. 21. Paulsson erroneously cites the general title of the pamphlet from which Lys Baldry's essay is drawn, rather than the title of Lys Baldry's essay.

25. Marius Vachon, *Le guerre artistique avec l'Allemagne* (Paris: Payot, 1916).

26. Paulsson noted here: "Cited from [Carl] Brummer and [Karl] Larsen, *Tyskernes Kamp mod den slette smak.*" *Der Deutsche Werkbund og dets arbejde* (The German battle against bad taste: the Deutsche Werkbund and its work) (Copenhagen: Krohns Bogtryckeri, 1918), p. 8. *Le Gaulois* was a daily newspaper (Paris: A. Meyer, founded 1868); General Cherfils was its military correspondent during the First World War.

27. The Österreichischer Werkbund was founded in 1912; the Hungarian equivalent, Magyar Muvészi Munka, was founded in 1913; the Schweizerischer Werkbund was founded in 1913; the Driebond in the Netherlands was founded in 1914.

28. *Hemutställningen* (The home exhibition), organized by Svenska Slöjdföreningen, was held from October to December 1917, at Liljevalchs konsthall in Stockholm. See Kåberg, Introduction, p. 65.

29. For the referral agency of Svenska Slöjdföreningen, ibid., p. 66.

30. Sw. *koloniträdgårdar*: lit. "garden colonies." In the last quarter of the nineteenth century garden colonies–groups of very small plots–developed in proximity to new urban apartment dwellings in Germany, Great Britain, and the Scandinavian countries. Sometimes leased by individuals, sometimes mandated by the state or municipal government at the time of new housing construction, such plots were cultivated by the families that held rights to them and provided fruits, vegetables, and flowers. Typically, each plot had a tiny "garden house" or cottage, sometimes self-built, for the storage of tools and for seating.

31. Nordiska kompaniet (also known as NK) was an exclusive department store in Stockholm. Founded by Josef Sachs in 1902, between 1904 and 1973 the company manufactured furniture at Nordiska kompaniets verkstäder in Nyköping, employing such designers as Carl Malmsten and Gunnar Asplund. NK was also an important exhibition venue.

32. On *graal* glass, see Kåberg, Introduction, n. 53 and fig. 5.

33. Heinrich Tessenow (1876–1950), a prolific writer, architect, and city planner, was later broadly influential in German architecture through his teaching at the Academy of Art in Dresden and the Technische Hochschule in Berlin. At the time of Paulsson's writing, Tessenow had built housing and the classicizing Jaques-Dalcroze Theater and Dance Institute (1910–13) at the garden city of Hellerau near Dresden, where he taught at the Deutsche Werkstätten; he had also published a series of works on house design, crafts, and carpentry. Paulsson states that he is quoting from what would become the most famous of Tessenow's writings, *Hausbau und dergleichen* (Berlin: Cassirer, 1916); translated by Wilfried Wang as "House-building and such Things," in *On Rigor*, eds. Richard Burdett and Wilfried Wang (Cambridge, MA: MIT Press, 1989), pp. 9–33, but the passage is not present there.

34. Paulsson noted here: "Cited from Jens Möller-Jensen's book *Tegneundervisningen, Haandverkerundervisningen og den nya Tid*. Copenhagen [Krohns Bogtryckeri] 1919." The editors were unable to verify the source of this quotation.

35. The factory of the Deutsche Werkstätten, Dresden-Hellerau, designed by Richard Riemerschmid (1868–1957), ca. 1910, produced furniture and household fittings destined for industrial production from models designed by craftsmen, artists, and architects.

36. Paulsson refers to Svenska Mässan, Göteborg. See n. 13 above.

37. For Kosta glasses, see Kåberg, Introduction, fig. 10.

38. Paulsson noted here: "Walter Lippmann. *Drift and Mastery* [*: An Attempt to Diagnose the Current Unrest* (New York: Mitchell Kennerley, 1914),] p. 29 and [45–]46f."

39. Knut Hamsun (1859–1952) was a Norwegian writer and Nobel laureate in 1920. Set in Norway, *Segelfoss by* is a critique of the commercialization, industrialization, and urbanization of modern society and the rootlessness it brings to people's lives. *Segelfoss by* (Kristiania [Oslo]: Gyldendal, 1915); translated into English as *Segelfoss Town* (New York: A. A. Knopf, 1925). Felix Moeschlin (1882–1969), the Swiss-German writer, lived for a time in Leksand, Dalarna. His novel describes life in a small village in that province in the 1870s and the tragedy that follows when Johan, a former villager, returns from America and introduces modern commercial ideas. *Der Amerika-Johann; ein Bauerroman aus Schweden* (Leipzig: Grethlein & Co, 1912).

40. The Nääs method of crafts education was developed by Otto Salomon (1849–1907), founder in the early 1870s of vocational schools for teenaged boys and girls and a teacher-training school for crafts at Nääs, a manor about twenty miles east of Göteborg. Salomon's teaching method required students to perform a series of carefully designed exercises and to produce specific models. By the end of the 1870s there were about a hundred similar schools in Sweden, and in 1878 crafts became compulsory in Swedish schools. The Nääs method also gained considerable influence in the United States, Great Britain, Germany, and Japan, but it came under increasing criticism from about 1900 on for its apparent rigidity. See Hans Thorbjörnsson, "Otto Salomon," *Prospects: The Quarterly Review of Comparative Education* (Paris, UNESCO: International Bureau of Education), vol. XXIV, no. 3/4 (1994): pp. 471–85.

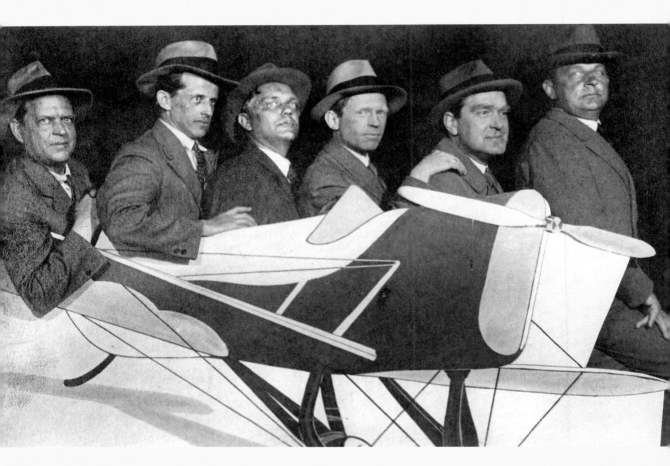

1. From left: Sven Markelius, Uno Åhrén, Gunnar Asplund,
Eskil Sundahl, Wolter Gahn, Gregor Paulsson.
Photograph: collection Arkitekturmuseet, Stockholm

An Introduction to
acceptera

Lucy Creagh

Acceptera (1931) is often referred to as "the manifesto of Swedish functionalism," an appellation that sets it into a long line of early twentieth-century avant-garde pronouncements on architecture, one of the major hallmarks of which is an antipathy to history and tradition.[1] Certainly, the event with which *acceptera* and its six authors have become synonymous—the Stockholm Exhibition of 1930, the program and reception of which *acceptera* provides something of a summary—has assumed almost mythic status as a radical and highly visible break with the architectural thinking that dominated Swedish discourse and practice in the 1910s and 1920s (figs. 1 and 2). The critique of historical eclecticism implicit in the unadorned surfaces of the Stockholm Exhibition seems to indicate an excising of history that concurs with the avant-garde's antagonism to tradition (fig. 3). Likewise, the authors of *acceptera* dispensed with the received wisdom of their cultural forefathers to the extent that the publication was considered by one prominent traditionalist as "the most insolent book ever published in Swedish—a fresh and boyish insolence to be sure, but altogether reckless and defiant."[2] The authors reinforced the idea of an intergenerational battle by representing themselves toward the end of *acceptera* as a schoolboy, injured but grinning after a "drubbing by an older pupil" from the school of conservative values (see p. 333). The punctuation of the text with bold-face aphoristic headings and captions and the striking use of photomontage, derivative of modern avant-garde publishing in Denmark and Germany, also contribute to the notion of *acceptera* as a radical manifesto associated with a transformative architectural event.[3]

Despite these initial impressions, *acceptera* lacks the aggressive posturing and utopianism of many of the avant-garde manifestos associated with early twentieth-century modernism, and its authors—art historian Gregor Paulsson (1889–1977) and architects Uno Åhrén (1897–1977), Gunnar Asplund (1885–1940), Wolter Gahn (1890–1985), Sven Markelius (1889–1972), and Eskil Sundahl (1890–1974)—were hardly radical interlopers on the Stockholm cultural scene. Paulsson's intellectual formation and rise to prominence has been set out in detail by Helena Kåberg in this

2. Crowd in central plaza, with advertising mast, press box, and Gunnar Asplund's Paradiset restaurant, at the 1930 Stockholm Exhibition. Photograph: collection Arkitekturmuseet, Stockholm

3. Hall 9, for metal goods and musical instruments, at the 1930 Stockholm Exhibition. Photograph: collection Svensk Form, Stockholm

4. Eskil Sundahl and Olof Thunström. KFs arkitektskontor, Kvarnholmen. 1928–30. Photograph: Carl Gemler, KFs bildarkiv, Stockholm

5. Uno Åhrén and Sven Markelius. Kårhus, KTH, Stockholm. 1930. Photograph: collection Arkitekturmuseet, Stockholm

volume. In his capacity as director of Svenska Slöjdföreningen (The Swedish arts and crafts society), a position he had held since 1924, Paulsson initiated the Stockholm Exhibition, the largest and most ambitious exhibition of applied arts ever staged in Sweden, and made architecture, and through its housing section the home itself, a central component of the exhibition agenda.[4]

 Each of the other authors of *acceptera* held key positions on the exhibition's organizing committees and brought their considerable practical experience to bear on its buildings.[5] Asplund, already internationally recognized as the foremost architect of his generation through buildings such as his Stockholms stadsbibliotek (Stockholm public library, 1920–28), was the exhibition's chief architect, responsible for its master plan and major buildings.[6] Sundahl, who chaired the working committee on architecture, had been since 1925 principal architect of Kooperativa Förbundet (The Swedish cooperative wholesale society, KF), running the largest architectural office in Scandinavia. KF's Kvarnholmen industrial buildings and workers' housing (1930) were some of the most architecturally significant buildings of the period, the latter a tangible example of many of the housing principles set out in *acceptera* (fig. 4; see also pp. 216 and 237).[7] Gahn, with Paulsson and Asplund, was one of about a dozen lead exhibition officials and served as the main consultant to exhibitors. As editor of the leading architectural journal *Byggmästaren*, Gahn played a crucial yet often overlooked role as a critic and was himself an architect of considerable accomplishment, completing what is considered Sweden's first functionalist office building at Drottninggatan 14 (see p. 329), in 1929.[8] Markelius designed model apartment 7 and house 49 for the exhibition, crowning a particularly productive year in which he had completed among other projects Sweden's first entirely concrete apartment building at Kvarteret Berget (1929), a number of middle-class villas (Villas Öhman and Engqvist, both 1929), his own house in Nockeby (1930) (see pp. 205 and 243), and with Åhrén, the Kårhus (Student union building) at Kungliga Tekniska Högskolan (Royal institute of technology, KTH; 1930) (fig. 5).[9] Åhrén, a prodigious writer who succeeded Gahn as editor of *Byggmästaren*, sat on two of the specialist committees for the Stockholm Exhibition and played a decisive role in the investigation for its housing section, to which he also contributed model houses 45 and 51. Åhrén had cut his teeth collaborating with all four of his fellow architect-authors over the course of the 1920s, and by 1931 had completed a number of buildings in his own right, including the apartment block and cinema at Kvarteret Tången (1929–30), and a large workshop and garage for the Ford Motor Company (1930–31).[10]

Together with Paulsson these architects represented the "new establishment" and an approach to architecture that was in some quarters officially sanctioned by 1931.[11] The Stockholm Exhibition, however, was an expression of this new architectural spirit on an unprecedented scale, executed with a single-minded attention to the potential of mass production, rational planning, and the eradication of historical references, all of which roused vocal opposition within sectors of Svenska Slöjdföreningen. This schism was amplified to the level of a public debate, both before and during the exhibition, through extensive coverage in the mainstream press, resulting in an often negative assessment of the new approach that Paulsson and these architects represented. As such, *acceptera* can be seen as an attempt by the authors to stand their ground. To a significant extent it is a reiteration of the content of many documents directly associated with the Stockholm Exhibition, from Paulsson's initial lecture on its program in 1928 to the brochures and catalogues to which some of the authors were signatories.[12] It is also clearly a rejoinder to criticism, evidenced strikingly in the text when the authors converse with a group of anonymous "gentlemen," even at one point with a certain "Mr. Traditionalist." Pressing the words of their critics into the service of their own arguments, the authors paraphrase, or cite directly, from a number of prominent opponents: the furniture designer and member of Svenska Slöjdföreningen Carl Malmsten, who considered the rationalization of the home according to functionalist principles a debasement of its traditional role as an intimate place for gathering and repose;[13] the cultural critic Torsten Fogelqvist, who viewed the Stockholm Exhibition as an extremist dictatorship of form;[14] the art historian Carl G. Laurin and the mayor of Stockholm, Carl Lindhagen, who both saw functionalism as responsible for the destruction of the cityscape;[15] and the writer Karl-Erik Forsslund, who believed the new architecture was nothing but a fashionable German import that would, after the cities, destroy the countryside as well.[16]

As the purpose of *acceptera* was, as Paulsson stressed in a letter to his co-authors written in December 1930, to present the principles of modern design in an optimistic light, their contributions were to be written in a "calm and positive tone, without controversy," and, as indeed evidenced at numerous junctures in the text, "sometimes with humor."[17] This populist approach is reinforced in the book through the liberal use of illustrative material. While complementing the text, the illustrations and their often pithy captions can also be read as a separate register of information, with a balance struck between photographs that attest to the tangible nature of the architecture being promoted, and collage and compelling juxtapositions that express more abstract points. Modern advertising techniques also influenced this approach, evident not only in the graphic design of the book, but perhaps also in the choice of title: "The whole reform movement is rather like an advertising campaign," Paulsson was to say in the same year that *acceptera* was published; "if you can get a selling slogan, you succeed."[18]

Contrary, however, to the manner in which the title has sometimes been translated—as a declarative, imperative "accept!"—the acceptance this book sought to win for the new architecture sprung less from an urge to agitate for something shocking and disruptive of the status quo than from a belief that the times in which the authors lived—"the reality that exists"—should be accepted as the inevitable outcome of historical circumstances. As Gotthard Johansson, a notable supporter of the work of Paulsson and these architects, was to observe, a fuller title, emblazoned in red, was inclusive of the name of the social democratic publishing house that released it: "acceptera Tiden"—"accept the times."[19] Concurrent with this sense of historical determinism, the authors would recast the concept of tradition, moving away from the fixations on technique and style that preoccupied their critics to a sense of functionalism as a continuation of the rational thinking already present in traditional Swedish building and handicrafts. More fundamentally they refer to a "tradition" of irresistible change over time.[20] Thus, as an architectural manifesto *acceptera* is one of a gentler sort. An attempt to mediate the simplistic yet divisive dualisms that had characterized public debate on architecture and design in Sweden at the time, it argued for art *and* technology, beauty *and* practicality, old *and* new, handicraft *and* mass production, and as was announced so strikingly on its very first page—and which in essence also underpinned the entire social, political, and economic program of the Stockholm Exhibition—the individual *and* the mass.

The initial impetus for the Stockholm Exhibition was, according to Paulsson, the great success of Swedish everyday wares at the Exposition internationale des arts décoratifs et industriels modernes, held in Paris in 1925, the first major international presentation of the progress of Swedish design under the program of Paulsson's *Better Things for Everyday Life* (1919).[21] While recognition of Sweden as a preeminent producer of quality glassware and ceramics can be dated to this event, the Swedish goods that aroused interest on the international market were of a decidedly exclusive nature. The Stockholm Exhibition aimed to redirect production back to the central message of Paulsson's 1919 work while simultaneously attempting to extend the socioeconomic importance of the industrially produced object to the house itself. The home would take on a real dimension in 1930: no longer a generic space in an exhibition hall that was simply a container for furnishings, but full-scale model homes and rental apartments where the functional, social, and economic implications of the home would be investigated with a degree of specificity hitherto unattempted in Sweden.[22]

While all six of the *acceptera* authors were involved in some capacity with the preparations for the housing section of the exhibition, it was Åhrén who, in establishing the guidelines for the types of dwellings to be constructed, perhaps exerted the greatest influence over its general program.[23] Since first encountering the work of Le Corbusier in 1925, Åhrén had agitated in numerous polemical articles, and in his own practice, for the release of architecture from the contingencies of personal expression in favor of a foundation in quantifiable, collective conditions. Le Corbusier put the home at the center of his architectural agenda and made it the fundamental building block of the new city.[24] In the face of acute overcrowding in places such as Stockholm, however, it would be the efficiently planned "minimal dwellings" of Germany and their combination into the parallel rows of the *Zeilenbau* (Sw. *lamellhus*) that seemed better suited to Swedish conditions, demonstrating an objective foundation for architecture that would greatly influence the housing section of the Stockholm Exhibition.[25] Ten houses and fifteen apartments were eventually designed—several of them illustrated in *acceptera*—each according to "need types" determined by the number of inhabitants and annual costs calculated at 20 to 25 percent of yearly income.[26] Implicit in this development of types was the notion of economy through mass production, and a constituent part of the presentation was plans that showed how these dwelling types could be arranged in the new suburbs of Stockholm.[27]

Once built, the architecture of the exhibition presented a complete functionalist exterior; the regular rhythm of pavilions along the main spine of the exhibition site, constructed in a waterfront park at the edge of the city, created an enclosed, almost commercial atmosphere, terminating in a capacious public plaza punctuated by an advertising mast standing some 260 feet high. There was, however, a distinct disjunction between this exterior and some of the goods and displays that filled Asplund's pavilions. This is acutely suggested by the embellishment of the naked structure in the display of Svenska hemslöjdsföreningarnas riksförbund (The national league of Swedish

6. Hall 23, home-crafts display at the 1930 Stockholm Exhibition. Photograph: collection Svensk Form, Stockholm

7. Svensk Hemslöjd pavilion, model living room with furniture by Carl Malmsten, at the 1930 Stockholm Exhibition. Seen here as published in *Svensk hem i ord och bild* (1930).

8. Uno Åhrén. Living room, model house 45 with furniture by Åhrén, at the 1930 Stockholm Exhibition. Mfr: Gemla Fabrikers A-B. Photograph: collection Svensk Form, Stockholm

home-crafts associations) and also in the hearth-centered model interior of the Svensk Hemslöjd (The association of Swedish home-crafts) pavilion, whose one-off furniture pieces designed by Malmsten were accessorized with books, Swedish textile pieces, and the Mora-type grandfather clock (figs. 6 and 7). The disparity is further evidenced in a comparison with the spare organization of the mass-produced pieces of Åhrén's interior for house 45 (fig. 8). Such variations were a tangible reflection of the division then taking effect within Svenska Slöjdföreningen, between those who viewed the organization as a guardian of Swedish traditional handicrafts, and therefore individual expression, and those who saw it as a force for technical and social change—for the modernization of artistic production and adaptation to the exigencies of a burgeoning mass market. Distilling the disagreement to its essential components, the respected novelist Elin Wägner argued that it was not at all about style, but fundamental social change: "the 1890s up against the 1930s, Ruskin versus Corbusier. The individualistic way of seeing things versus the collective."[28]

Such sentiments echoed Paulsson's own thinking from as far back as 1916, when in *Den nya arkitekturen* (The new architecture) he argued that having passed through a period of pronounced individualism and "a wandering circus" of architectural form in the second half of the nineteenth century, where patronage, paralleling society as a whole, was divided into "the great mass and the secluded little band of artists, flocking around an even smaller number of patrons," the era of the labor movement called forth a new form of collective work and a new monumentality.[29] Indeed, by 1930, Swedish society had been significantly reoriented through the rise of popular movements—the trade unions, the consumer and housing cooperatives—in which an "association" of individuals set out together to achieve social or economic goals. And perhaps most significantly, in 1928—the same year the law on collective bargaining was enacted—the leader of the Social Democratic Party, Per Albin Hansson, proposed that Sweden would take the form of the *folkhem* or "people's home," a metaphor for the

Swedish people as a nation-family living under the common roof of social equality and welfare solidarity. As Paulsson would later state, it was precisely the equality inherent in "*folkhems* thinking" that drove the Stockholm Exhibition and its efforts to ensure that the work of artists and architects was no longer the exclusive reserve of an elite, but available to the entire population.[30]

The writing of *acceptera* was certainly in progress before the close of the Stockholm Exhibition on September 29, 1930, and it is not out of the question that it was initially intended to counterattack a book-length account of the event that Malmsten reported in July was well underway.[31] Information on the exact writing process is sparse. It is known that various chapter topics were allocated to each author after an initial meeting, that these chapters were circulated and discussed as a group, and that this collaborative process seems to have continued well into December.[32] While Gahn would later report that the work was done rather quickly, Sundahl noted that the text was developed, off and on, over six months, culminating in a week-long working session at a hotel in Vaxholm sometime over the winter.[33] Paulsson and Asplund guided the content and tone of the work; Åhrén later confirmed that it was he who was responsible for the layout of the book and its cover design, as well as the concluding statement "accept."[34] Beyond this, the individual contributions of the six authors are unclear, and no record of the division of labor seems to have survived. When interviewed in 1979, Gahn, the only surviving member of the group, declined to discuss the authorship of *acceptera*'s constituent parts. While there is evidence for the speculative attributions presented by Anders Åman in the introduction to the facsimile edition of 1980, the working method of the group and the insistence on collective authorship were deliberate strategies to obscure their individual contributions, part and parcel of the very argument of the book itself.[35]

   Acceptera begins in much the same way as Paulsson's *Better Things for Everyday Life*, with a statement on the relative nature of social values, this time couched in a comparison of perceptions of sexual relations and the institution of marriage throughout the history of civilization. Just as social values are only true as long as they "exalt the status quo" of the age in which they emerge, so too are architecture and design deemed acceptable based on evolving cultural needs. In the historical continuum, each era brings forth a culture in which the theories it develops as much as the goods it produces reflect prevailing social relations, which for these authors are overwhelmingly class relations. Thus, and somewhat paradoxically, a fundamental truth is that truth is subjective; there can be no transhistorical absolutes in art or any other branch of culture. This argument anchors *acceptera*, as it did *Better Things for Everyday Life*, in Alois Riegl's overarching theory of *Kunstwollen*—that artefacts reflect the formative principles of the society that produced them. The authors of *acceptera* transform the inherent determinism of *Kunstwollen* into an operative strategy, and a fundamental theme of the book is that art and architecture should "endeavor to express the face of our age."[36]

   The work of Oswald Spengler is also strongly evident in *acceptera*, and there is ample evidence to suggest the influence of Spengler's decidedly spatial account of world history on some of the *acceptera* authors.[37] While Asplund would expound the spatial implications of Spengler's work in his inaugural professorial lecture, also of 1931, it is Spengler's philosophy of history that resonates most strongly in *acceptera*.[38] Spengler replaced the notion of history as linear progression with a "morphological" view in which all branches of culture—politics, ethics, religion, art, and mathematics— were intrinsically related as tangible expressions of the cultural soul of the age. As expressed in the chapter "New and old," culture must always be unified—architecture, clothing, or a way of walking are equivalent expressions of the motivating force of an era. Most notably, for Spengler history is seen as a series of independent episodes within which culture experiences a rise, apotheosis, and decline. Despite the inherent cultural pessimism of Spengler's schema, he gave to a great number of modern architects a scientific-philosophical framework (albeit perhaps of the quasi sort) to assert that all-encompassing cultural and architectural change was inevitable: "We are battling with a formidable force: the age itself and its will," the *acceptera* authors would write.[39] Spengler's pessimism is transformed into an optimistic sense of renewal in the closing chapters of *acceptera*, in which "the city as an expression of movement, work, life in a thousand different forms . . . is a living organism. Like everything that has life, all its parts develop from birth to death. The milieu is, and must be, subject to change."[40]

The chapters "The society we are building for," "What is required of housing," and "Industrialized housing production. Standardization" represent the core of *acceptera* as a document on housing, and together give a cogent account of the research and principles on which the housing section of the Stockholm Exhibition were organized. The simple message, repeated in various forms over the course of these chapters, was "the nature of the home has changed." The social and economic conditions sketched out in the first two chapters of *acceptera* are given statistical specificity in these three chapters, drawing directly on research for the Stockholm Exhibition, but also echoing articles written by Åhrén, Sundahl, and Markelius in the years before 1930.[41] When the authors ask "How much will I be paid?" and "What do I get for my money?" the collective "we"—mandated for use during the course of writing in an effort to reinforce group authorship, but also, it is sensed, to emphasize inclusion with the reader, the mass, the "90 percent"—has been replaced by the singular "I," in turn suggesting a solidarity with the working man.[42] Indeed, it is in this section that the new interplay between "we" and "I" in Swedish society under the force of labor-movement policies, and their impact on the home, is spelled out most clearly. The increased leisure and recreation time that were the benefits of modern industrial relations were now more often spent in a collective setting—in study circles, through organized groups and activities outside the home. The spatial legacies of class society are targeted, such as the persistence in overcrowded apartments of the un-functional hall or the seldom used *finrum* (parlor), replaced by the *vardagsrum* (lit. everyday room) as a spacious, light-filled, functional living room, a corollary of sorts to Paulsson's *vardagsvara* (lit. everyday goods) as the leitmotif of a new society unencumbered by social pretensions. With a characteristic sense of inevitability, the writers declare, "We have begun to be more natural and no longer care about demonstrating a wealth that does not exist, or a social status which at any rate is doomed to extinction."[43]

The rejection of ostentation and pretension in the home was the "soul" of beauty for figures such as Ellen Key, whose emphasis on the directness of expression that arises from the satisfaction of utility is a thread that connects her "Beauty in the Home" with Paulsson's *Better Things for Everyday Life* and *acceptera*. While for the *acceptera* authors the very word "beauty" had become problematic—sequestered by a movement that equated it only with historical and traditional forms, habituating a division between beauty and technology that was one of the major barriers to the acceptance of the new architecture—they never abandon its possibility, despite the memorable assertion "Down with beauty." In much the same way that Key would view nature as the elevation of purpose to "simplicity and ease . . . delicacy and expressivity," the *acceptera* authors allude to beauty as a higher form of "logical clarity" as yet seen most clearly in the "self-evident" form of bridges, automobiles, and airplanes.[44] But while the voice of Key seems to echo in *acceptera*, there are significant differences, not the least of which concerns the relationship of the home to society: for Key, the home was the fountainhead of social change, while for the *acceptera* authors, it was primarily a reflection of it.

As modern architecture and participatory democracy were extinguished in Germany after 1933, Sweden continued to test the ideas that had origins there, with *acceptera* standing as something of a brief for future developments. While the impetus for the "family hotel" that is discussed in *acceptera* could well have been Walter Gropius's lecture on "centralized master households" delivered at the Congrès Internationaux d'Architecture Moderne conference of 1929, which Markelius attended, in his collaborative work with the sociologist and activist Alva Myrdal, Markelius fused this concept with social issues under discussion in Sweden at the time: the welfare and education of children and the role of the working mother.[45] By supplying minimal dwellings connected to a central kitchen, a restaurant, and most importantly, professionally staffed child-care facilities, functional planning techniques would be used to ease the path of women into the wage economy. Two forces usually cast as opposites at this time—the emancipation of women from the domestic sphere and stronger institutions of marriage and motherhood—might then be reconciled. Markelius and Myrdal strove for a degree of individual choice within the collective framework. Thus, for example, meals could be self-prepared, ordered to the apartment from the central kitchen, or eaten in the communal restaurant. As suggested in *acceptera* and later reiterated by Markelius, this form of housing, founded on the balance implicit in the motto "individual culture through collective technology," could allay conflict and disagreement in the modern family, perhaps even preventing divorce (fig. 9).[46]

A "collective house," as it would become known, was eventually built at John Ericssonsgatan 6, Stockholm, in 1935, but never became the solution to mass housing it was suggested it could be in *acceptera*. Many of the other housing ideas set out in *acceptera* were realized, and at considerable scale. Parallel blocks of minimal dwellings were constructed in Stockholm in municipally directed projects in the Fredhäll and Kristineberg areas (1931–32) and also in Hakon Ahlberg's Hjorthagen development (1934–35), where industrialized construction techniques were also utilized. By the mid-1930s, however, the living environments engendered by this approach were beginning to be called into question, not least by the *acceptera* authors themselves. In 1936 Asplund suggested that while the *lamellhus* type offered great increases of sunlight and fresh air, the monotony entailed in these lengths of identical apartments standardized the lives of their occupants. Recalling Siegfried Kracauer's notion of the "mass ornament," Asplund warned of the dangers of lost individuality by evoking

9. "Will the central home prevent divorce?" Drawing after a lecture by Sven Markelius on a proposed collective housing development. Seen here as published in *Stockholms Tidningen*, December 6, 1932

10. Juxtaposition of unidentified *lamelhus* and the Tiller Girls. Seen here as published in Gunnar Asplund, "Konst och teknik," *Byggmästaren* 14 (1936)

11. Sven Backström and Leif Reinius. Gröndal, Stockholm. 1946. Photograph: collection Arkitekturmuseet, Stockholm

the popular dancing troupe the Tiller Girls, whose coordinated routine, while initially attractive, was ultimately a dehumanized surface effect where "the individual in the ensemble is . . . lost or degraded to ornament—an ornament of some hundred arms and legs and a hundred smiles" (fig. 10).[47] And in 1942, in his book *Arkitektur och demokrati*, Åhrén was to write that the great failure of the 1930s was the reduction of housing to purely statistical terms, emphasizing efficiency at the expense of individual needs and a sense of place and community. The social intention of 1930 had been partially lost, as indeed had the dialectical relationship of the individual to the group; Swedish architecture found itself in a state of general "disorientation."[48]

Yet it was through this process of self-analysis that the architecture of the 1930s would be recast into forms for a new age, with Sweden making a genuine contribution to the development of modern architecture in the postwar period. The term "New Empiricism" would be coined in 1947 to describe a Swedish return to a more informal approach to planning and a varied, more traditional palette of materials, all of which, as a foil to the predictability of the architecture of the 1930s, was said to introduce an element of "spontaneity" into modern architecture.[49] Markelius's villa at Kevinge (1945) was hailed as a significant example of this new direction.[50] The principle of "neighborhood planning," developed by Åhrén and tested in new suburbs such as Årsta (1943–53), put central community facilities at the core of new housing areas, very much in response to the failure of 1930s housing developments to incorporate a place for social interaction. Likewise the *stjärnhus*, or star-house plan, in which the through-apartments of the *lamellhus* were reconfigured to enable combinatorial possibilities, was an ingenious development that was at once a reaction to the uniformity of housing developments of the 1930s but also a permutation of it (fig. 11). While the developments of the 1940s called much of *acceptera* into question, they also stand as testament to the notion of architecture as an expression of ever-changing social conditions, as "an adaptable tool for life." And in the optimistic thinking about the future that permeated *acceptera*, failure was, after all, "only the opportunity more intelligently to begin again."[51]

Notes

1. *Acceptera* was first published in 1931 by Tiden, the publishing arm of the Swedish Social Democratic Party. With the addition of an afterword by Anders Åman, it was reissued as a facsimile edition in 1980 (Stockholm: Tiden, 1980). See the first note following *acceptera*, in the present volume, for further details.

2. Karl-Erik Forsslund to Eskil Sundahl, June 10, 1931. Arkitekturmuseet, Stockholm, AM 1989–17, box 2. On Forsslund, see *acceptera*, in the present volume, n. 28.

3. There is a distinct visual resonance between the graphic design of *acceptera* and Poul Henningsen's avant-garde publication *Kritisk Revy*, published in Denmark from 1926 to 1928, to which Uno Åhrén contributed. See especially issue 3, July 1928. On the cover of *acceptera*, the sans-serif, lowercase title bears obvious connection to Herbert Bayer's "universal" typeface, developed at the Bauhaus in 1925, and architectural photomontage was used in journals such as *Das neue Frankfurt*. In Sweden "functionalist" book design, with *acceptera* as a rather radical example, engaged influences from the Bauhaus, Russian Constructivism, and designers in Holland and Central Europe. See Marie-Louise Bowallius, "Tradition and Innovation in Swedish Graphic Design," in *Utopia and Reality: Modernity in Sweden 1900–1960*, ed. Cecilia Widenheim (New Haven, CT: Yale University Press, 2002), p. 217.

4. For a detailed outline of the program of the Stockholm Exhibition see Gregor Paulsson, "Stockholmsutställningens program: föredrag i Svenska Slöjdföreningen den 25 oktober 1928," in *Kritik och program: ett urval uppsatser, tidningsartiklar och föredrag* (Stockholm: Gebers, 1949), pp. 100–12. For a comprehensive account of the event in English see Eva Rudberg, *The Stockholm Exhibition 1930: Modernism's Breakthrough in Swedish Architecture* (Stockholm: Stockholmia förlag, 1999).

5. Information on the organizational roles played by each of the *acceptera* authors in the Stockholm Exhibition has been taken from *Stockholmsutställningen 1930 av konstindustri, konsthantverk och hemslöjd, maj-september: Officiell huvudkatalog* (Stockholm: Utställningsförlaget, 1930) and *Stockholmsutställningen 1930 av konstindustri, konsthantverk och hemslöjd: Specialkatalog över bostadsavdelningen* (Stockholm: Utställningsförlaget, 1930).

6. For a discussion of Asplund's work before the Stockholm Exhibition see Hakon Ahlberg, *Swedish Architecture of the Twentieth Century*, ed. F. R. Yerbury (London: Ernst Benn, 1925), pp. 25–27. Ahlberg's book was largely responsible for bringing Swedish architecture of the 1910s and 1920s to an English-speaking audience. This book also appeared in German as Ahlberg, *Moderne Schwedische Architektur* (Berlin: E. Wasmuth, 1925). There is an ever-expanding library of books on Asplund in English, most recently Peter Blundell Jones, *Gunnar Asplund* (London: Phaidon, 2006).

7. The work of KF from 1925 to 1949 is described in English in the three self-published books *Swedish Cooperative Wholesale Society's Architects' Office* (Stockholm: Kooperativa Förbundet Bokförlag, 1935), and the two-volume *The Swedish Cooperative Wholesale Society's Architects' Office, 1935–1949* (Stockholm: Kooperativa Förbundets Bokförlag, 1949). See also the recent monograph by Lisa Brunnström, *Det svenska folkhemsbygget: om Kooperativa Förbundets arkitektkontor* (Stockholm: Arkitektur förlag, 2004), which has a brief English summary, pp. 326–27.

8. There is unfortunately little scholarship in Swedish on Gahn, although Per Råberg discusses his contribution in a meticulous study of the years immediately preceding the Stockholm Exhibition. Råberg, *Funktionalistiskt genombrott: radikal miljö och miljödebatt i Sverige, 1925–1931*, 2nd ed. (Stockholm: P. A. Norstedt & Söner, 1972). For basic biographical information see Nils Ahrbom, "Wolter Barclay Gahn 1890–1985," *Arkitektur*, no. 9 (1985): pp. 43–44.

9. After Asplund, Markelius is the best known of the *acceptera* authors outside of Sweden, although he came to recognition in Britain and the United States almost a decade after *acceptera* was published: in 1939, through his highly praised Swedish pavilion for the New York World's Fair and then in the postwar period through his association with the so-called New Empiricism, a reaction against the perceived extremes of functionalism promoted by the British journal *Architectural Review*. Not long after Markelius began work as the Scandinavian representative on the design team for the United Nations Headquarters in New York, the idea of New Empiricism was debated at The Museum of Modern Art's "What Is Happening to Modern Architecture" symposium, held in February 1948. See the special issue "What Is Happening to Modern Architecture," *The Bulletin of the Museum of Modern Art*, vol. 15 (Spring 1948). For a complete account of Markelius's career in English see Eva Rudberg, *Sven Markelius, Architect* (Stockholm: Arkitektur förlag, 1989).

10. In addition to his collaboration with Markelius on the Kårhus, Åhrén worked with Sundahl on the cooperative shop at Storgatan 18–20 (1925) and a joint entry to the League of Nations competition (1927). With Gahn he completed a competition entry for Katarina realskola (1928), and he assisted Asplund on Skandiabiografen (1922–23). Åhrén is a key figure in the development of modern architecture in Sweden and without doubt functionalism's key theoretician; while his work has been the subject of a detailed study in Swedish by Eva Rudberg, his importance in the development of Swedish architecture has not been matched by coverage of his work in English-language publications, possibly because shortly after the Stockholm Exhibition he moved into the area of planning. See Eva Rudberg, *Uno Åhrén: en föregångsman inom 1900-talets arkitektur och samhällsplanering* (Stockholm: Byggforskningsrådet, 1981), which has a short English summary, pp. 249–53.

11. In 1930 Stockholms stadsplankontor (Stockholm municipal planning office) produced two projects for the Eriksdal and Fredhäll-Kristineberg areas, which can be seen to adhere to the principles of city planning promulgated in *acceptera*: parallel, equidistantly spaced narrow buildings, oriented along the north-south axis. See *acceptera*, in the present volume, p. 194, for Stadshagen, another municipal project that shows a similar arrangement. For a discussion of city planning in Stockholm around 1930, see Thomas Hall, "Urban Planning in Sweden," in *Planning and Urban Growth in the Nordic Countries*, ed. Thomas Hall (New York: Chapman & Hall, 1991), pp. 206–13.

12. See Paulsson, "Stockholmsutställningens program," Åhrén, "Bostadsavdelningens planläggning och tillkomst," and Markelius, "Smålägenheternas planlösningsproblem," in *Stockholmsutställningen 1930*, pp. 25–30 and 31–34, respectively. See also *Hemmet, Konstindustrien, Stockholmsutställningen 1930* (Stockholm: Stockholmsutställningen, 1930).

13. For a full account of Malmsten's criticisms of the Stockholm Exhibition and functionalism in general see Eva

Rudberg, "Rakkniven och lösmanschetten: Stockholmutställningen 1930 och 'Slöjdstriden'," in *Formens rörelse: Svensk Form genom 150 år*, ed. Kerstin Wickman (Stockholm: Carlssons, 1995), pp. 123–39. See also *acceptera*, in the present volume, n. 26.

14. Torsten Fogelqvist was the cultural and political editor of the left-leaning newspaper *Dagens Nyheter*. He wrote a number of articles on the Stockholm Exhibition, including "Lådorna på Djurgården," *Dagens Nyheter*, August 26, 1929, and "Schism inom Svenska Slöjdföreningen," *Dagens Nyheter*, September 21, 1930. For Åhrén's specific response to the criticism of Fogelqvist, see "Fogelqvist-Paulsson. Om journalistiskt ansvar," *Fönstret*, September 27, 1930.

15. Carl G. Laurin, "post funkis," *Svenska Dagbladet*, September 25–26, 1930. On Laurin, see Lane, Introduction, n. 34. On Lindhagen, see *acceptera*, in the present volume, n. 46.

16. Karl-Erik Forsslund, "K.F:s arkitektkontor och hembygdsvården: Dr K. E. Forsslund till angrepp," *Konsumentbladet*, October 11, 1930, pp. 8–9.

17. Gregor Paulsson to Sven Markelius, December 4, 1930, Gregor Paulsson Papers, Uppsala University Library.

18. Paulsson, "White Industry," *Architectural Review*, March 1931, p. 83.

19. Gotthard Johansson, "Acceptera: ett kulturprogram," *Svenska Dagbladet*, June 3, 1931. Johansson was the cultural critic for *Svenska Dagbladet* who crowned his significant support of the new architecture with the book *Funktionalismen i verklighet* (Stockholm: Albert Bonniers förlag, 1931), a collection of essays and articles that documented the development of the new architecture in both Sweden and Europe.

20. The argument that functionalism was a natural outgrowth of the Swedish propensity for straightforwardness and utility in building was fully developed in the previous year by Gustaf Näsström in *Svensk funktionalism* (Stockholm: Kultur och Natur, 1930).

21. Paulsson, *Upplevt* (Stockholm: Natur och Kultur, 1974), p. 113.

22. Paulsson, "Stockholmsutställningens program," pp. 107–09.

23. Sundahl, chairman of the housing section committee, was joined by Gahn, Asplund, and Paulsson in the judging of the limited competition for the housing units; Åhrén and Markelius designed four of the final house types.

24. See Åhrén's first published article for a discussion of Le Corbusier's work at the Paris Exhibition of 1925: "Brytningar," *Svenska Slöjdföreningens årsbok* (1925), pp. 7–36. An English translation of this article is forthcoming in Michael Asgaard Andersen, ed., *Nordic Architects Write* (London: Routledge, 2008).

25. At least five of the six *acceptera* authors visited Germany between 1927 and 1929: Åhrén in 1927 and Asplund and Paulsson the following year to visit the Weissenhof Siedlung, Stuttgart; Markelius in 1927 to visit Walter Gropius's housing at Törten, the Weissenhof Siedlung, and the exhibition "Die Wohnung," quite possibly also visiting the Frankfurt Siedlungen of Ernst May at this time, and again in 1929 as a Swedish delegate to the Congrès Internationaux d'Architecture Moderne (CIAM) conference in Frankfurt, reacquainting himself with Gropius; Sundahl sometime between 1928 and 1930 to visit the Bauhaus. See Rudberg, *Uno Åhrén*, p. 15; Paulsson, *Upplevt*, p. 121; Rudberg, *Sven Markelius*, pp. 48–50; and Brunnström, *Det svenska folkhemsbygget*, pp. 91–92. Further, Gropius visited Stockholm in March 1928 to deliver two lectures on the social function of modern architecture and industrial art and the necessity of adapting to industrial production methods. See Råberg, *Funktionalistiskt genombrott*, pp. 37–38.

26. Åhrén, "Bostadsavdelningens planläggning och tillkomst," p. 25.

27. The charts, drawings, and texts related to the housing section at the Stockholm Exhibition are held at Arkitekturmuseet, Stockholm: AM 1973–06, AM 1981–14, 01. See also Rudberg, *Uno Åhrén*, pp. 67–68, 267, n. 14.

28. Elin Wägner, "Revolution," *Svenska Slöjdföreningens Tidskrift* (1929): p. 156. Wägner was Paulsson's sister-in-law.

29. Paulsson, *Den nya arkitekturen* (Stockholm: P. A. Norstedt & Söner, 1916), p. 9. See also Kåberg, Introduction, pp. 63–65.

30. Paulsson, "Har man accepterat?" *Form* 5 (1940): p. 92.

31. In an interview in July 1930, Malmsten reported that part of his manuscript for a publication titled "Melodramen vid Djurgårdsbrunnsviken" had been completed. See "Skarp vidräkning med 'Traffikbarocken'," *Dagens Nyheter*, July 19, 1930. It can only be assumed that Malmsten never completed this book, as it was never published.

32. Gregor Paulsson to Sven Markelius, September 16, 1930, and Gregor Paulsson to Wolter Gahn, December 23, 1930. Gregor Paulsson Papers, Uppsala University Library.

33. Interview between Anders Åman and Gahn, "Om *acceptera*–efterskrift till 1980 års upplaga," in Asplund et al., *acceptera* (1980), p. 205. Interview with Sundahl, "Expeditens råd skall ersättas av förpackning," undated newspaper article, probably around October 1950, in AM 1989–17, box 2, Arkitekturmuseet, Stockholm.

34. Åman, "Om *acceptera*–efterskrift till 1980 års upplaga," p. 203; Rudberg cites an interview in which the closing statement of *acceptera* is attributed to Åhrén. See Rudberg, *Uno Åhrén*, pp. 75, 268, n. 9.

35. In 1980 Åman posited the following possible attributions: Åhrén, "Form," and possibly also the concluding remarks (the latter confirmed the following year by Rudberg; see n. 34 above); Asplund, "New and Old" (this chapter and "Form" were illustrated by assistants from Asplund's office and Asplund himself was responsible for the illustration on p. 304 of this volume); Markelius, the section on the family hotel; Paulsson, "It is hard to be objective," "The cultural situation," and perhaps also "Industry and handicraft"; and Sundahl, "Industrial housing production. Standardization." Åman does not speculate on the possible contribution of Gahn. Asplund et al., *acceptera* (1980), pp. 201–02.

36. *Acceptera*, in the present volume, p. 154.

37. Hans Sedlmayr has asserted the influence of Alois Riegl on Spengler; see Sedlmayr et al., *Framing Formalism: Riegl's Work* (Amsterdam: G+B Arts International, c. 2000). For a discussion of Spengler in relation to Åhrén see Eva Eriksson, *Den moderna staden tar form: arkitektur och debatt 1910–1935* (Stockholm: Ordfront, 2001), pp. 389–94. For the influence of Spengler on Paulsson see Gunnela Ivanov, *Vackrare vardagsvara–design för alla? Gregor Paulsson och Svenska Slöjdföreningen 1915–1925*, dissertation, Department of Historical Studies, Umeå

Universitet (Umeå: Umeå universitet, 2004), pp. 119–20. Spengler's *Der Untergang des Abendlandes* was one of the most widely read books in Europe during the 1920s. According to Eriksson, Spengler visited Stockholm for a lecture tour in 1924 and Gustav Strengell wrote a two-part account of his philosophy, "Spenglers historiefilosofi och arkitekturen," for *Byggmästaren*, nos. 16 and 17, pp. 186–88, 201–03, with which it is likely the authors of *acceptera* were familiar.

38. Asplund, "Vår arkitektoniska rumsuppfattning," *Byggmästaren*, no. 12 (1931): pp. 203–10; see also the forthcoming translation in Andersen, *Nordic Architects Write*.

39. *Acceptera*, in the present volume, p. 326.

40. Ibid., p. 327.

41. See in particular Sundahl, "Den moderna bostadens krav," *Svenska Slöjdföreningens Årsbok* (1929): pp. 3–28; Åhrén, "Elementär stadsbyggnadsteknik," *Byggmästaren*, no. 8 (1928): pp. 129–33; and Markelius, "Bostadsområde vid Dessau-Törten: ett aktuellt exempel på ekonomisk organisation av bostads-byggandet," *Byggmästaren*, no. 19 (1927): pp. 236–43.

42. Paulsson to Sven Markelius, December 4, 1930.

43. *Acceptera*, in the present volume, p. 202.

44. See Key, in the present volume, p. 34.

45. Gropius's argument is strikingly similar to that presented in *acceptera*–that the family as a unit of production had changed irreversibly and that women were now theoretically free to pursue work outside the home. This situation, said Gropius, "awakens thoughts about new forms of centralized master households which partially relieve the individual woman of her domestic tasks by an improved centralized organization which is capable of performing them better and more economically than she can perform them herself." See Eric Mumford, *The CIAM Discourse on Urbanism, 1928–1960* (Cambridge, MA: MIT Press, 2000), pp. 35–38. For a full account of Alva Myrdal's interest and involvement in this project see Alan Carlson, *The Swedish Experiment in Family Politics: The Myrdals and the Interwar Population Crisis* (New Brunswick, NJ: Transaction, 1990), pp. 60–66.

46. See Markelius, "Kollektivhuset: ett centralt samhällsproblem," *Arkitektur och samhälle* 1 (1932); Alva Myrdal, "Kollektiv bostadsform," *Tiden* (1932); and Claes Caldenby and Åsa Wallén, *Kollektivhus: Sovjet och Sverige omkring 1930* (Stockholm: Swedish Building Research Council, 1979), pp. 176–99. See also Markelius, "Kollektivhuset," *Byggmästaren*, Arkitektupplagan 6 (1934): p. 106.

47. Asplund, "Konst och teknik," *Byggmästaren*, no. 14 (1936): pp. 169–70. See also Siegfried Kracauer, "The Mass Ornament," originally published in 1927, in Kracauer, *The Mass Ornament*, ed. Thomas Y. Levin (Cambridge, MA: Harvard University Press, 1995), pp. 75–86.

48. Åhrén, *Arkitektur och demokrati* (Stockholm: Kooperativa Förbundet, 1942), pp. 5–22.

49. On New Empiricism and "spontaneity" in Swedish architecture see Lucy Creagh, "Asger Jorn and the 'Apollo and Dionysus Debate,' 1946–48," in *Architecture + Art: New Visions, New Strategies*, eds. Eeva-Liisa Pelkonen and Esa Laaksonen (Helsinki: Alvar Aalto Academy, 2007).

50. See Eric de Maré, "The New Empiricism: The Antecedents and Origins of Sweden's Latest Style," *Architectural Review*, January 1948, pp. 9–22.

51. Henry Ford, quoted with admiration by the *acceptera* authors, in the present volume, p. 337.

acceptera

den föreliggande verkligheten — endast därigenom
har vi utsikt att behärska den, att rå på den för att
förändra den och skapa kultur som är ett smidigt
redskap för livet. Vi behöver in⁺⁺ mmal kulturs
urvuxna former för att ⟍ älvaktning.
Vi kan inte smyg ⟍ Gunnar Asplund ⟍ bakåt. Vi
kan inte heller h ⟍ Wolter Gahn ⟍ besvärligt
och oklart in i en ⟍ Sven Markelius ⟍ te annat
än se verkligheten ⟍ Gregor Paulsson ⟍ den för
att behärska den. V. ⟍ Eskil Sundahl ⟍ d som
är mål i våra daga ⟍ Uno Åhrén ⟍ aldrig varit
någon verklig tvekai ⟍ ar de trötta och

Tiden

pessimistiska som på. att vi håller på att skapa
en maskinkultur som är sitt eget ändamål. Det är

Uno Åhrén
Gunnar Asplund
Wolter Gahn
Sven Markelius
Gregor Paulsson
Eskil Sundahl

acceptera—

The individual and the mass . . .

The personal or the universal?
Quality or quantity?
—Insoluble questions, for the collective is a fact
we cannot disregard any more than we can disregard
the needs of individuals for lives of their own.
The problem in our times can be stated as:
Quantity *and* quality, the mass *and* the individual.
It is necessary to solve this problem in building-
art and industrial art.[1]

Contents

It is hard to be objective.

There is an area in the cultural sciences in which opinions are as divided as in architecture, and typically enough this is research about the basis of human relationships and the organization of society—in other words, marriage.

In the nineteenth century an English scholar, [Lewis Henry] Morgan, on the basis of a number of facts, proposed a theory that marriage, like everything else in nature at the time, obeyed the laws of evolution.[2] Marriage thus developed from a primitive sexual union, the intercourse of all with all, through to what he called group marriage, the intercourse of some with some, to polygamy, the intercourse of one man with a few women, to polyandry, the intercourse of one woman with many men, and finally to monogamy, the intercourse of two individuals with each other.

This theory is acceptable as long as evolution can be considered identical with the unending chain of progress from primitive to higher forms, with modern civilization, private property, the family, and democracy as the ultimate perfection and concluding link. It is acceptable as long as it exalts the status quo.

But the concept of evolution then went on to acquire a relative meaning, in which development can just as easily be seen to lead to destruction as to perfection, with the present not representing the best of all possible worlds. Individuals who seek the overthrow of society attempt to adopt this theory as their own.

Later, society's leaders abandoned Morgan's doctrine, and instead another theory—one that showed that the concept of evolution is incorrect and that, having their roots in human instincts, current social values have always existed—received the full support of the ruling classes.

In 1891 one of the most famous works in the cultural sciences was published, [Edvard] Westermarck's book on the history of marriage.[3] Up until last year it was regarded as the standard work above all others on marriage and the emergence of moral concepts. It has been the bible of the social sciences. Its success is a textbook example of what it is that enables a social theory to be adopted.

Westermarck asserted that human marriage has existed as long as humanity itself, indeed is probably inherited from some apelike ancestors, and that the family is therefore an institution with which human social life is inextricably bound. Marriage is monogamous, founded in an instinct that existed long before humanity in the higher mammals, such as the apes. In other forms of social life, such as herds and tribes, male and female polygamy are deviations.

Now it is a remarkable circumstance that this author based his theory on highly defective facts. It is even more remarkable that the paucity of his evidence had not until recently been criticized by other scholars. For decades the author stood out as the authority above all others in his field and was never successfully challenged.

But this circumstance has its explanation. Westermarck's theory about the origin and development of moral concepts was opposed to Morgan's hitherto dominant sociological theory, which said that human beings originally lived in sexual community and subsequently developed to live in group marriages, a stage that still exists among certain primitive peoples, before finally attaining the current state of monogamy and family life.

Morgan's theory was a child of evolutionary thought, in which humanity was envisaged as developing from primitive states until the nineteenth century, whose society was seen as the culmination and ideal for human culture. This view also won general acceptance.

Because of the role Morgan ascribed to the concept of property in social development, however, his social theories were adopted by social democratic radicals such as Engels, Kautsky, etc. Now suddenly Morgan's theory seemed objectionable to the bourgeoisie. When the concept of evolution no longer described anything absolute but something relative, when the natural determination of the basic moral concepts of the laissez-faire system was challenged, when private property and the family were no longer regarded as indestructible and essential but in the opinion of the radicals were, on the contrary, doomed to disappear in the next stage of development, and when therefore the nineteenth century could not be regarded as the spectacular culmination of uninterrupted progress, the whole of this evolutionary concept was rejected and with it the social theories that had been based upon it. When, in other words, evolutionary theory turned out to harbor the possibility of both destruction and progress, it was considered harmful, and prepared the ground for scientific doctrines that argued that the prevailing values were inherent, that explained that private property was a fundamental instinct for all social life, that considered religion to be an impulse shared by both the savage and the civilized, that took as their premise that the family was the cornerstone of culture and regarded monogamy not as one form of marriage among others but as a form of coexistence that was fundamental for the human race and even for the mammals most closely related to it, and that declared that whatever direction evolution would take, private property and the family were unassailable values that no radical revolution could disturb.

Families.

In 1920 [*sic*] a Frenchman, Robert Briffault, published *The Mothers*, in which he marshaled a multitude of arguments and facts to demolish totally the volume by Westermarck that had been a standard work for an entire generation.[4] Now it was argued that far from monogamy being instinctive in humanity, on the contrary, hardly any primitive communities could be found without polygamy, and that where monogamy existed it had been forced on them by poverty.

The emergence of three contradictory accounts on the same subject can only be explained by unwarranted attention—no doubt unconscious—to certain facts and the suppression of others. Morgan probably viewed marriage primarily from its sexual aspect, Westermarck countered this by emphasizing the concept of family, children, and upbringing, and Briffault concentrated on the family not in terms of caring for children but as an economic factor in society.

It is not this set of contradictions that is of so much interest but rather the attitude of society to theories. The first held water only as long as development seemed to lead to the best of all worlds, in other words to Queen Victoria's bourgeois England. The second began to lose ground when individualistic bourgeois social values were generally questioned and collective economic factors were considered to be those that govern the world.

Not truth but social adaptability makes a theory powerful.

This circumstance is intrinsic to all social thinking; it can be expressed in crass terms by saying that it is not the truth of an idea that makes it powerful but its adaptability to other interests, mainly class interests. These interests draw down ideas from the vacuous world of abstractions and give them social significance.

On the other hand, social life provides the cultural sciences with their breath of life and raison d'être, and they cannot liberate themselves from the conditions imposed by life. Only in the natural sciences is there likely to be any possibility of thinking "in pure terms." (Though not necessarily.)

This thinking happens in the world of vacuous theories that are bound to no interests, where only facts are allowed to speak.

So what is it going to be like down in our world where interests govern?

What is building-art, one asks oneself, and the answers vary: Gothic temples, Classical temples, harmonious, rhythmic beauty and so on; during one decade in the nineteenth century this, during another that.

Amid all the vacillations to and fro in the world of aesthetic imagination, building-art suddenly became an "issue." This issue was the housing problem. In the same way, industrialization turned the production of domestic implements into an issue, the issue of how to acquire better household goods.

Lack of objectivity distorts
the solutions to social issues.

Our attitude to "issues" and our solutions for them are 99 percent based on our own interests. We seldom find the means to adapt *radically* to new situations. Social problems are solved as if we were remedying the symptoms of the illnesses and not the illnesses themselves. For instance if there is an increase in crime, most people feel this should be remedied by making penalties more stringent or increasing the police force. They argue like this: to prevent crime we have police forces and penalties, if crime increases these resources are inadequate, therefore they should be augmented. When corruption in the business world arises, then good old-fashioned honesty is sought, etc.

Generally speaking it can be said that when an "issue" arises it prompts dissatisfaction. The difficulty of solving it arouses thoughts of earlier times when it did not exist and when, by extension, everything must have been calm and tranquil. People therefore look to an earlier age for any possibility of a solution.

We forget the argument from sufficient reason.

So it is, at least, in building-art and applied art. It is clear that the radical changes in economic, social, and technological conditions during the nineteenth century placed these cultural areas in a temporarily insoluble conflict with these very circumstances, and one could say that architecture and the applied arts drifted around without direction. People attempted to resolve the issues in the way we have described, which was to look back to the lost paradise and seek to restore the relationship between art and handicraft, etc., that prevailed there. Consequently no attempt was made to adapt to the times. The conclusion was as follows: artistic culture can only flourish on the same terms as earlier, i.e., under the patronage of the propertied classes and produced by craftsmen. All social and cultural values must come from above and eventually be forced on to the lower levels of society. This is the way it used to be and always must be, this is the law of social evolution.

But this conclusion is after all merely a series of assertions and a mixture of *post hoc* and *propter hoc* reasoning and therefore lacks value. It is based on an autocratic perception of social life, i.e., that society is the society of the ruling classes, and if in any quarter something develops wrongly then it can be remedied with the patent medicines known to this society, wrested back into shape, excised, rearranged, so that it once again conforms with other approved circumstances.

In no other way at least can the stance toward the situation that arose in the nineteenth century in the fields of building-art and manufacture be explained. This

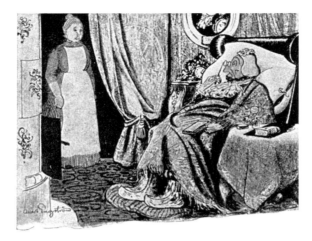

Mistress of the house and menial worker.

situation involved the dissolution of the guilds, the emergence of the proletariat, factory communities, railways, and cities with populations of over a million, the general use of iron and concrete as building materials, the practice of using machines to manufacture most household utensils that had previously been made by hand, and new synthetic materials for these objects. Moreover, it involved mobility among young people moving from their homes to early independence, and the conditions that ensued in housing, salary, work, and leisure, the decline in nativity, increasing comfort, etc., etc.

Instead of using logic, people resorted to emotional reflection with inadequate grounds. This is how people thought. Society used to be beautiful. Our society is ugly. What used to be beautiful? Yes, stylistic forms. What is ugly today? The lack of stylistic forms. *Ergo* we must return to the old styles.

The more perceptive attempted to probe more deeply and asked: Can there have been a reason why the earlier beautiful stylistic forms arose that will not emerge now? If so, this must rest with something that used to exist but no longer does. What is it? Indeed, handicraft. *Ergo*, let us revive the dying crafts. Anything else? Yes, kings and noblemen built magnificent palaces in which artists found haven. Through their forms these palaces also influenced the buildings and dwellings of the burghers and even of the poor. *Ergo*, if kings and noblemen no longer build palaces, let us nevertheless imitate what they built and in this way in spite of everything endow our age with flourishing art, refine the barbarians of this new era, and in fortunate cases "penetrate" as far as the lowest levels of society, who now live amid industrialism's worst forms and consequently without connection to cultured society.

These endeavors were prompted by the best of motives. But nobody noticed, firstly, that no progress was being made and, secondly, that the exchange of social values between different sectors of society is no longer one-way but takes place in both directions. Merely to take two aspects as important as our food and our clothes, it is from the "lower" classes that the tendency to buy mass-produced bread, tinned food, and ready-made garments has been acquired. Managing for oneself without servants is also a custom that comes from below. And in what is more important than anything else in our lives, how we earn our daily bread, the tone is undoubtedly set from below. This has been most obvious where women are concerned. Unmarried daughters and aunts, who were once "at the ready" around our homes, are now found in offices, stores, and workshops. (In conservative France it is said that so far clerical assistants have not been recruited from any sector "higher" than the daughters of concierges, but nowadays here in Sweden workers in an office are completely classless.) Even male occupations are at the moment undergoing significant

**Spinster daughter
living at home.**

changes, which aim to elevate practical skills and lower the status of at least the simpler "white-collar jobs."

In everything that is understood as prosperity, including art and architecture, on the other hand, the elevation of the masses is led from "above." **This is quite understandable. The masses confuse prosperity with the way of life of the propertied classes.**

There is belief in certain absolute aesthetic values just as there was in absolute social values.

Although modern society acquires most of its features from the new democracy, a number of values are allowed to remain completely intact as pure relics of a bygone cultural era. This is particularly the case with aesthetic values. Here belief in absolute values is virtually unshaken. Beauty consists of certain proportions and linear rhythms and found its highest expression during the classical period, from which other cultures have taken their maxims, supplemented by one or two of their own national traditions. Anyone who wants to assert that aesthetic values are relative and a function of the leading values of one's own age—the more independent of tradition the values of the age, the more independent of the tradition of classical aesthetic values—is regarded as a barbarian. This belief is so deep-seated that even those who have more than any others contributed to the creation of the current social structure, namely the social democrats, are able, with few exceptions, to stomach aesthetic doctrines that are expressions of cultures whose economic and social aspects they consider sheer exploitation. A minor but intriguing example of such reasoning: someone was invited by the city of Frankfurt am Main to travel out to see its *Siedlungen*, the most remarkable contribution of our age to the solution of housing problems, built in a modern and uncompromising manner.[5] In the same car sat a few other guests, communists from Hamburg. These communists did not at all appreciate the value of these housing solutions. When the visitor in question retorted that this housing was as practical an application of the principles of communism as could be, he was informed that it was "*ungemütlich*" [uncomfortable], that in all other respects communism was fine, but you want to live your private life at peace in an individualistic cottage and give full rein to your personality.

Out-of-date social values are allowed to govern building.

No one ever considers whether it may be possible to create new forms of housing that are better suited than tenant farmer's cottages to the economic conditions and patterns of thought and life of our society and its inhabitants. Similarly, it is taken for granted, indeed even demanded in some quarters, that the institutions created by our modern society, and to which there have previously been no counterparts, must don

Steam engine modeled on the Doric order.

the garb of earlier cultures, garb that will never suit them. How many department stores have been built in the Rococo style, the style of elegant craftsmanship *par preference*, how many of the labor movement's assembly halls in the Baroque style, the style of absolute monarchy?[6] This, in spite of the fact that the average workingman has a much clearer view of society, his relationship to it, and its probable development than the average member of the middle class. He allows nothing to conflict with his interests; he is in the process of molding society to the form he wants. He reads books that agree with his view of culture. But he builds what he opposes.

As we implied above, the probable explanation is that he seeks to gain prosperity but for natural reasons is incapable of immediately determining what form it is to take, partly from lack of alternatives, partly because it seems superior to adopt the forms in which prosperity once was clad.

Ducal palace or bourgeois dwellings?

Need these circumstances lead to skepticism about building-art? No!

Interest in the values of our own time engenders demand for objectivity. Radical building-art is sustained by the struggle for unconditional, objective embodiment independent of cultural borrowings.[7] This struggle is both a necessity and an interest. An interest in so far as it appears to us more stimulating and dignified to give form to the ideological and emotional currents that flow through and nourish contemporary life. We assert that the struggle for contemporaneity is a more valuable interest than moaning about the current leveling down of standards. It is an interest and a pleasure to affirm the features of the present that differ from other eras and to fearlessly allow new ideas of form to emerge. Creation for our times, the desire to be inspired by its brighter aspects, its dazzling technical inventions, its freer populace: this is all that can be meaningful. This interest, this endeavor to express the face of our age as its theme, itself makes demands that we attempt to fulfill. We cannot be inspired by an age if we feel no loyalty to it. We must place ourselves at its service, we must help to solve its problems.

B-Europe.

The cultural situation.

A- and B-Europe.

In terms of economic culture Europe can be divided into two main areas, which have been referred to as A-Europe and B-Europe.[8]

In the former the countryside under cultivation consists of a patchwork of roads on which a close network of railroads has been superimposed. In the latter there are a few long single railroads separated by extensive areas that are bisected by far-flung solitary roads and footpaths. Through A-Europe there is a broad ribbon, the black landscape of coal, which starts in Scotland, runs through Wales to northern France, then through Belgium and Poland to end in Serbia and Silesia. In this area the population density can reach four hundred per square kilometer while in the major industrial cities hundreds of thousands of inhabitants live cheek by jowl. In it can also be found green countryside, villages with their churches, and solitary farms. But from all these points, like the capillaries in a body, there proceed small byroads that flow into the major veins, the railroads and highways, which are in turn linked to the arteries, the principal international thoroughfares. Farmers send their crops, their eggs, their livestock to the city and receive in return tools, clothes, coffee, etc. The goods flow without interruption in two directions and are assembled in the large trading and industrial centers, from whence they are once again set in motion in two directions. The nerve centers, the major financial metropolises, register the movements in this circulation and attempt to regulate them.

So this A-Europe resembles a great organism in which all the functions are at the same time specialized and centralized and where all the cells, from the solitary farm to the immense factory or bank, are dependent on each other. This organic whole is also manifest in the appearance and conduct of individuals. Within this mighty circle, from Stockholm to Florence, from Glasgow to Budapest, men wear the same clothes of English cut and women the same dresses and shoes in the Parisian fashion. Perhaps not the same fashion among women, but sooner or later the Parisian models will be worn by the small-town housewife. The differences in food, household goods, and amusements are a matter of degree.

But cross the boundaries of this A-Europe: there are railroads but not railroad networks, there are large cities with trams, hotels, and women dressed in the Parisian fashion. But they are like isolated islands. The few poor highways are used to transport

Industry. A-Europe.

goods, but only occasional pairs of oxen will be drawing old-fashioned carts. Cut off from the rest of the world, the farmer builds his own cottage, eats crops that grow in his own fields, meat that comes from his own pigs and cows; his wife spins and weaves wool from his own sheep to clothe him. The village carpenter or village blacksmith makes the few items of furniture or tools that he needs for his survival. There is no agricultural machinery, occasionally an iron plow. He produces little and has almost nothing to barter. Once or twice a year he sets off to market with a calf or a couple of pigs, a few sacks of corn or potatoes: he takes home with him a scythe, a pair of boots, and a few meters of cotton cloth. He is rarely literate, does not know what a telephone is, hardly receives any mail. The circulation in the thousands of capillaries, veins, and nerves in A-Europe is reduced in this country to a few arteries, in between which millions of villages and farms stagnate like the tiny creatures in a coral reef. The behavior of the people has also stagnated. Their customs, clothes, and language vary from one province to the next.

Alongside A-Europe, with its specialized, centralized, and apparently uniform functions, B-Europe seems to be an amalgam of autonomous undertakings and alternating ethnic groups with no other unifying forces than religion and the powers-that-be, the latter often only by virtue of their swords. The difference can, as Delaisi points out, be expressed in one word: A-Europe is industrialized, even down to its agriculture, B-Europe is the domain of farmers even in its towns. B-Europe is what A-Europe was a hundred and fifty years ago.

Steam engines and coal have wrought this cultural change just as in the tenth century the invention of the harness, which enabled horses to be used as draft animals, provided the technical conditions for the emergence of the social, political, and artistic Europe of the Middle Ages. Today, the use of machines for the manufacture and transport of products makes it possible to produce and sell more than before. City-dwellers can buy the farmers' produce, farmers more goods from the cities. It has been possible to raise the living standards of every class. The fields can feed more people. In 1850 Germany fed thirty million people, today seventy-two million. Great Britain had a population of fifteen million in 1800, now it has forty-five million, and each one of these forty-five million consumes four times more than each of the fifteen million in 1800.

The correct measurement of the power of a population is not its size in numbers, but this figure multiplied by a coefficient of the country's aggregate horsepower. In this way, Belgium with its seven million inhabitants is a greater economic power than Poland with its twenty-nine million. With the help of horsepower, A-Europe has become the Europe of machines, banks, adult education, and science; without them B-Europe has remained the Europe of the rural, religious orthodoxy, and illiteracy.

The difference becomes even more prominent if one regards the **way of life** that both worlds have created. Outside the perimeter of A-Europe, undertakings consist of smallholdings on which one farmer lives with his family. To derive a livelihood for himself and his kin he has recourse only to his own hands, his horses, oxen, and

Agriculture. B-Europe.

sheep, his rye and wheat, his flax, spinning wheel, and loom. His horizon ends in the village to which he goes on Sundays or in the nearest town, whose market he attends. He has little to do with affairs of state other than to pay taxes and perform military service. Ideas are exchanged as rarely as goods. Keeping house, like thinking, focuses on the needs of the family. This is how he lives, and has lived for centuries.

In A-Europe specialization prevails. Workers in their factories, craftsmen in their workshops, and retailers in their shops make or sell a few types of goods. The farmer also endeavors to specialize in a few products that, because of the soil and market conditions, provide the greatest economic benefits. His farm does not comprise an economic unit, the self-sufficient household. He does not consume what he produces, he sells it to buy what he consumes. His wife does not weave her own homespun for clothes but fabrics for decoration. The occasional barter at the market has become a daily routine of exchange through the village shops, cooperative dairies, silos, and banks. And the flow of commerce is accompanied by a flow of ideas. The farmer belongs to the world, in good times and in bad. If circulation is obstructed in some distant spot, he notices it as well. The harvest in America affects the prices at which he can sell his own crops. And the remarkable thing is that this farmer, with the help of "mechanical agriculture," has raised the quality and the yield from his land, nature notwithstanding. The yield from naturally favored farming districts like the rich black earth of Romania and Hungary is half as much per square meter as from the much poorer soils of England, Belgium, and southern Sweden. Even in its farming, therefore, agricultural Europe is inferior to the industrial areas.

Agriculture. A-Europe.

From the population point of view this entire process has two aspects. Industrial manufacture attracts people, which explains the phenomenon of urbanization, the continuous growth of the towns (79 percent of the population of England lives in towns, in Ukraine 20 percent). Industrial agriculture drives people away (compared to a rural population of 80 percent in Ukraine, in cooperative Denmark it comprises only 55 percent).

Consequences:

   I. Population growth,
      urbanization,
      depopulation of the countryside;
  II. industrialization of the production of goods,
      increased production of goods,
      increase in wages and purchasing power;
III. interconnection of countries because of new forms of transport,
      interconnection through trade and banks,

are in the process of creating

a new world—

—a new type of individual.

Build for them according to the conditions that have created them!

Greater Norrland in Sweden—nature and culture.

Sweden-now and Sweden-then.

Every civilization has its own visage and involves an intervention in what came before. In the old Europe major revolutions had to take place and much of the cultural superstructure of the centuries has been challenged or directly imperiled. In actual fact in every country an A-Europe and a B-Europe still survives.

If we look at our own Sweden, it could be said that the new and the old have completely permeated each other. We have one culture that we have inherited from our fathers, of villages and market towns, and another that we have constructed ourselves, of railroad communities and factory towns.[9] We could call them Sweden-then and Sweden-now. If you imagine the maps of these two Swedens superimposed on each other, great differences will be revealed. Admittedly a population map of Sweden-now would in terms of **relative** population densities agree in certain substantial respects with one of Sweden-then. And if we could reconstruct the latter, we would probably see that the same density zones form a belt from southern Uppland through Närke down to eastern Västergötland and back east of Lake Vättern around the lakes of Boren, Roxen, and Glan out to the Baltic. We would see the same high levels of density in the counties of Malmöhus and Halland. But we would not find such dense zones in the uncultivated areas of western Västergötland or in Värmland, in Bergslagen or the coastal plains of Norrland. And above all, if we could draw up two maps to show the efficacy of the population, maps of **population x horsepower**, the agreements would be further reduced. We would see that the horsepower map of modern large-scale industries would only coincide to a very small extent with that of Sweden-then. For the sawmill industry this would be a complete reverse of Sweden-then: its black areas would occupy those once white; for the paper-pulp industry the effect would largely be the same, as it would for mining iron ore and for paper-making (note Värmland, Småland, and Dalarna). For ironworks the main black zone would be at the northern limits of Sweden-then (Norra Uppland, Gästrikland). The old mill- and foundry-Sweden and the new factory-Sweden do not share many zones. Their circulation and nervous systems differ.

In the Middle Ages the king made his royal progress through the most important towns: Uppsala, Strängnäs, Nyköping, Söderköping, Linköping, Skänninge, Vadstena, Jönköping, Falköping, Skara, Askersund, Örebro, Torshälla, Arboga, Västerås, and Enköping.

A royal progress today, if the king's route were to follow the major points on the horsepower map, would take him, for example, to Dannemora, Sandviken, Bergvik-Ala, Svartvik, Kramfors, Salsåker, Munksund, Gellivare, Kiruna, Porjus, Hammarforsen, Falun, Kvarnsveden, Avesta, Grängesberg, Västerås, Örebro, Kristinehamn, Uddeholm, Trollhättan, Borås, Göteborg, Tidaholm, Hälsingborg, Svalöf, Malmö, Trälleborg, Jönköping, Huskvarna, Motala, Norrköping, and Nyköping.

In this Sweden-now grows a new culture that provides the Sweden-then it encompasses with the livelihood and the material possibilities for its spiritual culture.

Two royal progresses: then and now.

A close-up of society.

This is what a picture of Sweden—and of Europe—looks like on such a reduced scale that only its main features can be perceived with no details at all. Let us approach the subject very closely, so closely that we can see how people lead their daily lives. We will then find that the people of A-Europe do not live in **one** society or in **one** era. In different areas society has evolved differently.

It is possible to divide social life into the six following areas:

work,
the home,
raising children,
recreation,
religion,
social concerns.

These six areas have not all reached the same stage of development; some have stopped at a certain point or have developed extremely slowly. In fact in only one or two of these areas can it truly be said that we are only now, for the first time, experiencing the most rapid changes that have ever taken place in history, and this applies mainly to our work. With only slight exaggeration one could say that we live, or have lived until recently, with

nineteenth-century **upbringing**
eighteenth-century **domestic life**
sixteenth-century **religious life**.

Work and amusements develop most quickly, then come upbringing and social issues, followed by domestic adaptations to the new circumstances, and finally religion.

Now it is of course not necessary for all the areas in which our social actions take place to be at the same stage of development. Some fundamental religious values, certain elementary principles of upbringing, etc., may remain the same for centuries. This need not lead to any dissonance in our lives. Dissonance will arise when the retrograde areas, the then-areas, put pressure on those that are up-to-date. This dissonance is not only a source of discontent but above all it makes it more difficult to find appropriate solutions to problems of the now-areas themselves.

Clear pressure of this kind can be found in the area of housing. One would like to think that the production of dwellings, like building-art in general, should know about life and provide designs that take different forms of life into account. It should be able to distinguish these from the forms that life once took, but in which it is now unable to thrive without friction.

But building-art is more conservative than life, for housing form has petrified while life has changed radically in important respects.

If one examines the route of the royal progress referred to above, one will find that the material centers of power in our country are largely places that account for the production of manufactured goods, of raw materials, semi-manufactured items, and machines. This is no coincidence. Consumer products are the Cinderellas of industry. No intellectual brilliance is devoted to them. Bad quality and bad taste is what characterizes them the world over. This is one of the strongest dissonances. Many blame this on industry, but they are wrong. In actual fact it is nothing but the consequence of failures in adapting between the old and new life. Europe-now produces the household goods of Europe-then. There is no clear conception of which of the latter's production methods and outcomes merit survival into the present.

It is a deplorable illusion to believe that artistic culture and at least the production of buildings and household goods can exist independent of economic, technological, and social circumstances. This culture must adapt to A-Europe or become meaningless.

An ideal villa in the eyes of the cynical observer.

The society we are building for.

Who works?

Nowadays 45 to 50 percent of those living in towns are gainfully employed outside their homes. Among every four workers, three are probably men, and one a woman. Thirty years ago the ratio was probably nine to one. An inquiry conducted among the three highest years in an American high school produced the response that 89 percent of the 446 girls questioned intended to look for work when they left school. Thirty years ago the same 89 percent would probably have continued to live at home. This change mainly affects the middle class. A large proportion of the women who work outside the home are married. This applies in particular to the working class. The reasons for this vary from downright need to the desire for a more comfortable way of living, an automobile, better accommodation, better education for their children, and in some cases the feeling of being independent of their husbands. It has been calculated that 75 percent of the mothers of these women never worked for gain during their entire lives; most of the remaining 25 percent worked in their homes as seamstresses, taking in ironing, etc.

At what age do people work? The age at which one takes up paid employment is now about five years older than it was a generation ago. This is due to the longer period required to raise and educate children. Compulsory elementary schooling ends at the age of fourteen, but those who then go to work directly are easily counted. We have vocational schools that pupils leave at the age of sixteen, other types of schools that children can stay on in until they are fifteen, and there are also continuation schools, middle schools, secondary schools, advanced vocational schools, etc. On the other hand young people play a more important role in places of work than they used to. The older workers are no longer necessarily the most proficient; vocational skills are not handed down by tradition from generation to generation, but in many cases trades are now better taught by schools than they were previously by master craftsmen; and machines replace the work of hands to make speed and endurance more important than all-around vocational knowledge. A twenty-five-year-old boy can work more effectively in many jobs today than his fifty-year-old father, which would hardly have been conceivable when his father was twenty-five. In this way young people, especially in the working class, have acquired a totally new and independent position. In the middle class this shift in favor of the young is not as clearly evident. There the young do not have the same opportunities, because their potential cannot be assessed as directly as it can for physical work. Thus long-standing promotion systems survive, based on "experience," "maturity," etc. But in the financial and industrial classes again we find that young people are more frequently appointed to managerial positions.

How much will I be paid?

The budget for a working-class family in the metal and manufacturing industries in Stockholm in 1922 to 1923 totaled about 4,880 kronor, and this figure is not likely to have changed appreciably for 1931. Most of this income came from the wages earned by the family's breadwinner, about 4,050 kronor, or 83 percent. The income of a corresponding family thirty years ago was probably about 1,100 kronor. At that time these were high wages. At a cotton mill in Stockholm the average wage during the same period was about 600 kronor. In the tobacco industry in 1899 only 7 percent of the full-time male workers earned more than 1,200 kronor per year, 40 percent between 1,200 and 800 kronor, 38 percent between 800 and 500 kronor, and 15 percent earned under 500 kronor. The average income for a married male worker was 880 kronor. Casual workers, unskilled laborers, were even worse off.

What do I get for my money?

In the 1890s those with high wages were spending about 20 percent of their income on rent, those worse off about 15 percent. The average rent for one room and a kitchen was then about 180 kronor and varied depending on the area. According to the survey of the housing situation in Stockholm published by Key [Karl Key-Åberg] in 1897, of 35,000 apartments occupied by workers, 14,000 comprised one room and a kitchen, 7,500 two rooms and a kitchen, and 2,000 three rooms and a kitchen. There were only 450 apartments with more than three rooms, and roughly the same number of the poorest kind of accommodation, consisting of a single room without a separate kitchen. Of the 19,000 apartments whose occupants were *not* workers, on the other hand, the majority, or 10,000, comprised more than three rooms, and then the frequency declined with 3,000 three-room apartments, 2,000 two-room apartments, and 500 one-room apartments. About half of the dwellings in Stockholm consisted of one room and a kitchen or less.[10]

Today some increase can be seen in the spaciousness of apartments. On the other hand there has been a reduction in the number of very large apartments. But no thoroughgoing change has taken place. A worker in Stockholm in the 1930s lives in the same kind of dwelling as his parents. Here we are talking about size, not the quality of the housing, which has improved considerably. Merely during the ten-year period 1915 to 1925 the percentage of one-room apartments with kitchens and bathrooms rose from 0.4 percent to 3.09 percent, for two-room apartments with kitchens from 3.27 percent to 9.35 percent. The proportion of apartments with central heating in 1915 was 10.8 percent but in 1925 22.3 percent.

The average rent for one room and a kitchen in 1897 was 180 kronor for apartments occupied by workers, for those occupied by others 216 kronor. In 1929 it was 628 kronor (without central heating, 1,062 kronor with central heating).

Today our worker spends about the same percentage of his annual income on rent, or about 20 percent, as he did thirty years ago. Both his income and his rent are now three times greater than they were then. Other living costs have, on the other hand, risen less. It is possible to determine that between 1913 and 1923 there has been a real increase in the prosperity of the working population of almost 20 percent.

This proves that housing standards have not kept pace with the rise in living standards and that I cannot afford housing of the standard that efforts to increase prosperity during recent decades entitle me to. If I want to raise the standard of my accommodation I have to lower my standard when it comes to clothes and food. Lowering the standard of clothing would mean a return to the scanty levels of the 1890s, and it is also obvious that few economies on food are possible for us in Sweden. And anyway this intellectual experiment need never be made, as the fact remains that the majority of the population has been unable to allow the standard of their housing to follow the general rise in living standards in other respects. Today, the typical Stockholm household of a well-placed worker can comprise a modern apartment of one room and a kitchen or an older one with two rooms and a kitchen, or roughly the same as it would have been in the early 1890s. If he is living in a house of his own in the suburbs, he may be living in the type of cottage that has one room and a kitchen and that offers the possibility of another two small bedrooms. In contrast, over 90 percent of his American brothers have four to five rooms, a kitchen, and a bathroom.

We believe that family dwellings should be larger than those we are accustomed to.

We demand not only the higher standard of comfort we have already attained but also higher standards of spaciousness.

What is work like?

Everybody knows that working conditions are enormously better than they were thirty years ago. Shorter working days have given us the opportunity for rest, study, and amusements. On the other hand, it is claimed that work has become more

The crafts-man's creative pleasure?

monotonous, that we are cogs in a machine, and that machines have destroyed the enjoyment the old-fashioned craftsman took in his work. If we take this enjoyment as the joy of creativity, then it was probably restricted to a select few in the past as well. In a pottery it was probably linked mainly to throwing the pots and decorating them. Preparing the clay, glazing, placing objects in racks, inserting them into the ovens, firing the oven, removing the racks from the ovens and the items from the racks, and then packing them and so on is tedious and at times arduous work. If we take trade after trade—baking, tanning, joinery, turning, glassblowing, and goldsmithing—and compare working conditions in the past and today, we will find that machines have led to a reduction of the heavy work and have also facilitated the application of genuine vocational skills.

There can be no doubt that the modern factory worker is no less fortunate given the assistance provided by machines. Certain tasks are, however, extremely laborious, particularly assembly-line production, where it is not the individual but the machinery or production line that sets the pace. If the reduction of working hours is taken into consideration, however, despite this exception it can probably be said that work today is generally lighter than it was a generation ago.

There can be no harm in listening to what workers themselves say about the machines. The French workman H[enri] Dubreuil writes in his book about American manual laborers: "If technological developments do not always require the same manual skills as in the past, they do, however, oblige the worker to acquire theoretical knowledge that extends far beyond the horizon of the day laborers of the past. A good workman today needs to know a lot more than a worker a hundred years ago. People who have never handled genuine machine tools have totally false conceptions of them. They exaggerate the legend that the worker is a slave to the machine. Just let them ask a gear maker to explain the work involved in shaping a cog!"[11]

Soul-destroying machine work?

Iron Rolling Mill, 1875.
Ingots are drawn on a barrow, ingots being rolled, workers eating breakfast in "fine" disorder.

Two film stills from an iron-rolling mill in 1930.
The ingots are transported automatically between and through the rollers. One man at the controls operates the entire machine.

The possibility of having a personal influence on the design, of making an individual contribution to a product's quality, has been claimed to be a major source of enjoyment for the craftsman, and the absence of such possibilities and the forced mechanical repetition of his work a heavy yoke for the industrial worker. There is naturally something to this point of view even though it is one-sided and exaggerated. The happiness of the individual is, however, not as dependent on his work as people would like to maintain. It can be just as dependent, perhaps even more so, on other circumstances. For out-and-out individualists a mechanical way of working may naturally be utterly taxing, and there are of course cases where a particular job is soul-destroying, but such is also the case in a number of the craft professions. The dissatisfaction and anxiety that industrial work is considered to provoke are not so much a question of an aversion to the work itself as the struggle for better economic and social conditions. This is a struggle that is also being waged by craftsmen and that also prompts their anxiety and concern. Those who believe that modern industrial workers fret about or are made passive by the lack of psychological stimulus in their work know nothing about the mentality of the worker and do not understand that such tendencies, if they exist, are usually due to the indifference of the management to the personal qualities and conditions of their employees. Wise managers avoid extending rationalization beyond the bounds at which human effort and enjoyment of the work begins to fail, and they are eager to find ways to ensure that workers derive pleasure in what they do and have economic security.

The places in which people work have undoubtedly been improved, but a great deal still remains to be done. This is natural, as refurbishments cost money. But these costs are only illusory because good premises offer a better profit from labor. Not only is more work done, but well-being increases, which in its turn counteracts the threat of monotony and can therefore itself also be valued in terms of money.

The changing conditions of our work lead to the following

consequences.

Through the increased number of workers in each family, through the greater independence of young people, through the rise in the standard of living in other respects, the character of our homes is being changed in ways that we will consider more closely.

The reduction in working hours offers greater opportunity for rest, study, and recreation.

Rationalized working conditions lead to greater possibilities of improvement in the place of work.

Radio in a log cabin.

Rest and recreation.

Two main factors create our possibilities for rest and recreation: on the one hand less arduous work, shorter working hours, and higher wages, and on the other, three inventions—the automobile, the movie theater, and the radio. The first factor entails that rest and recreation now form a given element in our existence, which is something that could not have been said a mere thirty years ago. The other offers us technical possibilities we could never have dreamed of.

For a long time we have had the following forms of recreation:

social life in and outside our homes, clubs, and associations,

reading and studying,

art, theater, and music.

In recent times we have added sport, scouting, weekending, and the like.

It is important to see clearly that the three inventions have had a radical impact on our leisure in multiplying our possibilities. In towns in the countryside once visited occasionally by touring groups of actors and where the usual artistic fare consisted of a barnyard comic in an assembly room, movies have, for instance, become the exponents of culture and antagonists of boredom. It is quite important to point this out on behalf of the much derided movies.

On the other hand the three inventions have no unified tendency in terms of their impact on the relationship of people to their homes. Automobiles and movies lure them away, radios keep them at home, taking the place of stories read by gaslight. It may well be that television will come to have an even greater influence in this second respect. It will certainly never compete significantly with the movies any more than radios can with gramophones, but it will become a new source of information and a new way of spreading knowledge. For instance, if one considers education, popular lectures will probably disappear when the lecturer can stand in a [television] studio and perform scientific experiments, demonstrate paintings, and so on, like a teacher in a classroom. This is probably what will happen first of all. It is within the bounds of possibility that television will soon influence the patterns of our movements completely. At any rate the function of the home will become more important because of it.

Radio also offers a counterweight to excessive collectivization. It addresses individuals and requires them to concentrate.

At the movie theater.

One may perhaps feel that our forms of recreation have little to do with questions of building, apart from when we are erecting movie theaters and the like, but as we shall see, this is wrong. If, for instance, we first look at social activities and the way in which we interact with other people, this has to a certain extent shifted from our homes to clubs, associations, and restaurants. The parties we give tend to be fewer or smaller and simpler. Friendships are cultivated in clubs and associations more than they once were. Food and drink is less important. What now occurs more often in our homes than it used to is dancing. But our dancing at home is now simpler and more spontaneous

Dancing to the radio at home.

with the help of the gramophone, not as it used to be at balls. If one wants to dance in more festive surroundings, one can go to a restaurant. In fact where dancing is concerned there have only been improvements, if we compare it to the past, when some old maid was hired to tinkle the keys of the drawing room piano. Generally speaking, the way in which social life is developing means that we need no longer entertain in our homes; this is more easily arranged in restaurants, town halls, and assembly rooms, so that instead it is possible for our homes to fulfill their roles in our daily lives as places where we sleep, spend time with our families, and seek privacy.

Does all this going out take us away from our homes? Of course it does, but is it not better to stay at home voluntarily than to have no other choice but to remain there? This used to be the case, if we admit the truth. Moreover, outside our homes we can find more artistic pastimes than before. We have already mentioned movies and their cultural significance. This is one definite factor. Many artistic pastimes are, on the other hand, now available in our homes through the radio and gramophone. The continual improvement of the latter in terms of tone and the quality of the repertoire is undeniable. If the gramophone and the radio are leading to the disappearance of domestic musical performances little harm will ensue, no more than in the reduction of dilettantish artistic endeavors resulting from the masses of museums and art exhibitions, photographs, and reproductions. The general trend for artistic pastimes is that technical aids are increasing their quantity while at the same time on the whole enhancing their quality.

One weakness in this mechanized distribution of art is that it leads to a passive approach to art, while the individual activities of the past are becoming less common. In the past one entertained oneself, now one is entertained by others.

Taken as a whole, all of these circumstances create a pattern of home life that is entirely new. Homes that are cultural settings—not only of the famous Malla Silverstolpe [*sic*] kind but those found all over the country in vicarages and military homes, etc.—are, **for the time being**, a thing of the past.[12] **This leads to the disappearance of a certain valuable type of individual and form of cultural life.** Their modern replacement, the more refined cultural hobbies, is not enough. The causes can be found in lack of time—while the working classes now work shorter hours, the old cultural classes now have to work longer—as well as in the technical inventions we have referred to and the passivity they give rise to.

It is of great importance that we bring about an improved activity in our cultural pastimes. It is, of course, impossible to say how and whether some modern replacement of the old-fashioned dilettantism can arise.

On the other hand the kinds of recreation that more than any others lure us from our homes, sport and outdoor activities, are of a very active nature. The few negative forms that exist—covert professionalism or the appeal to brutal instincts in boxing and football matches—cannot tarnish their merits to any great extent. We must not forget that the commercialization of sport has also extended its impact. When seen from the perspective of a previous generation, recreation today is unrecognizable.

The youth of today.

On holiday.

Gymnastic event.

Sunday afternoon walks or excursions to Hagaparken have become weekend trips, a game of ball in the backyard is now a football match or some other physical exercise at a large arena.[13] Boys and girls now have scouting, which is at once both training and outdoor activity. A few figures: there are 4,620 fair-size sports grounds in Sweden, and the production of skis has risen more than fivefold over thirty years. Healthy individuals, with a feeling of physical freedom and an instinctive desire for cleanliness, are now returning from the gymnasiums, tennis clubs, swimming pools, and athletics grounds, from the meadows, forests, and lakes. It would be natural for them to insist on homes that embody hygiene, sunlight, fresh air, light, and water.

All of this outdoor and athletic life results in a new relationship to nature. While a generation ago one hardly left the city limits or at the most undertook a three-mile walk once or twice each year, now it is customary to undertake some form of regular

Sunday morning.

outdoor activity. Here distances from the towns play no great role. It is obvious that this means that today people see nature with new eyes. Mastering the landscape through a combination of technical implements and physical and mental energy enhances self-confidence but also creates a feeling of the earth's power, because it is always greater than all our efforts. "The world is shrinking—the world is growing."[14]

We can also see that life outside our homes need not become superficial if we look at the development of studying. In 1917 68,000 people were members of study circles in Sweden, an impressive number if you consider how recent this movement is.[15] The production of books is increasing. One of the most important indications of the desire to study can be found in the holdings of public libraries and the number of books borrowed. In 1913 Sweden's public libraries possessed 540,000 volumes, in 1930 4,000,000. In 1913 the number of books borrowed totaled 1,070,000 volumes, in 1929 9,200,000.

Consequences.

Our modern forms of rest and recreation have the most far-reaching consequences for architecture. One can disregard the building types that arise directly from this, such as sports arenas, swimming pools, and movie theaters, and look at **the indirect consequences rest and recreation have for the ways we use the home**. Perhaps there are no factors more important than the requirement for hygiene presented by outdoor life, the isolation required for study, the gathering that takes place around the radio loudspeaker, and, conversely, the disappearance of the need for space in which to entertain as a result of the simpler lives we now lead in our homes.

Society's assistance to the individual.

Since 1913 there has been a fivefold increase in public expenditure to about 250 million kronor per year on health and medical services, looking after the poor, child care, pension insurance, and other activities that protect the less affluent from the financial consequences of accidents, illness, old age, invalidism, and unemployment.[16] In this way the state is paying to benefit the vigor of the population.

In all of these areas the relationship of the individual to the state has changed radically compared with the past. There is no need here to discuss the direct consequences for the building industry in the erection of institutional buildings, but the most important thing is that **society takes care of certain elements in the lives of individuals** that were formerly their own responsibility or that did not exist at all. This means that individuals have a greater chance of keeping their homes intact, both economically—they can be helped through crises they have not caused—and also functionally, as the home can be for rest and family life. Further, the old and sick are not solely dependent on the arbitrary charity of others.

Within the four walls of the home.

The question of who lives in today's homes, one would think, is an obvious one, but this is by no means the case. The fact is that thirty years ago it was the exception for a worker's family to have a home of their own, because in Stockholm there were lodgers in 47.4 percent of all the apartments with one room and a kitchen rented by workers, in 68.2 percent of all with two rooms, in 78.2 percent of all three-room apartments, and in 88.2 percent of all with four rooms. Those who were most able to live on their own were those with one room and no kitchen, as of these "apartments" only 37.6 percent had lodgers living in them. One can understand the nineteenth-century philanthropists who exclaimed that for people living in these dwellings the home must have been hell and the taverns and brothels heaven.

But family members have also changed. In normal economic conditions the father has the largest income; after his eight-hour day he can, without being exhausted, sit at home with a newspaper, a book, or the radio, and he can stake a claim to better food.

Those who have changed most are the children. If families have grown-up children living at home, they are independent individuals with good incomes. They have the right to demand better housing standards, expressed in more space and greater comfort.

Do they make these demands? No, for as pointed out above, it is in our homes that, next to religion, developments take place most slowly. Particularly in the working classes, people are conservative about the way they live even when they are not obliged to be. The clerical classes maintain a somewhat higher standard, spending a greater proportion of their incomes on their housing than the workers. This is perhaps because on the whole they have been brought up to expect a higher standard. Equally, it may be because at the moment they make greater demands than the working class to be able to spend their leisure time in comfort in their own homes and have a reasonable chance to sleep soundly.

How do people live in their homes?

Two functions are primary here: working at home and resting in the home.

The home is not only a home but just as much a workshop where the housewife does the housework that a home demands. Therefore we shall look at how the work is done there.

The three main areas of housework are cooking and the chores that go with it, sewing and repairing, and cleaning and laundry.

Cooking no longer occupies the same central position in housework it once did. This is not because mealtimes are any less a focal point for family life and that purely psychologically should be any less the object of care. The change has taken place in the technical field. Food is easier to cook and more is bought already prepared. This applies in particular to the working class. Their rising prosperity chiefly finds expression in more expensive food, and this food consists of easily prepared and often ready-made dishes. In this respect the middle classes are more conservative. It is difficult to produce any numerical evidence for this change of diet: where consumption can be measured, as for the purchase of bread, it has probably risen by 100 percent in thirty years. Where canned goods are concerned the change is even more obvious. Canned goods were once a luxury. In 1889 their production in the U.S.A. amounted to thirty million dollars, in 1919 four hundred million dollars. Home preserving is dying out. Admittedly every effort is being made to revive it through advertisements for newly invented preserving equipment. Formerly our diet was divided strictly into winter and summer diets. In the winter the main ingredient was meat and until recently was based in Sweden on salted produce, salt pork, salt beef, and salt herring.

Salted produce and preserves were based on the need to store provisions for the winter and between the slaughter periods. This led to a great deal of household work and large larders. Today this space is not needed.

Cleaning and laundry. In no area can there possibly have been greater changes than in the two other branches of housework.

Take cleaning. The following diary was kept by a married American man in 1887. "Wednesday 19. Bessie began cleaning yesterday. Friday 21. Cleaning still going on. Saturday 22. Still cleaning, parlor, downstairs hall, and upper floor finished apart from our room. Monday 24. Cleaning still going on, our room a great big mess. Tuesday 25. Finished cleaning yesterday evening." In other words a whole week's work. After hearing this kind of information one can understand the claim that "marriage condemns a woman to penal servitude for life in her own home. Her work is the most monotonous in the world and she cannot evade it." Under such circumstances it is a gratifying development, particularly noticeable among the working class, that in the vast majority of cases the mothers of the current generation did more housework than we do. In the middle class, on the other hand, for whom paid help was once cheaper, housewives probably have to undertake more heavy chores than the previous generation. They can find compensation in buying ready-made clothes, in the labor-saving appliances that have been introduced, and in the simplification of cooking. The equipment in the home, with its appliances and implements, has very little in common with the equipment of thirty years ago. These machines, however, are not completely the product of the effort to improve efficiency. The preserving apparatus in cooking has its counterpart in the electric washing machine, an expensive device that now risks reversing the trend for housewives to do less and less laundry themselves.

Sewing and mending clothes. There is less and less of this activity in our homes thanks to the increasing prevalence of ready-to-wear garments and also, to some extent, changes in fashion. Children are, for instance, dressed much more simply than they used to be; today they wear only half as many garments at any one time. In the summer perhaps only dungarees. For women as well, fashions have on the whole improved; working clothes, a skirt and blouse, are simple and attractive. Evening gowns forage around for styles from the present and the past, typically enough, but, unlike working clothes, seem to seek some form of analogy to the dinner jackets and tails worn by men. If only we could buy ready-made clothes, for women and children in particular, as cheaply as in America, sewing would soon disappear completely from our homes and they would have to house one less function.

To what extent have these changing circumstances for housework changed the home itself? Well, so far not very much. To begin with, the only consequences were the emergence of labor-saving appliances, general kitchen storage with room for everything and therefore for nothing, and many other things that industry, always on the lookout for the most up-to-date, delighted in supplying on the market. The entire "labor-saving" industry is paradoxical, since it is flourishing while at the same time developments are tending to shift work out of the home. Once people began to realize this, they understood that changes in work would require above all changes in building methods.

On the whole, it can be said that currently work in the home is a mixture of the old and the new, at once at a standstill, making headway, and going backwards. If we compare with the era when a family was not only a social unit but also an economic one, when women wove and spun, did the milking and managed the garden, when these tasks had the same economic importance as those of their menfolk in the fields and meadows or in the workshop, when even work in the home contributed to family finances, when tools and goods were simple and hardly changed, one realizes that housework in the past and today have very little in common. Housewives are generally not yet capable of assessing the value of all the machines advertised for them. The fact that older children do not contribute their labor directly to the household economy, but earn their daily bread outside the home in a trade different from that of their fathers so that they pay for their own room and board, has also played a role in changing housework completely.

Main trends in interior decoration.

Three trends predominate in the manufacture of household goods at the moment. The first is the endeavor to produce modern furniture of good quality, materials, and construction, where the aim is utility and where design is gradually and half-unconsciously evolving toward the clear restraint and objectivity of the utilitarian object.

The second is the outcome of our overdeveloped knowledge about and interest in history. It is a yen for the past that requires a home to be either a mishmash of period pieces or an all-embracing image of a specific style, copied of course, or at least to have an aura of history about it. In the latter case we are no great distance from pastiche. This whole trend is endorsed by the "lovers of beauty" in society. In this way they create "cultivated" homes. Many experience the annoyance of discovering that their period pieces are false so that what was once admired for the beauty of its form loses all value. Nobody seems to realize that what they admire and live in is a spectacle.

The final and most common category comprises the bulk of household goods that, forced on us by industrialism, are bought because they are cheap or to upstage Mrs. Andersson. This is, above all, pretentious and vulgar. As it constitutes nine-tenths of the market, at the moment most homes are pretentious and vulgar. It is against household goods of this kind that our struggle is mainly directed.

None of these trends, apart from the first, are based on any objective principle. It is by no means obvious that furnishing should primarily be planned to serve some objective function.

This is probably because in the little world that the home consists of, there are no longer any tried and tested standards against which one may measure one's actions. The older generation has its memories, the younger is breaking new ground. Nowhere else in life is there such friction between what is done by hand and what is industrialized as there is in housework and the home. Perhaps the most important factors behind changes in house-work lie in the altered relationships of the generations toward each other. Those who are apprehensive refer to this as the dissolution of the home. Since alongside their economic and biological roles homes have an important moral function, and as the vast majority of people always have a conservative attitude to all changes in moral concepts, the changes in human relationships in the home are equated with "the decay of the home." For this reason there is general opposition to every radical change in the design of the home.

But to raise this issue to the sociological level, is it certain that families will always be what they are today?

We are living during the transition to a new stage. This is characterized by three factors, the first being mastery of procreation, i.e., family planning, which has as its outcome the second, which is a rise in the value of children, and thirdly, also as a result of the first factor, release from perpetual motherhood and the possibility for women, without needing to perform routine domestic chores in return for the protection of a man, to earn their daily bread. It is clear that this places each member of the family, both father and mother, and the kernel of the family, the child, on a different footing in relation to each other, and that an **entirely new type of family is therefore almost certainly likely to develop** when routine chores disappear and children are no longer brought up by their mothers.

We will return later to the consequences for the planning of dwellings that this tendency entails.

The need to define the problems faced in housing construction.

The cost of housing swallows a good proportion of the resources of small wage earners, and the way in which it is designed plays a decisive role for the health and comfort of individuals.

If we consult the statistics, we are told that most households in the cities, or those with annual income between two thousand and five thousand kronor or less, have to sacrifice a quarter to one half of their earnings to acquire housing that despite this only barely meets reasonable needs.

Each year, new housing construction in Sweden has a value of close to three hundred million kronor, or the majority of the capital saved in Sweden annually. The value of people's health and happiness cannot be expressed in similarly precise figures but this does not mean that it is less important. Both are highly dependent on the quality of housing.

It is these circumstances that make the housing issue one of our greatest social problems and the planning of residential buildings one of the most important tasks facing the building industry. The fact that recently public discussion and the interests of professionals have focused seriously on these issues should therefore be considered more than a coincidence or a whim of fashion.

We now require objective justification for every technical undertaking. We do not start building a power station or a new road system without thorough studies of the needs they will satisfy and the cheapest and most efficient ways of meeting them. Nor does anyone question the justification of such measures. When we are building housing for millions, our approach should be the same. Perhaps we do not admit this readily and generally. But herein lies an inconsistency, for the technical solutions for housing must also be based on a thorough discussion of how to define the problem and on a clarification of housing needs.

These are the questions that we must therefore pose: Is the current form that housing takes the most efficient possible, does it give the best value for the money it requires, and is it adapted to the lives it will serve?

Without wishing to detract from the value of the highly commendable work devoted to the regeneration of housing in recent years, we have to believe that it is possible to progress further along the path that has been adopted. Above all, we must not rest on the merits of the results we have achieved, because many unsolved questions still remain.

We therefore have to react to the often encountered negative belief that claims that in building-art only slow, continuous development is permissible and that it will only allow cautious development based on what has gone before. One reason often adduced is that what was good enough for our forefathers should also be good enough for us, or that only good old-fashioned Swedish buildings, farmhouses and manor houses, are suitable for Swedish conditions and our Swedish landscape, where they have evolved through the experience of what is needed and what suits us.

Our rejoinder is that the old Swedish farmhouses and manor houses were certainly fairly consistent and thorough solutions in view of the problems faced and the technical aids available when they originated. They have also merged in our consciousness with the Swedish landscape, where they fit in well. But they are not therefore the most appropriate point of departure for the creation of modern dwellings, least of all when it comes to what we are mainly concerned with here, which is the question of housing for urban populations.

It is arguments like those presented above that prompt us to find that when we look at the homes in our society, on the whole they have not altered nearly to the extent as the lives led by individuals. And here we have not touched upon such incredibly deep-rooted aspects of home life and housework as raising and educating children and hygiene, areas in which the changes are much clearer to every observer than those we have dealt with. For most people social change consists of building more institutions, because so much has been taken out of the home, such as education, health, sport, etc. **But on the other hand not many realize that the way homes are built must also change as a consequence of the changing function of the home. We have acquired the technical equipment for all sorts of modern comforts. We have not been offered any change in the way the home is organized nor have we been given greater spaciousness.** A professor today and one fifty years ago do not belong to the same class in terms of where they live. Then an entire villa, furnished simply but with dignity; today four rooms and a kitchen in a banal tenement house. What differentiates the interior of today's home from those of the past is heating and running water, electricity, gas, and a bathroom. In addition there is a trend toward fewer and larger rooms for socializing. Externally, however, our homes have been purged radically, with the disappearance of the towers, porches, gables, and so on that made buildings resemble ancient palaces. Still, however, deliberate attempts are being made to match the appearance of buildings from the past. This tendency to imitate older buildings in particular means that appropriate trends prompted by current circumstances, such as the use of larger windows to provide rooms with increased light, have once again been abandoned. (It was not functionalism that invented large horizontal windows. They originated in England at the turn of the century and can be found in many of the large houses in Djursholm and elsewhere built around 1910.) For similar reasons the glazed-in verandas that were from many points of view highly efficient although undeniably ugly had to vanish without being given the time to develop a better match of form and function.

Previously we mentioned a professor's villa. Similar villas were occupied by most middle-class families. This was in the past. These villas were adapted for town-dwellers from a patriarchal way of life based on rural patterns. Now the community and commerce have taken over many of the duties of the patriarchal family. It is for this reason that we can never re-create or borrow the features of the old culture, no matter how much we admire it.

What is required of housing.

Regulations and the quality of dwellings.

We have already pointed out that housing now offers greater possibilities for variation than in the past. The possibility of satisfying individual demands in the design of
a dwelling must, for the vast majority of low-income earners, be limited to a choice
of type. Housing has become a commodity produced for sale, and as such must suit
as many buyers as possible. This **may** pose a danger. Not because individuality is at
risk of being eliminated, or because industrial production in and of itself necessarily
means lower quality, though at times, when demand exceeds supply, there is always
a risk that goods will deteriorate. When we are dealing with something as important
to people's health and well-being as housing, we must guarantee that it will fulfill
certain minimum standards in terms of quality.

To guarantee qualified medical care for those who live in housing we have registered physicians, to protect their savings we have a financial inspection authority, etc.
But we still do not have adequate protection against the production of inadequate
housing. Of course one should not rely too greatly on the effect of laws and regulations. They are not universal remedies. But our older town plans simply dictate that
a large percentage of dwellings never see sunlight. Nor do our building regulations
provide the inspection authorities with sufficient power to prevent unsuitably and
uneconomically planned housing. There are admittedly some regulations. We are not
allowed to have ceilings that are too low or rooms that are too small. But these regulations are inadequate and moreover not flexible enough. Nor are they always adapted
to recent developments in housing construction. New legislation has been announced,
however, and we must hope that it will better match today's requirements.

The most important housing requirements in terms of social well-being and public
health have hitherto often taken second place to questions of form and appearance.
This applies as much to public opinion as to the statutes and authorities. In the past

more concern was paid to how a building would appear to others than to one's own needs; in the home individuals wanted to impress guests, in local communities, traveling strangers, both perhaps wanting to boast and appear greater than they were.

At one time all was permissible, as long as one used the formula "where demanded by the style" or "for architectural reasons." An unscrupulous builder and a cunning architect could work miracles with these phrases. An architectural element could swell to comprise two-thirds of a building, which could then grow in height and hide the sun from its neighbors. A five-story house could readily support a sixth floor, provided that its shame was covered by a concealing roof.

The aesthetic benefits one expected of the system indeed never transpired, but no one understood that this was due to the separation of aesthetics and logic in urban building.

The current problem.

Answering the question "what is required of a dwelling" may seem relatively easy.

One could express it in a few words roughly like this: a healthy and sunny position and sufficient air and space for those living there. A separate room for each individual to sleep in, shared space where all can gather, preferably also somewhere in the fresh air, as well as a quiet corner for study. In addition, convenient and sufficient space for cooking and the appropriate aids to make the work easy, as well as sound hygienic facilities that will enable good personal hygiene.

None of these demands is, after all, unreasonable. Unfortunately one more has to be added that makes it considerably more difficult to comply with the others. The dwelling also has to be within financial reach, a condition that callously restricts the possibilities of satisfying the other requirements. Such a simple and natural state of affairs is not always taken into account, however, when it comes to assessing new attempts to solve the housing needs of the poor.

What may be dictated by stern necessity is generally regarded as fanciful and a desire for originality if it departs from the commonplace. For instance Carl Laurin was loud in his complaints about the small hip baths displayed in the housing section of the Stockholm Exhibition.[17] We would be the first to agree with him that it is more pleasant to be able to stretch out in a full-size bath. But had he known that for many ordinary people the choice is between a hip bath or no bath at all, his good heart and aesthetic sensibility would certainly have delighted in such an excellent invention as the hip bath, which also gives the poor the possibility of having a bath. The example can be multiplied. **No genius is required to draw up a list of what is needed for the ideal dwelling, but finding a genuine solution to the housing problem for the less affluent requires more. At the moment it is almost insoluble. What has emerged up to now must rather be considered desperate attempts to meet as many desires as possible without direct subsidies.**

In what follows, this question will be dealt with in view of the present situation, particularly in Stockholm where it is most acute.

If, therefore, we cannot satisfy all our justified desires in a dwelling, the natural thing is to determine what is primary, where no concessions can be made, and which demands may possibly be relinquished.

After all, there is a certain freedom of choice. A gain can be made through a sacrifice, and it is not always so easy to decide which one or the other should come first. Some would rather have spaciousness, others labor-saving devices. One thing that we should see clearly when we discuss these questions, however, is that an inevitable relationship exists between the possibility of meeting one demand or another. When the final total is fixed, you cannot increase one constituent without reducing another. Criticism that does not take this into account is worthless.

Therefore when planning a dwelling it is always wise to balance the different interests against each other and to attempt to create a harmonious and purposeful organism that will utilize the limited possibilities to the best effect. This then leaves hardly any room for romantic speculation or purely individual desires, because modern housing must be provided on the basis of the principle of frugality.

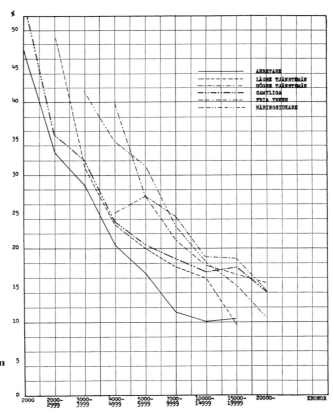

Rents paid in Stockholm as a percentage of incomes. Statistics for different social groups.

This state of affairs is best illustrated by the fact that the average Stockholm family cannot spend more than about 700 to 1,000 kronor a year on a dwelling, if the other equally important necessities of life are to be provided for. Add to this that the cost for constructing net floor area in Stockholm is between 250 and 500 kronor per square meter, which corresponds to a rent of 20 to 40 kronor per square meter, or 750 to 1,500 kronor for a one-room apartment, and you will realize the difficulty.

Now the rejoinder may be made that our task must primarily be to unite all our efforts into working for sounder conditions in the housing market so that decent accommodation will be available for everyone. Of course we concede that this is an important task, but until it has been completed architects must make the best of the situation as it is. With the incredible production of new housing taking place at the moment, this is no small task either.

Housing and town planning.

Local planning largely determines the quality of individual towns. We have already pointed out that older town plans required the construction of a large percentage of dwellings that never receive direct sunlight. Today one imperative demand must be that when housing areas are planned they must guarantee every apartment an adequate supply of sunlight and air, a requirement that completely reverses the older concept of town planning, which dealt with closed building blocks and street layouts that defined space.

Streets and squares were once the basis of town planning, and the role of buildings, from the planner's point of view, was mainly to provide walls for these spaces, sometimes forming a backdrop for a perspective view down a street.

Jakob Westinsgatan seen from Norr Mälarstrand and the poor-quality floor plans resulting from this contrived street backdrop.

The Stockholm we should demolish.

But the social justice demanded of our age, and the awareness that it is no longer good enough to allow people's homes to be nothing more than a motif in the townscape, mean that we must abandon the closed block system in new housing areas.

It is no longer good enough to use a formal scheme to determine the exterior framework of our cities and then squeeze into it the individual cells, dwellings, as best we can. A radical change of approach is necessary in which—as with the planning of the dwellings, to which we will return later—we begin to work from the inside outward, and with the perfect apartment as the building block construct the entirety, the body of the city.

Developments in recent decades reveal a clear progression toward a totally new type of town plan. The interiors of the blocks have been cleared of overshadowing protrusions. T-shaped buildings have vanished and instead of a patchwork of small yards and protruding wings, there are now one or two large communal courtyards per block, often with gardens. Certainly, there has long been hesitation about taking this tendency to its conclusion and abandoning the closed block. The inmost sections of their four interior corners can never be built economically because they cannot be used for well-lit apartments. The sections that run from east to west overshadow the north-south sections unfavorably. In addition the buildings normally have a depth of fifteen meters, which, given the type of small apartment that now has to be built, cannot be used for through-apartments.[18] The outcome is that along the northern walls a large number of dwellings have been created that get no direct sunlight. In addition the distance to the building on the opposite side of the street is less than to the building on the opposite side of the yard, so that apartments facing the street are darker than those facing the yard.

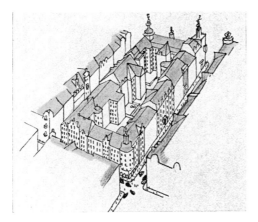

Evolution from the old closed-town plans to the new open-city planning system.

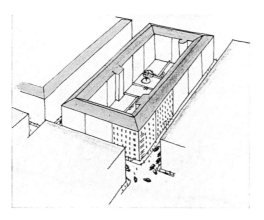

New York.

Skyscrapers.

Recently there has been quite a lot of discussion about various ways of clearing out undesirable housing areas. Skyscrapers have often been advocated as one means of doing so where land is expensive and has to be exploited intensively while at the same time meeting demands for space and light. We do not know whether they can compete on economic terms with lower building types. Probably not, given current collective agreements and organization of labor. But if we must accept skyscrapers, it should be where, despite possibly higher costs, they can really be justified on the basis of their hygienic advantages. Let us therefore be cautious about idolizing them in a romantic and provincial manner by placing them in the middle of dark and dense parts of the city as town planning features without demolishing the buildings around them.

The new city plan for
Stadshagen in Stockholm.

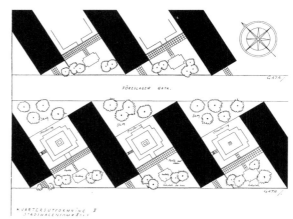

The open city-planning system.

If in terms of hygiene we must demand the same standard of housing for everyone, **the worst and not the best dwelling will set the norm for city plans.** In this way the demand that all dwellings get direct sunlight has endowed modern housing areas with a completely new character. It has necessitated an open style of building, with parallel blocks whose orientation is determined with reference to the sun, east-west if there are through-apartments, otherwise north-south. The first building type is preferred as it permits cross-ventilation and provides a side that is genuinely sunny. But it requires through-apartments which, reducing the depth of the building, lead to longer facades as well as fewer apartments on each stairwell, such that this system is

Project for a housing area.

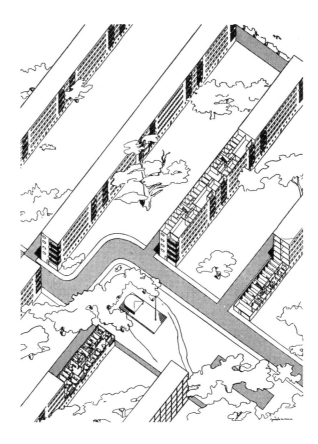

economically inferior to blocks that run from north to south. In addition, if the sun is to penetrate to the lowest stories during the darkest times of the year when it is most needed, the distance between the buildings must be greater. Because the buildings are not as deep, streets cost more per unit of floor area.

As long as building operations have to focus mainly on the production of apartments of the smallest type and while production costs remain so high, we must probably continue to erect relatively deep buildings that run from north to south, unless we consider ourselves able to make further sacrifices in terms of the conveniences or spaciousness of housing, in return for southern sunlight and the possibility of cross-ventilation.

Diagram showing the variation in height and distance separating buildings offering total living area one-and-a-half times greater than the site area with a building depth of 14 m.

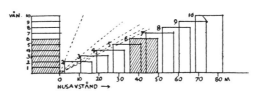

Project for a housing area.

The new cityscape.

But it is not only the arrangements of blocks of flats that are to be opened up in this way to ensure that every apartment gets its ration of air and light. Housing must be supplemented by parks for adults and playgrounds for children, which will further open out the entire urban area.

If you build cities on this new open building pattern, and at the same time want to produce just as much usable floor area per unit of ground area as in the older parts of the city with their closed blocks and narrow streets, the height of the buildings has to be increased, as does the distance between buildings on each side of the streets and yards.

We see therefore how radical compliance with the primary demands for housing quality give rise to a complete regeneration of the cityscape itself and a deviation from tradition. But we also believe that it will provide us with new aesthetic values even though they differ from the type offered by the spatial relationships of Baroque town plans. The increasing general acceptance of the open city-planning system strengthens our belief that it is futile to oppose radical and logical building.

Row houses in Basel.

Three types of housing.

In the previous section we established how the role of housing has to some extent become very different from what it once was. The home is no longer a unit of production, not even in the countryside, and self-sufficient households have completely come to an end. As a place of work and also as a place for entertainment, the home has by and large lost its importance. Work, recreation, and social life have to a great extent shifted outside its walls. But conditions have changed in other respects as well. In the past we lived close to our place of work, in an apartment if the office or workshop was in a city, in a cottage if we worked on the land. Fifteen minutes walk to work was considered very far. How astonished we were in the past, for example, to see schoolmates who every day had to be taken to and from school from some farm five kilometers outside the town by horse and carriage.

Thanks to modern transport, housing has now become less dependent on proximity to our places of work, which means that individuals have greater freedom to choose the form of housing, apartment building or suburban villa, that best suits them.

If a **rented apartment** was once the only choice open to a city dweller, it still predominates.

But for a generation now a **home of one's own** has been the ideal for the city dweller, one that perhaps initially only lay within the reach of the affluent.[19] Today it is beginning to pose serious competition to the city apartment as the usual form of housing for all social classes. So far these two types virtually reign supreme, but we can already glimpse a third, **the family hotel**, which in various forms is making inroads in capitalist America as well as communist Russia.[20] There collectivity has been taken further than we are used to in Sweden.

In the future we can probably expect all three forms of housing to be common, and perhaps in between there will be some intermediary forms.

The plan of the dwelling.

If sound conditions are laid down by the city plan that can enable decent dwellings to be provided in an apartment block, there still remains the far from easy task of laying out the individual apartments in the best way possible within the restricted floor space permitted by economic constraints. This is a matter of ensuring that at least the most important requirements can be met and that the minimal cube can be used for maximum benefit. The fact is that thirty to seventy square meters must suffice for a family home in Stockholm.

We have maintained above that the role of the home now differs in essential respects from that of the past. Even if, from a psychological point of view, it may have the same significance for the individual today, in material terms it no longer plays the same role. If, therefore, the home has largely lost its importance as a place of work and also as a place to gather and to entertain, construction costs and people's pretensions, on the other hand, have grown considerably. The housing problem is therefore more difficult to solve than it used to be, regardless of the minor significance attached to housing as a social problem in the less democratic societies of the past.

Differentiation of the plan.

Even though the role of a dwelling differs to some extent today from that in the past, it must, however, still serve three main purposes: to provide space for housework, cooking, etc., to enable the family to gather for meals and spend time together, and to offer a place to rest and to sleep at night. We have already pointed out that a shift has taken place in the mutual relationship of these three functions, however. The space required for housework has been reduced, perhaps also for members of the family to meet, while the role of the home as a place of rest is probably still the same. Whatever the case, a dwelling should, as in the past, provide a place for gathering and a place for privacy.

A clear trend toward differentiation of the plans of dwellings in view of these three functions is a fundamental feature in building modern housing. The earlier type of plan, which exhibits two or three more or less equivalent areas, the kitchen and one or two rooms, is increasingly being abandoned because it no longer seems able to serve life within the home in a suitable way.

This differentiation of the layout of a dwelling with respect to these main functions should apply to all housing. Some variation among plans for apartments of the same size must be permitted however, even though from an economic point of view it could be advantageous for the plans to be as general as possible and suitable for all families within a certain income bracket.

Of course the same plan type cannot be suitable for a family with many children, a family of only adults, or a single person. We must also take into account the increasing number of households in which both husband and wife are working outside the home and who do not earn enough to employ a servant to look after the youngest children, if they have any.

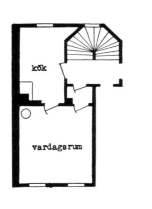

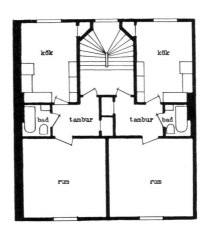

Older floor plans, where space is not differentiated to the same extent as in modern dwellings.

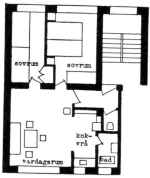

Germany.

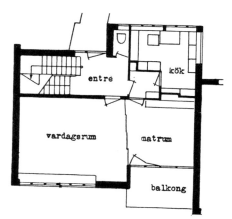

Swiss floor plan.
(See illustration opposite
page.)

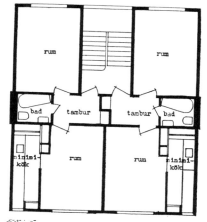

Göteborg.

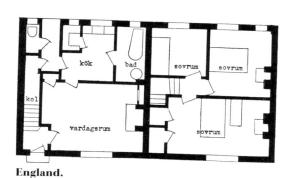

England.
Some minimal dwellings.

The Netherlands.

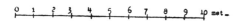

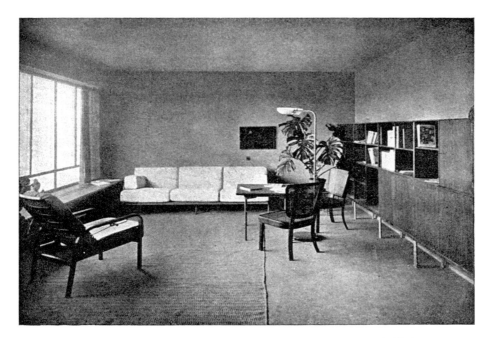

A living room.

The living room.

Gathering, work, and rest were the three main tasks for the home. Earlier, and indeed still today, the family often gathered in the kitchen, while the largest room, the "best room," was rarely used but served for entertaining and to display the family's prosperity. This applied to the simpler homes.

In bourgeois circles homes had parlors. These contained some comfortable chairs and sofas, often with silk upholstery, well concealed by loose cotton covers, as well as thousands of small useless knickknacks, which the womenfolk spent a great deal of their time dusting. This room stood empty and unheated except for once or twice a year, when friends of the family were allowed to occupy it. Often there was no comfortable room in which the family could gather every day.

This is a state of affairs to which our unconventional generation has reacted strongly. The room in which the family meets every day has become the most important room in our homes. Today the living room is the major central room, around which the other rooms are grouped. Here all the members of the family and their guests should be able to gather for meals and spend their spare time. Often it is the only room in which we can afford to retain some of the spaciousness of dwellings of the past.

A living room should be pleasant and comfortable, spacious and full of light. It should not primarily be a room for show. We have begun to be more natural and no longer care about demonstrating a wealth that does not exist, or a social status that at any rate is doomed to extinction. To the contrary, we want a room that is pleasant to be in and where we can feel comfortable. We do not want furniture for its own sake. But the furniture we own should be agreeable and fulfill its role with modesty.

What then should a living room contain?

There should be somewhere to eat with a good connection to the kitchen, unless that is where we prefer to eat. A reasonably roomy seating area with pleasant places to sit makes an important contribution to the comfort of the home.

But living rooms must also offer space for some work.

A well-lit spot must be arranged for the housewife's sewing and other tasks. Preferably it should provide room for a sewing machine. Homework, writing letters, and other tasks require somewhere to write. If room can be found for storage, a cupboard or a sideboard, preferably a place for a musical instrument as well and a bookcase, the space will be filled and the room's most important function satisfied.

Unfortunately, far too often the living room is the only room. But it becomes necessary in other cases when families have many children and little income to use it as a bedroom for one, or perhaps two, people. To make full use of the space, sleeping arrangements must serve as seating during the day or via some mechanical device, wall beds, "Murphy beds," or the like, be concealed from view. In the most difficult cases even living rooms will be cramped, and each item of furniture required is to serve a number of purposes. Somewhere to sleep can, as mentioned, offer seating during the day, a place to write has to be combined with furniture for storage and perhaps with a bookcase as well, and so on.

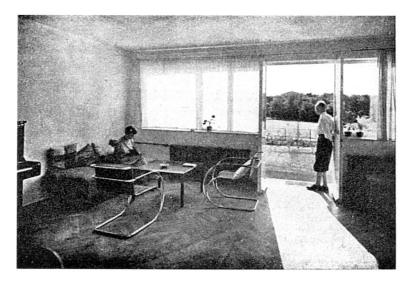

Living room.

Living room with dining area, Stockholm Exhibition.

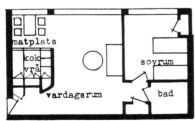

Murphy bed.

What is therefore important in planning a dwelling is to give great consideration to how easily a room can be furnished. Far too often rooms are planned without taking this into account. The walls must not consist solely of doorways nor the floor merely of paths for circulation. Furnishing must be envisaged when the floor plan is designed. A small, well-planned room can often serve its purpose better than a badly arranged larger one.

An outdoor space.

Modern people appreciate open-air life more than their parents did. This finds expression mainly in sports but also in the requirement for a more open design in housing. Today's ideal is no longer a form of fortified enclosure. We have no fear of the outside world and do not withdraw into our shells. We do not obscure daylight behind layers of thick drapes but instead add to the spaciousness of our living rooms by opening them out with large windows to embrace the unrestricted views offered by our modern city plans. We allow the room to interact with the landscape outside to create a feeling of space and freedom, and we open our homes to the fresh air, sun, and the city's greenery.

Our climate is admittedly harsh and for much of the year we have to think about protecting ourselves from it. But technological developments have enabled us to close out the cold without having to lose the feeling of contact with the outside world. And in the spring and summer when the days start to become warmer, we long to spend as much time as possible in the open air. For this reason a modern dwelling should always possess some outdoor space that supplements the living room.

Unfortunately, for reasons of cost, this desire cannot always be fulfilled. At the moment, at any rate, it does not seem that the cost of providing a balcony can be compensated by the extra rent it is able to attract. We appear still to be so unaccustomed to such a benefit that it is not included as one of the primary requirements

Roof terraces are not only justified in the Orient.

when renting somewhere to live. Perhaps this circumstance can be partially explained by the fact that the balconies of older buildings were on the whole less appealing because of the narrow and dark streets of the earlier town plans.

Bedrooms.

The second main task of a dwelling is to provide somewhere to relax and sleep. This is probably what has been neglected most in Sweden's building tradition in the last century, in contrast, for instance, to what has been the case in the Anglo-Saxon countries.

A separate place to sleep for each member of the family is a requirement that should not be overlooked. Unfortunately we are still far from being able to realize this desire. On the contrary, it seems that Sweden, because of the high cost of building, is probably the country in the civilized world that is furthest from achieving this aim. Far too large a percentage of families in this country still have to content themselves with dwellings that do not have separate bedrooms. At best these are replaced by an alcove in the living room. The plans of minimal dwellings from some other countries illustrated here are examples of housing intended for wage earners who in Sweden would have to settle for one room with a kitchenette or at best one room with a kitchen.

In order to fulfill the requirement of a separate bedroom for the different members of the family as far as possible, one is obliged, when there is no other option, to reduce the floor space of the individual bedrooms to a minimum. The result, however, is that

Bedroom, Stockholm Exhibition.

the volume of air is small. How far it is possible to go in this direction without jeopardizing hygiene has probably not yet been established. It depends to a great extent on the possibility of effective ventilation. With central heating and the declining fear of sleeping with an open window, one could probably justify a minimum area of six square meters for one person, if the ceiling is of standard height.

With suitable furniture and a correctly placed door, in addition to somewhere to sleep, this area can also provide room for a small writing space, if it can be combined with storage.

Standards of hygiene have risen and therefore the sleeping area of a dwelling must be provided with a bathroom, something once only found in more affluent homes. Today this is to be considered obligatory in every dwelling. In more difficult cases it may possibly be replaced by a shower room.

It is universally acknowledged that one of the most positive contributions of the modern age is greater attention to bodily care and hygiene, and a bathroom is no longer considered a luxury.

But bathrooms are not only places to take a bath but for all personal care and grooming. The old washstands that used to adorn every bedroom have disappeared, replaced by washbasins in the bathroom, so it has to be close to the bedrooms. It is this that has made it easier to manage with smaller bedrooms, as they no longer have to provide the space required for personal hygiene.

The invention of hip baths mentioned earlier has also given us the possibility of arranging bathrooms that require very little floor space, to the benefit of the other rooms.

Finally, the bedroom area requires storage space for clothes—wardrobes or cupboards. These are best located, where somewhat larger dwellings are concerned, in a corridor between the bedrooms and the bathroom. Or it may be appropriate to arrange a wardrobe for outer clothes and the like next to the entrance.

The kitchen.

The kitchen may well be the part of a dwelling that has to undergo the greatest change in comparison with earlier types of housing. Of course when a reduction in the total floor area is to be made, some element has to be trimmed.

It has previously been maintained that both the bedroom and the living room have on the whole retained their importance in home life. On the other hand it is undeniable that the role of the kitchen has been curtailed considerably. For a long time there has been a tendency to reduce its area but to add to its technical equipment, so that the work that still has to be done there will take as little time as possible.

Voices have admittedly been raised against the tendency to make kitchens smaller, and it may be that at times things have gone too far in this respect. This could be the case when a kitchen, as sometimes happens, has been reduced to a diminutive kitchenette without any daylight.

In all fairness, we must clearly realize, however, that one room with a kitchenette is better than one without, or a kitchen alone, and that it should not be compared to one room with a kitchen.

We readily admit that it is also desirable for a kitchen to be well lit, airy, and spacious. But when floor area has to be limited at all costs, there is hardly any other option than to take the desired reduction from the kitchen, whose significance has after all declined more than any of the other areas in the home.

How much the area of a kitchen should be reduced depends completely, however, on the degree to which it remains a place of work. One cannot, of course, require a housewife who does all the cooking for a large family to spend much of her day confined to a kitchenette with an area that barely exceeds two square meters. On the other hand it would be poor economics to sacrifice a major proportion of the living space for the kitchen of a dwelling when those who live there spend eight hours a day at work, eat one of their meals there, and then prepare the other, which may consist of purchased ready-made dishes, as simply as possible.

There are also other arguments against large kitchens. If the kitchen is large enough to enable the children to spend time there, this is what they will do while the housewife is in it. This is not desirable. Kitchens contain gas stoves, which are dangerous playthings. The air is always stuffy and unhealthy. For these reasons arrangements should be made that drive children out of the kitchen into the airier living room, which should be put to use even when there are no guests in the house.

One acceptable and increasingly common way of solving the kitchen problem is to create a relatively large and well-lit kitchen but to divide its inner half off from the rest by a glass wall with a door. The actual cooking occurs, and the kitchen equipment is placed, in this inner section, which is provided with effective ventilation. A dining area is arranged in the outer section, which is connected to the living room by a sliding door or some other device. This can also provide somewhere to sleep or a secluded place for work when there is no cooking going on or meals being eaten and has the advantage over a kitchen dining area in being protected from the coating of grease that is otherwise inevitable.

In other countries, Austria for example, totally different approaches have been adopted. For the smallest types of apartments, for instance, living room and kitchen have been combined to form what is called a "Wohnküche" ["living-kitchen"]. This system offers obvious advantages but also drawbacks. The advantages are greater spaciousness, which is always the outcome of combining two spaces, and also the

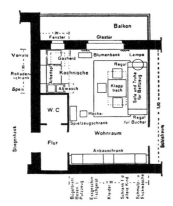

"Living-kitchen," Vienna.

contact offered to the housewife with the rest of the home, the children in particular, while she is doing her housework. The drawbacks consist mainly of the difficulties of preventing cooking fumes from penetrating the entire room and the impossibility of arranging a separate space to sleep linked to the kitchen as described above.

The hall.

The area known as the hall is probably one we could sacrifice in order to increase the area of the living room or bedrooms.[21] Its task in recent years has increasingly been to make a dwelling seem to have a higher standard than it has, rather than to serve any real need.

For the very smallest apartments, instead of a hall, an attempt should be made to enlarge the living room by a few square meters and to turn this additional area into a sleeping alcove that can also provide seating during the day. However undesirable it may appear, this twofold use of space and furniture is, as has already been pointed out, a necessity in the smallest types of dwelling. Experience also tells us that if a hall is provided in this type of dwelling, and there is any possibility of placing a sofa there, it is invariably used as a place to sleep, an arrangement that cannot be condemned too strongly.

Mezzanines.

All possibilities must be explored in the effort to utilize the cubic space of small dwellings as efficiently as possible.

Given the premise that it is cheaper to build a deep building than a shallow one but that the disadvantage is that the interior will be badly lit, plans have been made

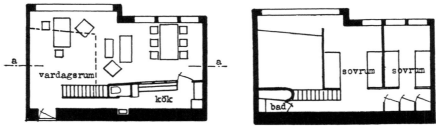

Apartment with mezzanine, Stockholm Exhibition.

to build deep blocks of apartments with relatively high ceilings—four to five meters. The living room has been given this height, while bedrooms and the kitchen have been placed one above the other. Calculations show that the floor area that can be gained by these means is somewhat cheaper than in single-story apartments, and the contrast between the high ceilings of the living room and the smaller rooms affords a new and different sense of comfort.

Yet the system probably also has its drawbacks, one being that because of the low ceilings in the smaller rooms, the volume of air may be too small. What this means in fact is that these areas, the bedrooms in particular, must be open to the volume of air in the living room at night, so that the desired privacy cannot be achieved. If the question of ventilation could be solved, then this problem would be eliminated as well.

Windows.

Earlier we touched upon the requirements that should apply to city plans in terms of the correct alignment of buildings to ensure that all the apartments in a block will have access to direct sunlight. An equally important and no less discussed issue is the way in which the light should be admitted to the rooms or, in simpler terms, the arrangement of the windows in the plan and elevation.

The optimal quantity of light in hygienic terms for an apartment block probably cannot be exactly determined. Here physiologists' opinions differ, or at least they are unable to provide any exact information on where to set the limit for what is directly beneficial.

Some examples of earlier norms for the ratio of window area to floor area may be mentioned here: in dwellings 1:10, hospitals 1:7, schoolrooms 1:5. The building regulations laid down for the city of Görlitz stipulate that a room in a dwelling with a volume of thirty cubic meters is to have a window area of at least one square meter.

There does seem to be agreement, however, in considering that light is beneficial and stimulating to the system. Large windows are preferable to small ones.

But the significance of light is not merely directly physiological. Indirectly, especially in the case of sunlight, it influences our health through psychological stimulus.

The function of daylight is not merely to improve our health, any more than it merely exists to delight our eyes with the beautiful interplay of highlights and shadow. Its most obvious task is after all to assist us in our work by providing agreeable and effective illumination. It may seem ridiculous to mention such a simple fact, but nevertheless it is often more honored in the breach when it comes to designing and placing windows.

A schematic division of the facade with identical windows placed at great distances from each other must be rejected. This has been cherished for many years for the calm and handsome facades it provides. About ten years ago one inspection authority is even said to have virtually required a regular placement, with four meters from the center of one window to the next if a facade was to be approved. Otherwise it was not considered to "meet reasonable demands of taste and order." Whether or not the dwelling behind such a facade met reasonable demands in terms of illumination and hygiene obviously meant less then than it does now, nor did it mean much that it became unreasonably expensive because of the inflexible plans imposed by the system.

One objection that can be made to large areas of windows is that they form large cold surfaces that give rise to drafts. Obviously there is a risk in going too far. The disadvantages can, however, largely be remedied with effective and suitable heating systems. Certainly this will result in a somewhat higher cost but not one large enough to be decisive when it comes to determining the size of windows. According to some calculations, for instance, increasing the window area from 20 percent of an apartment's floor area to 30 percent would involve increased heating costs that correspond to one-third of one percent of the rent.

Quartz glass.

Attempts to provide housing with light that is as healthy as possible have resulted in recent years in the trial production of a type of glass, quartz glass, that also admits ultraviolet and infrared rays. Hitherto these experiments have not, according to reports, been completely successful, as after some time the glass loses its beneficial characteristics. Moreover it is fairly expensive.

In England, as well as other countries, experiments have been conducted in which the windows of certain classrooms were fitted with quartz glass, and others with ordinary glass. A significant difference in the health of the children is said to have been observed in favor of the quartz glass. We should therefore hope that attempts to produce a cheap and enduring glass of this kind are successful.

The family hotel.

We have previously pointed out how the functions of the dwelling have been reduced to some extent. Much of the preparation of food that used to take place in the home is now carried out in factories, as is the manufacture of clothes, and so on. The recreation that it was once the task of the home to provide can now be found in the theaters, movie houses, club activities, or other more or less public entertainments.

In other respects as well, in the future homes are likely to be supplemented by collective arrangements of various kinds.

Let us take some examples. When parents are working outside the home and lack the possibility—or in certain cases the desire—to keep servants, their children cannot

The smallest type of "cell" in an American family hotel.

The beds are folded down at night from their vertical position between the living room and a well-ventilated dressing room. This makes it possible to avoid the hygienic drawbacks connected with tightly enclosed Murphy beds.

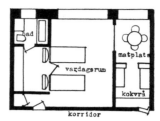

From the new Russia.

Plans for a totally collectivized housing complex linked to a factory in Moscow. The arrows in the diagram show the route taken by the individual from infancy to adulthood. He is born in this complex and lives his adult life there. There are shared kitchens and social areas, a lecture room and a movie theater, etc. He spends the years from 4 to 8 in the building bottom right (7), and then goes to school until the age of 16 in the building in the top right-hand corner (8).

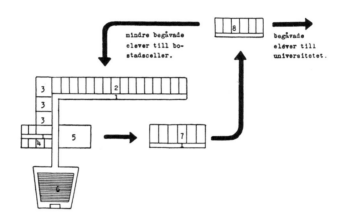

be left without supervision in their homes during the working day. Kindergartens and day nurseries will then have a role to play. Under the supervision of trained staff and in airy and spacious premises linked to a major housing complex, children can often be guaranteed better care than at home, where their mothers are obliged to entrust the supervision of the youngest to some older brother or sister, a neighbor, or some other relatively unsuitable person.

Shared laundries are not new, and heating has for many years been supplied from a joint central heating system. In other countries, housing complexes already have shared gymnasiums.

As pointed out earlier, however, an even greater degree of collectivity, the family hotel, will soon be a reality in Sweden as well.

Either entirely or in part, cooking and even eating is transferred from the private dwellings to communal rooms. Communal lounges are provided as well, and the

Playroom in an H.S.B. building, Stockholm.

main task of the home is to offer somewhere to rest during the night and a place to withdraw to when complete privacy is sought.

Even within the housing type that is called the family hotel, various degrees of collectivity can be found. Often the apartments are provided with simple kitchen facilities to enable water to be boiled for tea or the preparation of simple meals. Many families prefer to have their meals sent up to their rooms, where they have arranged a separate place to eat.

What form this housing type will finally take when it seriously begins to make inroads in this country we do not know. One thing is certain however, that in families without children or with grown-up children, where the wife lacks interest in or aptitude for housework, is perhaps involved in some intellectual occupation and has a well-paid job, the family hotel could well save the family from many conflicts and grounds for disagreement.

From an economic point of view as well, the family hotel should be competitive with other forms of housing, at any rate when the housewife, once freed of house-work, can earn a decent wage by going out to work. As the food can be prepared on a large scale in a communal kitchen, the costs of its production should also be reduced. Experience suggests that at the moment this is not the case. These cal-culations would only be completely correct, however, if the work of a housewife in

**Single-family house
outside Copenhagen.**

**Single-family
house,
Stockholm
Exhibition.**

Row house at Hästholmen, Stockholm.

the home were valued in terms of the wages she could earn through getting another job, and this amount included in the expenditure of the individual family.

A home of one's own.

What has been dealt with up to now in this chapter has concerned housing in the inner city. Owner-occupied homes in the suburbs must however in many respects be preferred to rented city apartments, and probably represent a more ideal solution to the housing problem.

The demand for light, fresh air, and peace and quiet can be satisfied there more easily.

The longing for these priceless assets, which compels us to seek the outskirts of our cities, has unfortunately often been linked to certain far too romantic perceptions of nature and stubborn preconceptions about agrarian forms of housing. The result has been that the completely logical design of garden cities and owner-occupied homes has been thwarted.

Many have believed that they would be living in a cabin in the forest when they moved out to the suburbs. But as the sites must be exploited so intensively, buildings, not nature, will predominate. In cities, in both their outer areas and their centers, it is therefore a case of using nature, not vanishing into it.

And, above all, let us not believe that because we are living on the periphery of the city we are farmers and therefore must at any cost live in buildings that resemble farmhouses, unless we are so aristocratic that we prefer the shrunken manor houses that one can see here and there.

Life in a farm cottage or a manor house has very little in common with life in a suburban dwelling, and there will be little success in trying to revive these once rational and appropriate housing types.

The simple floor plans of manor houses and farm cottages, with their few but large and symmetrically arranged rooms, are also most unsuitable for the homes of modern city dwellers. Some exterior features of these earlier dwellings can be retained, but thanks to changes in proportions and other circumstances, the most valuable aspects of the exteriors of rural buildings, their calm rhythm and natural form, is lost.

What is required of suburban houses must after all on the whole be the same for a rented apartment, as the somewhat lower building costs allow greater spaciousness and the openness around them makes it easier to arrange contact between the living room and outdoors. But affection for the ideal, the cottage, was so great for so long that we were happy to sacrifice this possibility to retain the seclusion of the original, once justified by the high price of glass and fear of marauders as well as inadequate knowledge of hygienic factors.

The same applies to the firm resistance in Sweden to such an economical and natural type of owner-occupied home as the row house.

View from a Copenhagen window.

The row house meets the demand for a home of one's own with outdoor space. It provides the same possibility as a detached house for a clearly differentiated plan with facilities and living rooms on the ground floor and bedrooms above. They can be arranged to offer greater seclusion from the prying eyes of neighbors than in totally detached houses. In addition, as they require less space to build and the street frontage is shorter per house, they can be built on more expensive central sites. Those who live in them therefore do not need to undertake such long and tiring journeys to and from work.

Industrialized housing production. Standardization.

The route to economical production.

Every worker can afford to own a bicycle. This complicated device, with all its small parts manufactured with precise accuracy, is not too expensive.

Its perfection and reasonable price is the result of mechanical processes and industrial organization.

This is what has happened with most of our necessities, from pins to automobiles; thanks to industry they have come to play a role in public consumption that would otherwise be inconceivable.

But our dwelling, the most important of our necessities, is still too expensive. For the vast majority it is impossible to provide the space, number of rooms, and conveniences they are entitled to demand at a reasonable cost. The only choice is between old-fashioned, inferior dwellings or living in cramped conditions with all the irritation and hygienic and moral perils this entails.

Why this contrast? Why does modern life offer us classless comfort in most areas but not when it comes to our housing? The answer is not so simple, but this much is true:

In our building we do not utilize the resources of our age as we do in most other areas of production.

Only with the help of industrial production can we under prevailing conditions meet the demands for the greatest possible efficiency at the lowest possible cost. It is admittedly true that, for various reasons, the goods produced by industry are often inferior in quality to handicraft. But in most cases industry has a decided advantage over handicraft when it comes to reconciling the demand for quality with the demand for affordability. We already have proof of this in the extent to which industrial products play a role in our daily lives.

Study the following figures, which illustrate the difference in time and cost between different ways of producing books.

I. Handwritten.

A. Time used for:

Preparatory work . . . . 0 days
Writing out a volume of 100,000 words . . . . 14 days
Writing out 100 copies . . . . 4 years, 25 weeks, 2 days
Writing out 1,000 copies . . . . 44 years, 45 weeks, 2 days

B. Cost in kronor for:

Preparatory work . . . . 0:—
One volume . . . . ca. 200:—
100 copies . . . . ca. 20,000:—
1,000 copies . . . . ca. 200,000:—

II. Hand-printing.

A. Time used for:

Preparatory work . . . . 80 days 1 hour — mins.
Printing one copy . . . . 1 hour 20 mins.
Producing the first copy . . . . 80 days 1 hour 20 mins.
Producing the first 100 copies . . . . 96 days 5 hours 20 mins.
Producing the first 1,000 copies . . . . 246 days 5 hours 20 mins.

B. Cost in kronor for:

Preparatory work 1,397:55
Printing one copy 2:42
Producing the first copy 1,399:97
Producing the first 100 copies . . . . 1,694:—
Producing the first 1,000 copies 4,325:75

III. Rotary press.

A. Time used for:

Preparatory work . . . . 96 days — seconds.
Printing one copy . . . . ¾ (0.72) seconds.
Producing the first copy . . . . 96 days ¾ seconds.
Producing the first 100 copies . . . . 96 days 72 seconds.
Producing the first 1,000 copies . . . . 96 days 720 seconds.

B. Cost in kronor for:

Preparatory work 6,621:16
Printing one copy 0:00007
Producing the first copy. 6,675:61
Producing the first 100 copies 6,675:68
Producing the first 1,000 copies 6,676:31
Producing the first 5,000 copies 6,679:20

Machines assist us. They represent cheap labor and perfect precision. The principle on which they work is

reproduction.

Herein lies the secret of the increasing possibilities for economical production.

Reproduction is the mechanical duplication of an object. Handicraft requires the creation of each object anew, even if one resembles another. Industrial production only creates patterns. The manufacturing process reproduces them.

Indeed the more often the original pattern is reproduced, the cheaper the product becomes. For each new example the actual manufacturing costs are insignificant. The major expenditure is on the patterns and the machines. As production becomes more extensive, the smaller the proportion of these one-off costs each example has to cover. Manufacture on a large scale therefore makes it possible to devote scrupulous and extensive preparatory work to the original pattern and the manufacturing method without adding appreciably to the cost of the product. In this way industrial production allows a product to be developed to a technical and functional perfection that production by hand can only achieve, as a rule, in pure luxury goods.

Only industrial production can make quality goods available for the vast majority.

The principle of reproduction in industrial production presupposes limiting manufacture to certain fixed types of products. In other words it presupposes **standardization.**

Standardization, for the purposes of production, is the utilization of

a natural tendency to develop types.[22]

This tendency has existed in all cultures. In different forms of societies, similarities have developed in the way people live and give form to things. Mutual exchanges among individuals led to the perfection of tools that could meet common or similar needs. What one individual produced was improved by another.

Generations of improvements and refinements honed objects to their **typical forms.** They became **types.**

Classical temples, churches, dwellings, books, and automobiles are a few randomly chosen examples of the multiplicity of such types, types that embody the development of material culture.

In every cultural era it is possible to trace the development of objects toward increasingly distinct and perfected types. This natural tendency to develop types was evident in earlier periods. It was the result of distinct craft and stylistic traditions. Local traditions, in particular, contributed to their uniformity. The choice of type was extremely restricted where the home and household goods were concerned.

Deprived of the support of these traditions, the modern craft of building, with its connections to arbitrarily chosen traditional examples, gave rise to irresolute individualism.

It is also certainly a mistake to interpret the motley variety in today's housing as the expression of varying, deeply felt personal inclinations. If we examine the issue more closely, we soon discover that at the heart of all this individualism there are very similar living habits. Now, as before, the vast majority conform to certain shared patterns in their way of life. These enable us to create common forms for our necessities. Standardization of the home and household furnishings is possible in so far as we have "standardized" living habits or can adapt to new ones without difficulty.

As in the past, today there is also a tendency to develop types. It is an economic imperative to make use of this through standardization. Only in this way can all the best features of a product be developed under the most favorable terms for its manufacture. Only in this way can the best products be manufactured in sufficient quantities and at the lowest possible cost.

Standardization is the deliberate development of types.

The natural development of types did not involve any conscious endeavor to attain common forms. Types emerged as common forms because in every age, in every place, and for every function there is one way of doing something that is considered better than others. In standardization today, for economic reasons, we are **consciously** attempting to establish common forms for certain necessities. We are looking for, striving to create, common forms. Herein lies the difference between standardization and the natural development of types, where uniformity developed of its own accord. This is what makes standardization difficult. The natural development of types did not lead to anyone feeling that some individual requirement had been repressed. In so far as such feelings did exist, they resulted in a deviation from the type.

The ideal for every standard should be that in this respect it resembles the natural type, that it is not experienced as forced uniformity but accepted as the best form to fulfill a specific need.

First and foremost, a standard has to be kept "alive." If it fails to change when needs change and methods improve, it will pose an obstacle to development. The best way of doing something today may not be the best tomorrow. "To decree that today's standard shall be tomorrow's is to exceed our power and authority. Such a decree cannot stand. If you think of 'standardization' as the best that you know today, but which is to be improved tomorrow—you get somewhere. But if you think of standards as confining, the progress stops."[23]

By offering a choice of types and possible combinations, standardization should be able to satisfy varying needs. Restricting the number of types is not something that is desirable in itself. It is something that is necessary for economic reasons. The degree of restriction is dependent on economic conditions and the development of production. It is likely that with greater industrial development we will be able to meet all the demands that generally exist in most areas of production. There already exists on the open market an extensive choice of types in terms of price, size, detailed execution, etc.

"Small-cottage" being erected. The wall unit is being positioned.

Can our housing become an industrial product?

Yes, most certainly. It already is to some extent, and not only can it be but it must be to a much greater degree than is currently the case.

The type of cottages now being built in the hundreds in Bromma and Enskede under the management of Stockholm City Council are already being produced industrially in part.[24] They are constructed of ready-made wall units that are manufactured in a few different versions at various factories in Sweden where labor costs less than in Stockholm. They are loaded onto railroad wagons and trucks and assembled in a few hours to provide the building's shell. Window and door openings can be inserted in the appropriate wall units in the factories, and correctly proportioned frames and doors fitted with locks and hinges can be supplied at the building site. The kitchen fixtures arrive ready-made from the factories. And the inhabitants of these little cottages are happy and content. Their "fabricated houses" provide them with three rooms and a kitchen. And they can afford to live there.

This type of cottage is the first large-scale example in Sweden of industrialized housing construction. Industrial principles, while undeveloped, have also proved appropriate for the production of apartment buildings. When it comes to simple dwellings, it is comparatively easy to come up with universally applicable types. Here standardization can be taken further than it can for larger dwellings for those with higher incomes who presume they have the right to make greater individual demands. But here too some degree of industrialized production could well help us to attain better conditions and cheaper financial terms.

Differing degrees of standardization.

Industrial production can take place to varying extents and be based on different degrees of standardization. In principle, industrialized housing construction entails minimizing craftsmanlike work on the building site.

Standardization may be limited to comprising only a certain range of building components and interior details, such as doors, windows, fittings, bathroom and kitchen fixtures, cupboards, and furniture. In this respect there is already some degree of standardization, which only needs further development. Far too many unnecessary and impermanent variations still hinder effective exploitation of standardization in reducing costs and raising quality. The aim is for these various details to be produced in an industrial manner, in a limited but adequate number of types that can be supplied from their warehouses by the manufacturers. Standardization of this kind allows great freedom in the design and fitting out of the buildings themselves.

The material for the "small-cottages," laid out on site. Factory-finished joists, wall units, floor beams, and floorboards.

The next step is to allow standardization to extend to the construction elements—walls, beams, joists, and the like. These are produced in the largest units that it is possible to transport and assemble. The elements are produced industrially—in factories or on site—and assembled ready-made to form the building. This procedure would enable the combination of different standardized building elements to produce various house types. This would also allow a certain freedom of choice in terms of the number of rooms and the organization of the plan. But freedom of choice would be restricted here to a larger or smaller number of fixed types.

House with a skeleton frame.
The load-bearing frame consists of iron sections that
are delivered to the site in suitable lengths. Assembly.

The wall units are faced with lightweight concrete tiles.

The finished product.

Housing project in Frankfurt am Main.

Standardized wall units of light-weight concrete are positioned with the help of cranes.

Mass production.

From an economic point of view, the possibility of using a limited number of house types to create large housing developments is of the greatest significance. The volume of the work makes it possible to use mechanical equipment for assembly and transport. The building elements can to a large extent be produced on site, often using material that is available close at hand or no great distance away.

Frankfurt am Main. Groups of standardized dwellings.

Where standardized house types are simultaneously constructed in large numbers, out-and-out industrialization can be applied. The work of the builders will correspond to the "production-line assembly" of the factories. We have already seen remarkable examples of this from a number of foreign construction companies, particularly in Germany. Following the production-line principle, teams of workers move from building to building to complete their own specialized tasks. Excavations are made for the foundations of the first building to be erected. In the next stage the same team of workers excavates for the foundations of the second building, while another team lays the foundations for the first. In the following stage the excavators have moved on to the third building. Foundations are now being laid for the second building and work has begun on the insulation of the first. And so the work continues, with new teams of workers arriving one after the other. The size of the different teams is adapted to the amount of work involved, so that they can take over from each other without wasting time or having to work hastily and so the work proceeds at an even pace. The same workers or teams of workers carry out the same tasks in each building, and this makes it possible to speed their work up gradually and increase its precision. Thus it has been possible to apply the principles of industrial organization to housing construction.

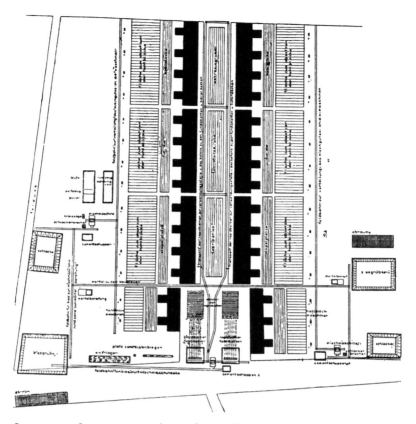

Large-scale construction of row houses.
The site plan demonstrates the careful preparation before building starts.
Areas for manufacturing and storing wall units and beams, tracks for cranes,
and material transport are indicated. (Törten, Dessau).

In our circumstances industrialization to this extent remains difficult to implement with any economic advantage. This is because we rarely undertake building on such a scale. In Sweden housing is generally built by a number of entrepreneurs who organize the work in their own way. Another difficulty can be found in the system of wages imposed by the building trades, who stubbornly resist most reforms intended to increase the use of labor-saving materials and machines. One typical example: concrete could be used as a building material far more efficiently than is possible today if, for instance, standardized formwork could be used for pouring concrete for larger housing projects. At the moment this formwork is generally constructed of planks of wood for each section of wall to be poured. Identical formwork is constructed again and again instead of using sections that could be reassembled and moved from building to building as soon as the concrete has become firm enough to allow its removal. It is easy to understand the entrepreneurs' lack of interest in labor-saving methods for erecting formwork when the cost of constructing new formwork

Stockpiling materials. (Dessau-Törten).

is the same as for reusing standard formwork. One repeatedly encounters this kind of example of the difficulty in taking advantage of the resources now offered by modern technology and modern organization caused by the prevailing system of wages and piecework payment. It is clear that the economic development of housing construction will depend to a great extent on sweeping changes in current conditions in the labor market.

This is not to say that this development will be guaranteed simply through better and more efficient building methods. Production techniques are only one detail, however significant, in the complex of issues that must be dealt with in any rationalization of the way in which housing is built. But to go into problems such as finance and credit, land acquisition, profit margins, unsound speculation, and the like would be going into too much detail for this discussion.

Conversation with a skeptic.

"You mean in other words we have to accept these possibilities: industrialization, standardization?"

"Of course. We already have when it comes to most of our daily needs, from shoes and sweaters to suitcases and automobiles."

"That's totally different! Our dwelling is after all our home! For the entire working day I am a cog in a machine. When I get home I want to feel like a real **person**!"

"That's easy to understand. And you're perfectly right. You need a sound, spacious and comfortable home where you can rest and feel free and happy. But it must be inexpensive, otherwise you cannot afford it. Where we live, the home, is not 'totally different' in the sense that it can evade the current laws of economic production. It will only be cheap in the same way as all the other things that you definitely would not be able to afford if they were not industrial products, standardized . . ."

"Hateful words!! I want a home and you offer me a standardized house with standard furniture!!! . . . a machine to live in . . . *funkis* . . ."[25]

"Slogans."

"I want my home comforts! I do not want my personality stifled!"

"And you should stick to that. But let us discuss things in more detail."

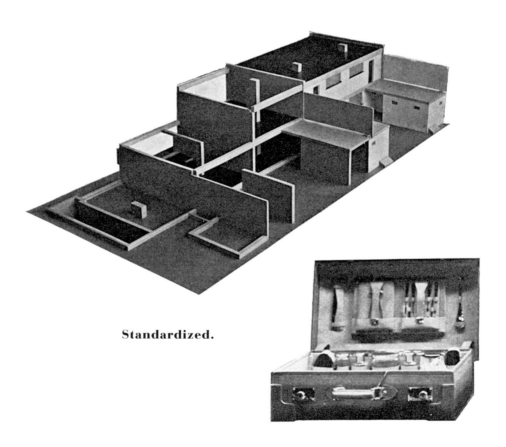

Standardized.

A chapter on home comforts.

The standing objection.

Those who believe in the potential of improving the way in which people live through the consistent exploitation of current possibilities often encounter the objection that they have a one-sided, material view of things. This is what they are told: rationalization, economics, and all that goes with them is all very well, but do these gentlemen ever consider that there is something called comfort? And that what is important in a home, surely, is the beauty, comfort, and feeling of tradition that it can offer? Are we not giving in to crass materialism when we place convenience, spaciousness, and hygiene before the opportunity of allowing our homes to be characterized by our own desires, our own taste? Comfort depends, after all, on having a home that suits me alone and nobody else. Rather, let us go on living in slightly cramped and inconvenient conditions—all that about hygiene is not that dangerous after all—but do not deny us comfort. Leave us the beautiful—that suits our own tastes!

Yes, this is the standing objection. It may take various forms, but the content remains the same. All that goes under the name of rationalization, industrialization, and standardization poses a threat to the feeling of well-being and individuality. To this we could respond brutally, "It is very unfortunate but necessary, alas." We could indeed choose to respond like this because as a rule the objection comes not from the 90 percent for whom a decent, affordable dwelling is a demand that can no longer be suppressed, but from the prosperous member of the bourgeoisie and the eloquent custodian of "good old-fashioned culture." And it is, after all, not their housing problem that needs solving but that of the far less affluent gentleman with an income of two to five thousand kronor and a family to support, in other words a gentleman who is certainly unable to perceive the picturesque charms of miserably primitive dwellings to the same extent as the aesthete strolling through the city. Despite having reason to believe that this often heard objection does not come from those who really need inexpensive housing, we shall nevertheless examine it closely. We do not want to be found guilty of defending a development that offers material benefits at the expense of spiritual values. We therefore intend to scrutinize the idea of comfort and personal taste to see to what extent these factors conflict with the rationalization of housing production.

To begin with . . .

You object that it is not possible to standardize housing. You for your part would not put up with living in a house or apartment that was identical to those of your neighbors on your right, on your left, and across the street. You want a dwelling that suits you alone and nobody else. Thus far, you are of course right: your home should satisfy your needs.

Let us, however—to start with something concrete—take a closer look at the housing currently available on the open market. What possibilities do we now have of satisfying our particular needs? Let us disregard the dwellings intended for the more affluent, who under current circumstances already have no difficulty in acquiring a sufficiently comfortable and spacious home. So we shall concentrate on small apartments. If we want to live in the city itself, we go to take a look at apartments for rent in some of the new buildings. To begin with we look at the smallest types of apartments, with one or two rooms and a kitchen. We will discover what a modern one-room apartment looks like. We walk into an entry vestibule or what is called a "hall." It has room for outdoor clothes, a closet, and three doors, one to the main room, one to the kitchen, and one to the bathroom. The kitchen has a larder, a serving area with cupboards and drawers below, a sink and slop sink with a cupboard beneath, a work surface, and a gas stove. This is not something we may have thought about in any detail earlier, but now we are struck by how little the one-room apartments differ from each other, as we go from one building to the next. The main room may be on the right and the kitchen on the left, or vice versa, the rooms and floor space vary somewhat in size. But the variations are few. During recent years a new type has emerged in which the kitchen is divided into an inner section, which contains the kitchen equipment itself, and an external section close to the window, separated from the inner section by a glass partition and intended as a dining area. This is a variant of the previous type, but this too is repeated with minor differences. We have already dealt with different kinds of plan types in the chapter on planning dwellings.

What we find, therefore, is that modern one-room apartments have, with no conscious attempts at standardization, taken the form of a few relatively distinct fixed types that can be found with insignificant variations in one building after another,

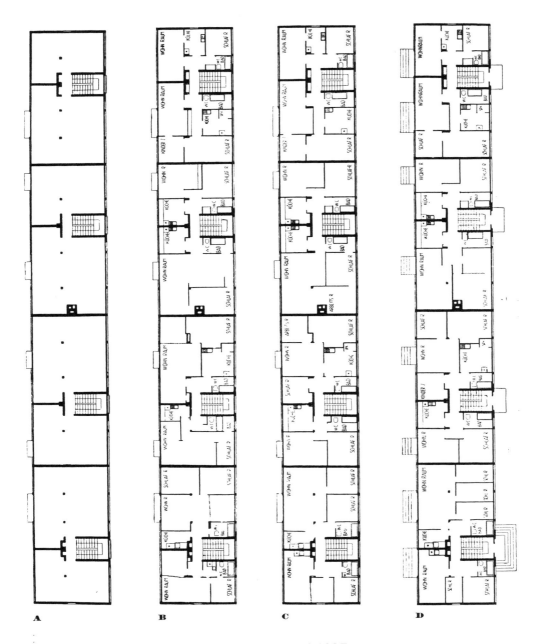

Apartments at the Stuttgart Exhibition of 1927.

A. The fixed elements of the plan.

B.
C. } Options for laying out different apartment types according to varying needs
D. } in terms of the number of rooms, different room sizes, etc.

one area after another. We also find that this is the situation for two-room apartments and also, to some extent, three- and four-room apartments.

These apartments have, however, been produced speculatively. The producer has no other desire than to rent out his apartments on the most advantageous terms possible. His endeavor has merely been to adapt to the wishes and needs of the public. If, despite this, only a limited number of types come about, we are obliged to conclude that the few types that exist on the general open market satisfy needs within a given economic framework. At any rate the need for other types is very small. Otherwise the desires of the public would soon be reflected in the production of buildings through the emergence of new types.

The type formation that on the whole already exists could, if only it were utilized consistently, provide a basis for a rationalization of the city's housing constructions. Indeed, there would be no obstacle to extending the choice of types that already exist. Making the light dividing walls inside an apartment moveable to some extent would allow for variations in room size and floor plan that are not possible in apartments available today. Flexible adaptation to the varying needs of tenants could be offered to a greater extent than ever before. In various countries, work is already under way on technical solutions to allow these "flexible" floor plans. One noteworthy attempt is displayed in our illustration of an apartment block erected at the Stuttgart Exhibition in 1927.

If we look at current housing construction in garden cities and suburban residential areas—still with our attention focused on the small dwellings—we will find the same trend as with rental apartments toward type formation. Certainly there are more variations here because of the differences in the relationship to roads, orientation, or the terrain, but on the whole we can without difficulty apportion the various houses to a relatively limited number of different types. Here as well, and with no external pressure, a development of types has occurred, indicating that a fairly high degree of standardization is feasible without encroaching on the individual demands that housing of this category is generally considered to satisfy. Even if the industrial production of housing can, through various combinations of prefabricated elements, be organized to offer a great range of variation, the possibility of more stringent limitation of the choice of types, particularly when it comes to the simultaneous development of large, contiguous areas, offers major economic advantages. Only then can we count on considerable savings in building costs. In view of the economic aspects of the housing problem, it is therefore gratifying to know that conditions clearly exist that would make it possible to limit the types available even further.

What creates home comforts?

It is true that the feeling of comfort is something subjective, variable, and often dependent on highly intangible conditions. But this does not mean that it is independent of strictly material factors.

The feeling of comfort in a home depends to a great extent on how well a dwelling can satisfy the needs of those living there in terms of practical functions.

It is first and foremost dependent on adequate space. If there is too little room, annoying conflicts can occur. The members of a family cannot enjoy as much independence from each other as they need. Their opportunities for organizing things as they would like are restricted by concern for others. In the long run this enforced dependence breeds annoyance. It becomes a source of irritation that in many cases makes home life intolerable.

In the organization of dwellings, in their practical usefulness, there is also value in comfort of a more universal nature: the comfort the average person

Housing layout. Hästholmen.

feels when faced with the well-arranged, the well-organized, and that which functions well. Everything in its place and easily accessible, adequate and suitable lighting, both natural and artificial, sunlight, peace and calm both in places for relaxation and for work, good furnishing possibilities—all these are organizational considerations of fundamental importance for comfort that do not conflict with either the rational planning of housing and housing areas nor the principles of industrial production, but which can on the contrary be greatly enhanced by them.

Are there greater differences in personal taste today than there used to be?

It is obvious that in the past housing culture was more uniform than it is today. One striking example can be found in the houses once built in the countryside. Characteristically there were only a few types. These could vary widely in various regions—the farms of southern and northern Sweden are very dissimilar—but within a certain limited area there was almost stringent consistency in the types used. Earlier bourgeois housing culture displays similarly uniform features.

This uniformity has vanished for a number of reasons. The most fundamental of these is a decidedly romantic attitude to building problems, nourished by our increased knowledge of historical forms. The old farmhouses embodied the abstemious satisfaction of needs using highly restricted resources in terms of material and execution. Today's attempts to imitate them offer a superficial resemblance to their romantic charm. We learn nothing from the practicality of the old farmhouse, with its effort to make the best of what the period could offer. We imitate the external effect. And the result offers an image of conflicting conceptions of taste, as reminiscences of this traditional building-art from various parts of the country and periods are all mixed together in the houses we build today.

The homes in the garden cities, whose forms alternate between borrowings from manor houses, farm cottages, Italian villas, and the like, demonstrate how the desire to turn our environment into a stage set has prevented us from coming to terms with our own era and the obvious conditions in which we live.

Plan of a village showing the similar arrangements of the various yards set next to each other along the main street.

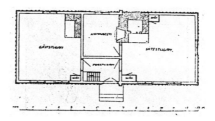

Plans demonstrating the similarities between different two-room cottages from Västmanland. The similarities even apply to the position of the various items of furniture: cupboards, benches, tables, stoves, beds (compare with the interior views, overleaf).

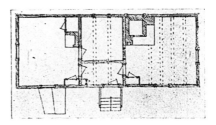

**Two-room cottage cor-
responding to the plans
on the previous page.**

Our romantic and individualistic attitude today has been inherited from what was in itself a natural reaction to the emergence of unbridled industrialism. It was the revolution in technology that gave us unimaginable possibilities. The fixed forms of handicraft, hallowed by centuries of tradition, were not least the outcome of the limitations imposed by technique. Machine technology was not bound by these restrictions. The old traditions of form disintegrated. Technological development went hand in hand with the decline of form. This is how industrialism came to be regarded as the sworn enemy of beauty. At work, in the factories, offices, stores, and in public life, economic laws prevailed. This was the victory of the machines, organization, standardization. The home became the last stronghold against "barbarism" and "leveling down." The romantic infatuation with farmer's cottages, antique furniture, and four-poster beds was a reaction to the cold, sober reality of industrialism. Personality suddenly assumed value in the face of the uniformity threatened by industrialism.

It is from this period that our current anxious overemphasis on the individual, the personal, can be dated.

And the romantic who, fully aware of his own individual personality, is now at work building a home of his own need feel no lack of nourishment for his imagination. This is provided by the weekly magazines, which provide an unceasing supply of pictures and descriptions from the homes of other idiosyncratic individuals. He is offered an unfailing source of inspiration: Rococo homes, Louis XVI homes, interiors in the peasant or manor-house styles, and finally homes in the "functionalist style." If he wants more he need only glance at the bookseller's display: *Das schöne Heim*, *Old English Cottages*, *Neue Villen* . . . Indeed he need not despair about finding expression for his own personal taste. There is more than enough to choose from.

There can be no doubt that the current situation has given rise to a romantically tinged individualism that has left its stamp on today's building to such an extent that it is easy to understand why so many are asking if any standardization in the field of housing is at all possible without suppressing something valuable in human terms. Do rationalization, organization, and standardization mean that we necessarily deprive people of important and deeply felt values?

If, without any further concern, we were to allow ourselves to be convinced by this conservative opinion, our answer to this question would be yes. But if instead we attempt to look more closely at these various expressions of the individualism that today prevails, try to make clear what is genuine and what is false, superficial, and transient, which needs are genuinely felt and which are whims, we will not answer yes. We do not believe that the existence of architectural variations between different cottage porches, roof forms, or window frames has the kind of relationship to the individuality of the occupant that leads to harmful effects on spiritual well-being and personal development when they are eliminated. We believe that these variations are in most cases on the one hand fortuitous, dependent on the individual forms in which housing building is currently organized, and on the other blandishments offered by speculative builders who are psychologically astute in expecting it to be easier to sell a house that looks as if it were built specifically for the buyer and not—as it usually really is—a commodity for an unknown consumer. The speculative builder is a psychologist. He builds—to some extent—a standardized house, but he knows that "the personal" is in demand while standard products are despised. With handcrafted building methods, variations themselves add little or no extra cost. It is natural for him to take advantage of this. Furniture manufacturers are also psychologists. They sell mechanically produced standard furniture with added ornaments that give the false impression that they are made by hand. The ornaments are made to pattern, they lack all artistic decorative value but they conjure away the irritating fact that the item of furniture in question is a standard industrial product and not a hand-crafted piece. Again we encounter this desire that things should preferably seem to be what they are not, to seem better and finer.

If we are to be able to make productive use of the standardization that we have in fact to a very large extent already accepted, we have to abandon this predilection for replica effects. Furniture that is not merely a standard product but also allowed to look like one can be both better and cheaper if the false impression of it being made by hand disappears. And in this way it can be more beautiful, at least according to a healthier attitude toward taste that demands the genuine.

If we can afford it, let us give preference to good handicrafts and really outstanding applied art and acquire furniture and household items that also meet our requirements in terms of individual form. If we do not have the money—and this applies to most of us—then let us choose from cheap but nevertheless good and well-designed standardized furniture. A great deal is already available of this kind and there will be more, if only we manage to overcome our prejudice against making use of it.

We really have only these two possibilities to choose from—what lies between, quasi-artistic imitation, has nothing to do with sound domestic culture.

And let us not believe that in being confined to inexpensive industrial products we have to give up our home comforts or the personal touch. This may well be the case if we blindly go in for "three-piece suites," "complete" interiors for drawing rooms, bedrooms, or smoking rooms that consist of—and here you are correct—stock combinations that can be found in dismal repetition in the homes of our friends and acquaintances whether they meet a specific need or not. **If we furnish our home with the things we really need, the selection will be an expression of the life in the home as we live it.** In this way the personal home evolves naturally and authentically—just as much if each item is also one in a series of humble, impersonal manufactured pieces of furniture.

But what about stylistic coherence?

Do not worry so much about it! With an ounce of judgment and discrimination we can easily combine furniture of varying character and of different periods—old and new. The implementation of stylistic coherence is more a question of ostentation than of home comforts. If you like sitting in grandfather's rocking chair, then do not throw it out to make room for a "complete suite" of furniture in some period style. The loss will be yours.

Standardized furniture.

Beauty can be attained in many ways. But what is false and untrue is rarely beautiful in the long run, even if it can dazzle for a moment. Beauty is not bound to a certain schema of form. It depends on the way in which something is done.

Comfort. The same applies here as to individuality. It cannot be bought. Who believes, despite the contradictory assurances of smart advertisers, that one can for instance buy an individualized automobile or individualized suit fabric, and while gone with the family to the country, acquire an individualized home by entrusting it to an interior decorator?

Comfort is something that a home acquires first and foremost from those who live in it. If they possess so priceless a talent, the home will be cozy, if not, then it will hardly help to place, like Carl Malmsten, a sofa in the center of the wall, flank it with two chairs and hang a painting above it, or, like the architects in the housing section of the Stockholm Exhibition, position the sofa in the corner of the room.[26] One thing is certain, however, which is that comfort vanishes if a home is not suitably organized to allow life to be lived with the minimum of friction.

Traditions and sentimental values are the feelings that bind us to the old familiar forms and things that we have seen since our childhood. Are they not something that we should benefit from? For many this is certainly the case, but let us remember that we cannot through imitation endow what is new with the sentimental values of the old or the mood it inspires. These values are not created by architects, engineers, or artists; we ourselves and time create them through the memories we attach to the objects we have surrounded ourselves with during our lives and which have gradually become part of us.

Industry and handicraft.

Popular opinion.

We often believe there to be an important difference between handicraft and industry in the character and sentimental value of their products. We then readily equate handicraft with the handmade and industry with the machine-made. It is obvious that a conception such as this is not totally correct. Nonetheless, it often unconsciously colors our judgment. It also merges with other obsolete conceptions in our spontaneous appreciation of the items produced. We can trace these conceptions back to known historical causes.

As we still judge a product in the following way:

if it is handmade	if it is machine-made
then it is beautiful	then it is ugly
and sturdy	and of poor quality

we are undoubtedly influenced by the change in opinion toward the outcomes of industry and handicraft that was propagated by Ruskin and Morris during the second half of the nineteenth century. In the middle of that century handicraft began to encounter competition from industry, which had on the whole succeeded in attaining sound and refined designs for its products. Ruskin's preaching aroused, however, some degree of suspicion of the cultural value of industrial products. Only handcrafted production methods were, in his opinion, fit for human beings. Only handicraft could create harmonious individuals.

As we know, Ruskin's view gained many adherents and gave rise to widespread regeneration of the applied arts. Influenced by Ruskin's way of thinking, public opinion changed and the idea arose that industrial products were of less value. The methods by which they were produced denied workers their liberty, and their manufacture led to severe disturbances in social conditions. Handcrafted products were seen as the outcome of a freer and—it was considered—more human way of working. Their production was felt to enrich the producer's personality. They were therefore more valuable. This change in the attitude of the public to the two forms of enterprise made the situation difficult for industrialists. They were, however, convinced of the greater possibilities offered by their production. They therefore attempted to secure the share of the market they had already captured by allowing industrial products to imitate handcrafted goods. For reasons that can easily be explained this imitation resulted in products of a lower quality than before.

Product collection of a traveling salesman.

The grounds no longer exist to warrant this approach. But it is still practiced. It has even acquired certain support from our slightly irresolute worship of the artistic forms of expression of the good old days. We hardly react when our machine-made household goods, decorations, and souvenirs have a handmade appearance. On the contrary, many of us are quite content with the false impression of handicraft they give. The general feeling is also probably that industrial products that imitate handicraft add an air of prosperity to their owners that neither modest nor first-class machine-made goods can impart. The misconception here can be traced in part to Ruskin. It is also linked to the erroneous belief that an industrial product that is not disguised looks cheap: **we do not want people to think that we have cheap things in our homes**.

False generalization.

To say that a handmade product is good and a machine-made one bad is today a false generalization. Both machines and human hands can produce goods of high quality. With full recognition of Ruskin's noble purpose at a time when industrial production first brought about severe sanitary and social evils, we must nevertheless maintain that the Ruskinian belief cannot be applied to our circumstances. In most occupations today, industrial work has developed into a job wholly befitting human beings. It fosters humanitarian and social progress and a relatively high standard of living for those engaged in it. Instead the point of view in question is an incontestable obstacle to the sound development of both forms of production. It thwarts endeavors to develop high-quality machine-made household goods. And it ruins the market for advanced handicraft by producing banal imitations.

Popular opinion encourages artificiality.

We often attempt to give factory goods the appearance of old handicrafts. This effect is achieved by imitating defects in their execution that were natural during earlier cultural periods with their inadequate technical resources. The most consistent application of these efforts can be found in the modern mass-production of "antiques," which has brought us the blessing of being able to make a newly furnished home look as old-fashioned as we want it to.

One episode from the history of this industry shows that its rationalization is the outcome of deliberate effort. As long as Italian "antiques" were only being made in Italy, many Americans traveled there to buy the country's inexhaustible stock of "artistic treasures." When the number of Americans with a hunger for antiques rose, a branch of production moved to the U.S.A. In this way the demand for "antique" Italian objects increased even more, while, on the other hand, unnecessary expense for their production could be reduced.

The production of "oriental" decorative objects has developed in the same way. Richly decorated Eastern handicrafts are now reproduced more or less accurately in European workshops. From there, catalogues and imitation products are distributed to prospective buyers. If you travel to Siam to buy a genuine Siamese bronze urn, nine times out of ten you will get an imitation made in Birmingham.

The artistic quality of the imitations is usually poor, however. Their sculptural work and hand-painted decoration are second-rate and uninformed. But they are in great demand. For the uninitiated they still have the lure of the unusual.

We cannot absolve ourselves of a certain involvement in this artificiality. We imitate the rural crafts of the past industrially. We embellish machine-made everyday

**Four little brushes
set out one day . . .**

things with handmade dents and artificial patina. We decorate our homes with false furnishings expecting to make them homey.

If we ask our salesmen we will learn that these imitations of handicraft, and the even less distinguished hammered metal goods and items of carved furniture, are still highly marketable in furnishings stores.

What is the reason for the incontestable success of these imitated goods? They are cheap and yet, at the same time, offer us the spurious illusion of being rare and valuable. They appeal to our vanity and desire for novelty. This kind of production may be organized with psychological astuteness, but its success will come to an end when the psychological grounds disappear—in other words, when we tire of its products or discover that we have been deceived. All of these pretentiously false goods, which we now cherish, will sooner or later reveal their emptiness and sicken us. We will be ashamed and displeased by our gullibility. Most of us have certainly found ourselves in this situation.

"We have to sell what people want."

The buyers and salesmen involved in distributing these industrial products that largely imitate handicraft normally argue as follows: "It is not up to us to reform the taste of our customers, we have to sell 'what people want.'"

Hardly anyone will find this argument totally convincing. "What people want" is a slogan sometimes used to deceive oneself and others. In fact only a few customers definitely know what they want. The others can easily be guided by a skillful salesman. Nor can we ignore the fact that both buyers and salesmen order and promote, to some extent, products they themselves prefer.

Nevertheless, retail trade cannot be based merely on what the salesman "prefers" and what he believes "people want." Objective knowledge about the products must be the basis of every successful commercial undertaking. This knowledge is often possessed by the buyers for the large companies but not as frequently by their salesmen. In the small stores the salesman is often the buyer as well. Even so, too often they lack knowledge about the products. This is undoubtedly one of the difficulties in the struggle against inferior industrial goods. The influence of furnishings salesmen should therefore be matched to a greater extent by knowledge about the products they are selling. They need to know how the goods are produced and how they attain a natural form.

This does not mean that inferior goods cannot be combated more effectively. Increased knowledge about the products among salesmen selling furnishings is a preventive measure and as such not infallible. We find the affirmative measures elsewhere.

Consumers value quality, especially if they can acquire it at a reasonable price. **Producers should therefore manufacture goods that are better and less expensive than imitations. Cheap and bad products have to be driven out of the market by cheap and good ones**. To achieve this we must make use of both domestic and foreign production.

Is there a dividing line between industry and handicraft?

We implied above that the concepts of industry and handicraft cannot merely be defined by classifying the outcome of production as machine- or handmade.

Industry comprises something more than machine production, and handicraft is more than making things by hand. If we think carefully we will be forced to admit

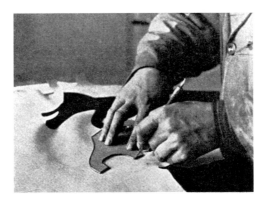

Cutting out the uppers for a pair of leather shoes.

This is how "new furniture in antique styles" is made.

that **first-rate** industrial and handicraft products are not so particularly different in character. It would be unfair to blame this situation on Ruskin. It is due, rather, to the way in which both industry and handicraft often work using the same means and similar methods. It is also because they collaborate with each other. Working by hand and the use of machines alternate continually in both handicraft and industrial production.

Handicraft makes use of machines more and more, while in certain industries a great deal still has to be done by hand. Carpenters use mechanical saws and lathes. Contemporary craftsmen use machines when they carve or do intarsia work. On the other hand cutting out leather for the uppers in a shoe factory is still carried out by hand, and even today the industrial production of household glass goes on according to the working methods of handicraft. These examples could be multiplied.

The use of machines for making products therefore tells us nothing about whether an enterprise should rightly be classified as industry or handicraft. Here other factors must be taken into account: speculation and organization.

What is industry?

The industrial process involves, as a rule, the production of a series of standardized, interchangeable parts assembled as units through the rational division of labor with as few different actions performed by hand as possible. Certain industries, however, are engaged in mass production without assembly. Others adopt a production process that is the opposite of the rule: the object is taken apart and then each of the parts is processed (the food industry, processing raw materials). What the majority of industries have in common, however, is that their production is based not on the preferences of individuals but ultimately to satisfy broad and general requirements. Industry produces on a large scale and has to dispose of its products through high-volume sales. Rapid technological progress and incessant

Production-line assembly.

Knitting machines.

**Automated food production. This is a detail from a cereal mill.
The cereal is stored, purified, steam-treated, and packaged without
any contact with human hands.**

changes in human needs over the course of a generation have continually given rise to new industries. Lacking the support of tradition and experience, they have had to blaze their own trail. For this reason the forces on which industry has been obliged to rely for its consolidation have been far from conservative. Its success has to a large extent been due to the speculative capacities and organizational talents of its leaders.

What is handicraft?

Handicrafts are usually executed on commission and cater to a relatively small group of customers. They attempt to satisfy the specific desires of individual purchasers. They generally produce unique objects, which differ from each other in their dimensions, form, and use. They have no organizational costs to speak of. Craftsmen often

Glassblowing.

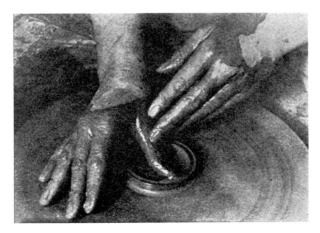

Pottery-throwing.

sell directly to their customers. The demand for the utensils and decorative objects that handicraft has been supplying since time immemorial has changed very slowly. In effect the skills of craftsmen are the outcome of an uninterrupted tradition. But this tradition not only provides support. It is also a constraint. Handicraft can easily become conservative.

The development of industry from handicraft.

Within handicraft, however, it may happen that speculative interests can burst the shackles that normally apply. This usually occurs when a craftsman discovers or otherwise perfects some form of specialization. Eventually, he will then turn the production of this specialty into manufacture on a larger scale (mass production). The transformation from handicraft to industrial production is then strikingly completed and demonstrates the fundamental significance of the speculative mentality for the development of this form of undertaking. Handicraft and industry are not so different in essence that coherent development from one form of undertaking to the other is impossible.

Examples of this kind of development can be found in home industry and large-scale industry today.[27] In various parts of the country, home industries that are derived from the handicrafts of earlier days are still operating. Småland in particular, with its increasingly industrialized production of furniture, toys, purses, cast brassware, and the like, provides examples of this kind of change.

Karl-Erik Forsslund describes how even the production of the old-fashioned Mora grandfather clock was already shifting in the early nineteenth century from handicraft to a form of industrial organization.[28] At the same time he quotes a comment by an earlier writer who says that "the people of Mora are generally recognized and famous both for their aptitude for the mathematical and the independence of their characters." The ingenious, calculating menfolk of Mora obviously discovered that some degree of division of their tasks facilitated production. Some of them specialized in the details of the clockwork, others made the cases, others again did the painting and decorative work, and so on. Each clock was finally assembled by the maker whose name it bore. In other words the parts were still entirely handcrafted but the organization of the manufacture became, as demand for the clocks grew, industrial—mass production.

Similarly the textile industry in Borås has gradually evolved from what had been sheer handicraft. The development in this instance is more typical and takes place over a longer period and on a larger scale. During the seventeenth century the first serious inroads into the old guild system could be perceived, and these were to play a major role in the disintegration of the earlier regulatory system and the introduction of commercial freedom in the middle of the nineteenth century.

There can be no doubt that it is thanks to speculation, or commerce if you prefer, that this development has taken place. The earlier barter economy was by nature based on private concerns. It was restricted to the various towns and parishes, a direct transaction between producer and consumer. When handloom weaving in Västergötland attracted the interest of merchants and the government at the beginning of the seventeenth century, output soon became greater than it had hitherto been possible to dispose of locally through barter trading. Home industries arose. The surplus products were distributed to other places by intermediaries. The prospects of greater earnings for both the merchants and the individual producers encouraged a putting-out system in which merchants supplied the raw materials to the producers, who in turn delivered the finished goods to the merchant for sale. The next development involved the movement of the producers into workshops provided by the merchants. The emergence of manufacture in Borås meant that producers began to work completely for agents and became their paid employees. In principle this was the implementation of one of the first major industrialization processes in Sweden. It was completed during the eighteenth and nineteenth centuries with the introduction of the division of labor and mechanical operation.

Similar developments from handicraft to large-scale industrial production can be seen in our iron industry and in the manufacture of shoes.

These examples testify to the fertile interaction of developments in industry and handicraft, and show that on the whole they have supplied demand jointly and in collaboration. They still need to function together in this way. In contemporary production, however, we can observe an even more explicit division of their roles, with separate modes of operation. This is due to technical developments and their continuing influence in supplying human demand. Before discussing this, however, we would like to stress that our national demand coincided in important respects with that of the rest of humanity.

The purpose of production.

Our needs vary in intensity. Insofar as they are based on human nature, their satisfaction influences our spiritual and material existence. The primary needs, which are linked to the maintenance of life and its mechanisms, are firmly defined and require relatively regular and straightforward satisfaction. Of course, the less time and effort we have to devote to satisfying material requirements, the more we can commit to the satisfaction of our deeper needs. In addition to primary needs, there are an infinite variety of other more or less latent needs that demand satisfaction less regularly. What particularly characterizes modern people like us is our need for change and novelty. Another typical category of need is based on social self-assertion. We acquire things and objects to indicate our social status. We need because others need. We imagine that we have certain needs.

When new needs arise, our assets have to be augmented if these new needs are to be satisfied without having to repress others. Where material resources are concerned this augmentation has taken place through the industrialization of production. The assets of this country have been greatly multiplied in one lifetime.

We are therefore considerably more affluent than the generation immediately before us. (Affluence includes not only the total amount of capital we have saved but the aggregate of our material prospects.) We can for this reason satisfy new needs without exceeding our assets. This development is similar for the other populations in A-Europe.

Information about the number of bankbooks and account balances, etc., in savings banks in Sweden.

Year	Total Swedish population	Number of bank accounts	Balance of accounts in kronor	Average balance per citizen	Average balance per account in kronor
1860	3,859,728	182,675	27,291,937	7	145
1875	4,383,291	685,962	132,714,531	30	193
1900	5,136,441	1,228,930	437,391,160	85	356
1913	5,638,583	1,717,694	952,605,043	169	555
1928	6,105,190	2,763,866	2,793,440,060	458	1,011

Human needs continue to increase, however. Can this rise persist? Let us try to answer that question.

Our inability to be satisfied, our speculative mentality, continually drives us to new improvements. We invent things, and we compete with each other for economic advantages. The population of the world is increasing. As a natural consequence of these circumstances, production also increases. **Our efforts to produce things as cheaply as possible create new needs.** In contrast to previous periods we can pursue these ambitions, since we are free to take on new scientific work and experiment with new forms of organization in our enterprises. Industrial mass production, with its mechanical operation and specialization, is one outcome of these endeavors.

There are, however, phenomena that lead us to suspect that demand will always grow faster than production. At times when there is a surplus of money, production can be stimulated that exceeds consumer demand and creates new needs. The consumption of toiletries, patent medicines, ornaments, working materials, and the like is often magnified by exaggerated advertising that in no way corresponds to the value of the products. On the whole, advertising often stimulates consumption that is not based on any genuine need. Our weakness for novelties is readily exploited for this purpose. On the other hand we must, in all fairness, admit that advertising also adds to our prosperity. By increasing consumption of high-quality products advertising actually enables further rationalization of their production and therefore reductions in price.

The more natural and simpler way of life of the current generation is, one could believe, one of the factors that should encourage greater restraint in the increase of demand.

What remains, however, is the indisputable fact that the vast majority of the world's population is still living in such primitive conditions that any lull in demand would be unnatural. Nor are we likely to be ready to submit voluntarily to any restriction of our needs.

It is more probable that demand will continue to increase. The continuous reciprocity between consumption and production will lead to continuing industrialization and rationalization in the world of production. At what rate this will take place is impossible to predict. We can, however, definitely foresee that every form of production that has no counterpart in our needs must eventually come to an end. **No form of production can survive for its own sake or be maintained for any length of time by artificial means.** This law applies to the same extent to the forms of enterprise dealt with here.

The efficiency of production.

In his book *Men and Machines* Stuart Chase used the statistics he collected to illustrate how machines and organizations have increased the yield from human labor.[29] He also shows how machines have increased our manufacturing possibilities and compares the production of various countries with China, where in many areas handmade production is as it was three thousand years ago. A Frenchman produces eight times as much per day as a Chinese, a German twelve times as much, an Englishman eighteen times as much, and an American thirty times the figure.

These statistics illustrate the differences in capacity between industrial operation and production by hand, which increases in proportion to the degree of rationalization. The difference is decisive for the extent to which both forms of production can contribute to the satisfaction of demand. This still means a continued increase in the possibilities open to industry at the expense of handicraft. Today a shoe can be industrially manufactured in two hours. But it takes at least nine hours to make a shoe by hand. Certain articles of clothing are still likely to last longer if they are handmade, but the quality of industrially produced garments is continually improving. Hundreds of thousands of brains are working on this. For the majority of people industrial mass production means a higher standard of living. For instance, more people can afford to dress well, and ready-made garments save time, work, and money for the consumer.

Everyday things and luxury products.

If we consider the production of goods, we can divide our needs into everyday needs and luxuries. The former coincide to a large extent with the basic necessities of life, daily chores that must be facilitated. The latter with public and private display, our inclination for the exclusive or the extravagant and impressive. Inasmuch as production satisfies these needs, it supplies everyday things in the first case and luxury items in the second.

We can see, however, that it is impossible to make a firm distinction between these two categories. What is an everyday thing for one person is a luxury for the other. But we all need everyday things, and everyone seeks luxuries. Some need things rationally, others with no common sense.

Everyday things—our servants.

Everyday things consist of the items we need to be able to work, run our homes, and dress ourselves, and some simple items of fashion and ornaments. This category also includes widely used sporting goods and means of transport. The first demands we make of all these items are efficiency, affordability, and good form. These demands are already accepted for our clothing, household utensils, and the everyday things directly linked to our jobs, transport, and sport. We have accepted certain standards for products in these areas of production. In our conception the affordability and utility of these goods is unquestionably linked with their objective form. We take the efficient form of overalls, a frying pan, a typewriter, or a hockey stick for granted.

For many of our household goods, however, things are different. We usually think about them in the following way.

"Of course they should be affordable and useful. But these characteristics may not prevail at the expense of their ability to impress."

"The appearance of an object, what it says about its owner's personality and affluence, is, after all, almost the basis of our feeling of hominess."

"The idea of objective form sounds far too crude. We need to get away from crude utility, at least in our homes. That's where we want to enjoy what is beautiful."

This is an argument that is often heard from those who place a great deal of stress on the impression made by their homes. And they continue:

"We have managed well with things that are perhaps terribly impractical. They have even become dear old friends of ours."

We answer: "Keep these familiar old friends and enjoy them. They have sentimental value that we do not despise. But do not be surprised that **we want to create objects that we can both feel an attachment to and that work well and beautifully.**"

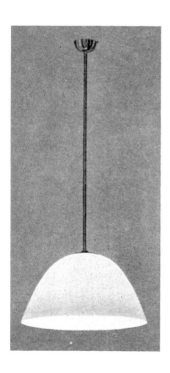

The obvious task for everyday things is to be of service. Our aim when we produce them must be that they will not merely serve adequately but irreproachably. We must also recognize that the better something serves, the less fuss it makes. Everyday things should be utilitarian, unpretentious, calm, and appealing.

But only in exceptional cases have we produced and imported goods in this spirit. The servant has usually been superior to his master. We have shown more interest in appearances than efficiency.

In this way the general public's interest in good form has been linked to goods intended for ostentatious display. We have devoted an incredible amount of effort to devising and varying objects intended to impress. In doing so we have encouraged artificiality instead of unaffectedness. We have produced and imported household goods as if we were a nation of shopkeepers and dubious art dealers. It is not only our "cultural enthusiasts" and "American friends" who have competed with each other for the distinction of supporting such a sterile trend in production. Our hacks practicing in the traditional and "*funkis*" manner have not been much better.

We must escape this blind alley. If we are to set the stamp of our age on the production of utilitarian things, we must begin with the elementary tasks. This may not always be rewarding, but it is necessary! Then we will find the true course to what is genuinely representative.

It is natural for everyday things to be standardized. They are intended to serve general and widespread needs. They are typical industrial products. But when we make this statement, have we not then become guilty of far too rigid a generalization? We know that everyday things are not only manufactured in factories. Home industry, handicraft, and home-crafts are also involved in supplying us with utilitarian things.[30] Enterprises of this kind operate without any real organizational costs. Certain kinds of products can under favorable conditions be produced that surpass those from factories in quality and value for money. (Basketwork, knitted woolens, certain items of cabinetry, etc.) It is not impossible that these small enterprises will experience a revival. The availability of cheap electric power in the countryside also enables their continued development. In certain areas of production, home industries provided with automatic machinery are certainly better suited to satisfy some needs than large-scale industrial production.

A change of this kind would also lead to social benefits. It could offer consumers cheaper goods and raise the earnings and the living standards of many producers. They could, in fact, with the help of their families, also find additional means of support—farming, raising cattle, and the like. At any rate, similar combinations have been sought in other countries. A development of this kind has after all begun in this country in Småland and Dalarna and, it should be possible in other parts of Sweden as well. This is a change that it would be obvious and beneficial to test on a larger scale, to make up for the decline in the opportunities offered today by farming.

Luxury goods.

The category of luxury goods consists primarily of products that serve our need for display, for the exclusive and the unique. Here we include for instance jewelry, ornamental objects, expensive fashion items, and the kind of utilitarian objects that verge on the decorative. This is where outstanding examples of applied art belong, as do superior industrial products that are manufactured using methods similar to those of handicraft. A rug from Handarbetets Vänner [The association of friends of textile art] or a Rolls Royce are different but typical examples of luxury goods.

Alongside these more unusual creations, however, the market is overflowing with inferior luxury objects with hackneyed decoration and dilettantish form, whose only tangible feature is that they are expensive. They are the present-day offspring of barbarian luxury and are therefore not restrained by any real interest in culture. They pretend to be something other than they are, something superior.

The time is past, however, when luxury objects can make false and boastful claims with impunity. Today we require honesty and high cultural standards from a luxury item. We are attracted by the luxury that finds expression in technical perfection, fine materials, and superior design. **For us luxury is the highest standard of quality and not magnificence.**

We claim that the opinion of our contemporaries on this subject expresses a higher culture than one in which luxury items are merely the result of the desire to embellish. Industrialization has quickened the pace of life for the people of A-Europe and created a calculating type of human being. It may well be that this explains why the decorative urges of these people do not have the fresh originality required if the outcome is to be beautiful. The desire to decorate has turned into a mania for ornamentation, which has given us a commonplace and sterile kind of decorative luxury.

It goes without saying that industry is not the place for the manufacture of unique objects where its processes involve reproduction. Here handicraft is preordained because of the individuality of the process, which allows the involvement of the creative imagination and spontaneous judgment at every moment of production.

The situation.

We have already shown **that development tends to limit the production possibilities of handicraft and increase those of industry. This is a change we have to accept as one of the basic foundations of our work.** We can hardly endeavor to sustain the earlier division of labor between the different forms of enterprise. Technological progress and the needs of increasing populations, which determine developments in this area, regulate the real division. We can only partially

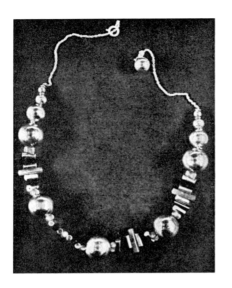

Luxury is the highest level of quality.

govern the development of production. But insofar as we can, our goal in doing so should ultimately be the satisfaction of deeper needs than the material.

At present, it may be that this goal has been undertaken somewhat too exaggeratedly and unilaterally by the applied arts. We shall return to this in another context. But in other respects as well, the applied arts do have a tendency to demand a greater share of public interest in their production than circumstances warrant. When increased industrial production is viewed from applied arts quarters with dislike and it is claimed that much of the encouragement and interest that should be devoted to the applied arts focuses on industry, no notice is taken of the fact that the production that supplies perhaps 90 percent of our necessities is of incredible importance for social and cultural development and must rightly predominate in our concerns. It is true that a great deal of this 90 percent consists of imports. But here too we should be interested. We could certainly lay down certain elementary quality standards for them.

Turning industrially produced everyday things into reasonably priced quality items without the stamp of social class, within the reach of the families of agricultural laborers, factory workers, and shop assistants, is an ambition that can well match in importance the endeavors of handicraft to preserve in its field an uninterrupted tradition or a continuous development. Indeed, these endeavors are at different levels and should not be set against each other. **This is not a question of "either-or" but of "both-and." Yet with the situation that prevails in our country it is impossible to acquire from the different commercial companies simple household furnishings of good quality at a price and to the extent required to set up a home for a family belonging to the most common income category (two thousand to five thousand kronor).**

What were called "better things for everyday life" nearly became the pet concern of the exclusive shops and their customers, and almost failed to attain the social purpose for which they were once intended.[31] Why? Well, many artists and manufacturers aimed more at an exclusive audience than the general public. Attempts have been made to set things right again. But **affordable and elegant everyday things**, those that most of our population need and can afford, **still play a very minor role in production and consumption.**

We cannot force a development that we consider correct, but we can encourage it and indicate the conditions required. In doing so, let us not forget that a large new group of customers has come into being as a result of industrialization, whose purchasing power cannot be ignored and whose consumption potential is increasing incessantly. There is an obvious need within this group—as yet perhaps not clearly recognized or understood, but no less significant—for inexpensive, high-quality consumer goods.

While we wait for these everyday things to become available we are largely using inferior products, often with banal, showy decorations intended to conceal that we have bought them cheaply.

Handicraft and the consumer.

Handicraft's demands for a more favored status are hardly based on its ability to meet our needs better than industry. We believe that these demands have arisen because, for many practitioners of handicraft, production is, to a certain extent, an end in itself. For them, the desire to satisfy existing needs is not of primary importance. Their work has multiple aims. As in Ruskin's day, therefore, this work should provide its practitioners with enjoyment and delight, foster personal development, give us happy, sound individuals, and so on. It is not certain, however, that the assertion of general human interests will contribute to the progress of handicraft.

During a discussion of business ethics we heard the following narrative. A shopkeeper in a mill town happily advertised his general human interests. Among his customers he founded a society to prevent the misuse of alcohol, another against the abuse of tobacco, a third to work for peace, and so on. The outcome was that his business collapsed.

It is probably indisputable that many of today's craftsmen see the products of their work more as examples of their skills than as things that people need. Several applied artists have intimated that they consider it a public duty to support the applied arts, for instance.

Understandably, these and similar demands arise when production loses its firm foundation in human needs, or when these needs can be supplied by other goods more effectively and cheaply. It is not only handicraft that can face a similar predicament—this can happen to far more important enterprises if they fail to adapt to needs and the circumstances of the time (agriculture and industry, for example). It must be admitted that the current situation is difficult for many applied artists, but it cannot in the long run be improved with the help of privileges or artificially fomented interest when the basic need declines.

It is better to find other approaches. And in fact these have already been initiated. In many cases the surplus of labor from handicraft has been absorbed by industry, which offers employment in the preparation of patterns. Other possibilities can be found in the fact that the markets for handicraft are not restricted by national boundaries. Surplus products that are considered particularly "Swedish" can be conveyed by willing hands to Americans. Unless after careful consideration they decide to restrict imports to protect their own national culture.

Craftsmen, both those with and without claims to artistry, are now discussing what measures could promote a resurgence of their trade. Government aid and self-help are mentioned. Self-help means, for instance, mutual loan funds, exhibitions, and cooperation with the press. All of this is excellent and should be of some use. **But even better would be a living attitude to the age, production that corresponded to the needs of a new generation. The earlier predilection for handicraft products was mainly an upper-class phenomenon. What was** sought in these items was originality and display. We no longer value items in this way. We are more interested in their utility. We take what suits us best, regardless of whether it is a result of handicraft or industry. In handicraft's struggle against changed contemporary circumstances, it will be this kind of consumer that passes judgment.

Machines.

So far our survey of circumstances has led us to the conviction that we must accept the ongoing industrialization of production, and here we anticipate the following objection:

"If we accept the state of things as they are today, will we not run the risk of becoming slaves to the machines?"

We face the same risk if we do not accept it. Specialization has already left us dependent on numerous technological processes that only a few technicians understand in detail, and nobody has complete control over their outcomes. We depend on these processes for our supplies of nourishment, water, and other necessities, our communication systems, etc. In spite of these circumstances we cannot say that human beings are governed by machines, although at times they may be allowed to operate with somewhat loose reins. Let us not close our eyes to the dangers of mechanical developments. Technology and speed must not become ends in themselves. One important task is to oppose the unreflecting worship of the attributes of modern production that is becoming more widespread among us and which leads to superficiality and folly. The aids we make use of are so complicated and powerful that we must employ them wisely. Tamed, they are—like fire—one source of progress and of happiness; untamed, they will lead to destruction. The progress of human production has something of the power and momentous tension of a natural force.

"We have to learn that machines are public servants—that they only benefit insofar as they serve," in the words of Henry Ford. And a Swedish writer, Thorsten Odhe, has developed this idea further in roughly the following words.[32] Every attempt to establish the mastery of machines without taking into account human needs, both material and spiritual, is doomed to fail. Human beings need their work to be made easier, they need flexibility, change, leisure, a thousand things around them, constantly new things: all of which machines can in time provide for everyone. But human beings also need to create, to partake of and share in spiritual values. These are needs that machines cannot fulfill. If we believe in human development, then we must also believe that a time will come when machines, inventions, disciplined cooperation, indeed all the fruits of human intelligence and capacity to organize, will be utilized to provide us with the possibility of increasing our self-worth and not to bind some of us in fetters. So said Odhe.

Indeed, the more we comprehend the deeper purpose of production, the more we also realize how necessary a different appreciation of collective labor is from what is common today. The specialization of human labor is continuing, and seems to reduce the number of those who can find satisfaction in their own work. It also reduces the number of those who are able to experience the approval or even admiration of their fellow man for their work. The pleasure taken by the craftsmen of yore in their work, which was based to a great extent on stimuli of this kind, is something that few have the benefit of feeling today. It is futile to believe that this pleasure could be extended if more of us became craftsmen.

We cannot oppose the division of labor and specialization. All we would achieve by doing so would be a chronic state of tension about our own era that would in the long run be fatal for the individual. We must accept the principle of rationalization and find in it the possibility of a higher form of enjoyment of our work through joint effort and inspired cooperation.

Mass production still has almost unexploited possibilities for contributing to the creation of a new and liberating conception of the value of work. Although perhaps slowly, and resisted by many, industrialism will alter our perception of work as mainly an individual undertaking and enable us to appreciate it as the joint employment of our powers. If we perceive work like this, then the actual mechanization of working life will offer the possibility of a higher form of pleasure in work than the handicrafts of old. But to experience this, a more advanced kind of human being, which will only evolve after some time, will be required. Experiencing work like this will not make the delight in personal creation any less valuable or desirable a reward, it merely places it in a truer context.

Quality and quantity.

Many people hope for but cannot put their faith in a change of attitude toward work. And one may perhaps perceive a risk that personality will be eliminated by the inevitable attempts to attain standardization in mass production, a belief that cannot be offset by benefits in the area of industrial psychology. Those of us who think in this way should find consolation in considering that standardization and mass production offer not only a way of making everyday goods cheaper but also of raising their quality. As has already been pointed out in the preceding chapter, industrial reproduction, if it takes place on a large scale, makes it possible to devote a high standard of preparatory work to patterns and machines without adding appreciably to the cost of the product. Handicraft production cannot on the whole permit preliminary work of such high quality without its products becoming more expensive. The greater the distribution of a product, the greater the chance of raising its quality.

Swedes are people who value quality work. We are therefore better qualified than many others to promote efforts for quality in production. It should be easy for us to understand that standardization and mass production offer great possibilities as well when it comes to nurturing and refining public taste. Acceptance of these conditions of production is in fact necessary if we are to attain a high level of material culture.

The development we have tried to elucidate may perhaps involve the gradual waning of handicraft skills in some areas of production and the complete disappearance of certain handicrafts. Not merely from the point of view of the craftsmen but also from that of the general public, the current situation therefore prompts a few questions.

The question of the future of handicraft must therefore, as has already been shown, be answered by another question: In what way can we best meet, culturally and economically, our increased material needs? We have found that strictly speaking there is only one answer to this question: through superior production at the lowest possible cost. If this definitely consigns handicraft to the production of home-crafts and luxury goods, it would seem to be a matter of public interest to encourage as far as possible a renewal of its quality, but a renewal of this kind must be well grounded given the resources and needs of today.

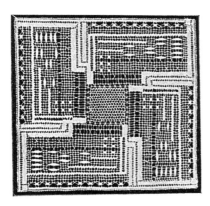

Home-crafts.

The kind of home-crafts that city dwellers usually come into contact with are not those that one makes for personal domestic use, though these are still being made in the suburbs of the cities, albeit in a more dilettantish manner. Our conceptions of

Handwoven cloth.

home-crafts are mainly linked to the type of handicraft objects specifically produced for sale, or in other words with the products of our home-crafts associations.

The housing conditions offered by apartment blocks do not, as we know, encourage families to pursue handicrafts. It is only when people have a home of their own and their own plot of land that the human impulse to work with one's own hands develops to any appreciable extent. The endeavor to acquire a home of one's own is the mainstay of home-crafts: it may well be worth remembering this fact. It is therefore natural that home-crafts should be based in the countryside.

Home-crafts as they operate today, with the support of agricultural societies, county councils, and private organizations, can hardly be described as sole sources of income. Their function in offering secondary incomes has been firmly established by developments during the last sixty years. At the moment they are mainly practiced by women, who are usually engaged in spinning, weaving, sewing, lace-making, braiding, and knitting, while men mainly work as smiths, basket makers, metalworkers, potters, and woodworkers.

Cultural holiday.

Oh, that nice old culture!

When the production in these different branches of home-crafts is undertaken for sale, it can easily shift from secondary occupation to handicraft production and acquire a more general significance. Thus home-crafts have a certain role to play in the production of our household goods. As the practitioners have no artistic training, they quite rightly stick to their traditions. **In this way much that has been handed down to us today is universally meaningful and ageless in design.** This is particularly obvious in textiles craft (for instance fabrics sold by the meter). We admire the creations that still survive, often the result of many centuries of tradition. Tranquil and undemanding, they transcend the vicissitudes of time. The confusing, "functionalistic" zigzag patterns we are now blessed with are put to shame by comparison with their timeless predecessors and vanish from the market.

If we therefore want to retain most of our home-crafts, this does not have to mean that they should petrify. Except for the restricted number of home-crafts products with perpetual life, some degree of development would probably be justified. We have previously mentioned the technological and organizational resources that could be used for this purpose.

It is probable that one or more branches of crafts will likely die out because they lack any basis in the needs of today. This will not be a moral or cultural catastrophe. Meanwhile we can look for new viable forms of work in the home based on today's prevailing conditions. Electric power makes it possible and natural that home-crafts to a certain extent will become home industry. Compared to home-crafts, a well-organized home industry might well find it easier to appeal to consumers. Only time can bring about a change of this kind, however.

We want to hold onto all the old traditions that can enrich our existence. But we also want to work for new benefits and look ahead. This approach is the only fruitful one in any form of production. Handicraft and home-crafts can survive on their traditional foundation insofar as they can adapt to our own age. That which is valuable but no longer viable belongs under the preservation of cultural relics.

The situation is now in no way the same as when the guild ordinance was promulgated in Thorn in 1523.[33] It stipulated:

Nobody is to devise or invent anything new
nor use nor exploit anything of this kind,
but each and everyone is in civic and brotherly
affection to act in concert with his neighbor.

Form.

Practical and/or beautiful.

In discussions on building-art and the industrial arts, a distinction is made time and again: the practical is differentiated from the beautiful. This means that something might be a product of technology **or** art, or else of technology **and** art.

We have become so used to seeing things in this way that we do so without reflection. After all one can maintain with some justification that this is a practical distinction in everyday use, but there is something more behind it that we should make clear to ourselves. It is by no means unknown for our words and ingrained definitions to become obsolescent so that they no longer address what they originally did or they confine our thinking to positions that in reality we have already abandoned. There is therefore no harm in occasionally putting our most common words and ways of thinking to the test.

This being so, we must observe here that it is not merely difficult, but impossible to distinguish what is art from what is technology. In our use of language we employ the word "art" as if it still referred exclusively to the "recognized" arts: architecture, painting, sculpture, and the like. Meanwhile, however, we have more or less consciously adopted an approach to many modern phenomena—trains, automobiles, airplanes, various forms of "technical" apparatus—in a way that leaves no doubt that we appreciate their forms as artistic.

Technology or art?

We unresistingly accept a whole world of form, and as a matter of course we experience it as beautiful.

At the same time we discuss these things in speech and writing using the concepts of technology and art, and merely succeed in confusing the concepts and inhibiting appreciation of these new forms.

As we have already pointed out, it is not difficult to see that the essentially moral opposition that exists between the concepts of technology and art must be based on the cultural situation during the first, brutal phase of industrialization. It is fairly natural that the "technological" was seen as inferior, simple, prosaic. People still say that this or that is merely technical, no more than technology. On the other hand it is natural for art (that is the fine arts such as painting, sculpture, etc.) to

Aqueduct.

be regarded as the flower of the culture that at that time took up the cudgels (and still does in some places) against industrialization. Art was something that came like manna from heaven.

Today the cultural position is different. Industrialism is the major fact of our new culture, if we want one. We must accept it to be able to use it for our own good. To see our situation clearly and arrive at a new and fruitful conception we must cleanse ourselves of all the old, purely aesthetic perspectives that in reality we have outgrown.

Fine art—utilitarian art.

We must then begin with a very elementary study of concepts. As we have already observed, painting and sculpture remain the prototypes for what is meant by art. It is therefore extremely common, even among those who claim to understand art, to contemplate the beauty of buildings and other amenities in the same way as painting and sculpture. But if we think more deeply it will soon become clear that here we are dealing with things that differ in essence and can hardly be compared directly.

To begin with, even though it may seem redundant, we will not hesitate to point out the simple fact that one has a practical purpose, the other not—most of the uncertainty depends on a lack of distinction in this respect.

The artistic quality of a painting is determined primarily, regardless of any of its other attributes, by its degree of harmony or perhaps more accurately the organization of its various formal elements, such as color, line, and surface. Each element is placed in direct or indirect relationship to the others and together they form a whole. Stated in these general terms, this is an elementary, universal truth.

If we then look at what we call the utilitarian arts, this cannot merely involve the organization of volumes, lines, surfaces, or colors. Here the object also has to be used for some purpose, not merely contemplated. Thus the user of the object in question becomes part, a very important part, of the whole. From this one could conclude that there is something wrong with a utility object that seems to be complete even when it is not being used. When we see an object of this kind we must feel the desire to make use of it—"at your service" in a pleasant way.

Composition.

In the utilitarian arts, therefore, beauty cannot be of the same type as in the fine arts. Its form must express its purpose and provide a clear visual embodiment of its functions. This is exactly the kind of beauty that we acknowledge without reflection or resistance in an airplane or an automobile. The ease with which we accept this while finding it so difficult to approve of new, purposeful forms in buildings, for instance, must be due to the fact that automobiles, and airplanes in particular, are new phenomena whose forms are subject to no traditions, or only to very vague and untenable ones.

In this connection it should also be pointed out how mistaken it can be to judge utilitarian art on the basis of first impressions. One cannot really grasp the beauty it may possess as an expression of its function before one senses its intended purpose and how it works. For example, it was not that long ago that fierce resistance was encountered even in Stockholm's building permit committee to a proposal for a commercial building in which the supporting columns had been set back from the facade at street level to allow more space for display windows, so that on first impression the building seemed to be supported by panes of glass. Once one understands how the structure of a building like this functions, the sense of shock will disappear and the form will be seen as beautiful and expressive. It is much more beautiful in its explicit purposefulness than the department store, which for "architectural" reasons is constructed with wide columns of granite facing the street—columns that are soon for compelling commercial reasons bedecked with display cases anyway.

Department store, Rotterdam.

**Röjeråsen lookout
tower near Rättvik.**

Self-evident form.

The demands that we are making—that what we call utilitarian art should possess a beauty of its own that springs from the desire to give logical clarity to the workings of its form—constitute in reality a rejection of the dualism between technology and art. In recognizing the functionally beautiful, we repudiate the opinion that art is something that is added to the technological in order to produce a result that is "utilitarian art."

The cultural movement that has aimed at "refining" the products of technology all over the world has more or less committed this mistake. In the civilized world people are working eagerly to endow our existence with beauty, although they do not know what it consists of and they do not know where it can be found, now that the historical styles have been exhausted. Major industries live by supplying all the beauty with which we feel obliged to endow our buildings, our furniture, and our household goods. At the same time, amid this confusion into which we have been

As the robust frame is completed, "architecture" creeps up like moss to conceal it. This is admittedly a particularly grotesque example . . .

thrown by a handful of aesthetes who possess cultural consciences but lack awareness of the realities of life today, we can spontaneously appreciate bridges, automobiles, and airplanes as beautiful things, with their own self-evident, liberating beauty. A sense of clear functional form is beginning to take root, but we dare not acknowledge it, assuming instead that it is something separate, namely "technical form" (we have also heard someone warn against "machine romanticism").

On the other hand one often hears the opinion that "if something is really practical then it is also beautiful." This is a ridiculous slogan. It is just as wrong to believe that technology will be able to cope with every aspect of utilitarian art as to believe the opposite statement: that utilitarian art is the same kind of art as sculpture and painting. It is very easy to establish that the work of an engineer in planning a bridge also involves the creation of form. Calculations do not provide all the answers. There are many possible alternatives and combinations, and the constructor has to choose. If he has the talent to display how it works with logical clarity, he can therefore also turn his bridge into a work of art, in which the technologically appropriate form is at the same time a worthy expression of its function.

All this talk of the practical on the one hand and the aesthetic on the other has totally confused our ability to see simple, clear reality. It is therefore tempting to do as some do, in particular German architects, and simply eliminate the words "art" and "beauty" from our vocabularies and instead use the concept of "organization," or "Gestaltung von Lebensvorgängen [giving shape to the processes of life]."[34] It would be nice to simply withdraw from aesthetic discussions, with their never-ending drivel. But we should not forget that there is also no shortage of drivel about "the practical." Nor should we overlook the fact that it is the aesthetic conventions that obstruct to such a great extent the development of a new understanding. The correct method, albeit not the least troublesome, is probably to expose, as we have done, the real grounds for the misconception.

We mentioned in passing that we find the form of certain modern objects self-evident. Here we have something to build on. Should not everything, art or non-art, appear self-evident, otherwise it is simply not yet finished? Thorough working out, complete ordering, yields finished, self-evident form.

Art is order. This is a proposition that we need to establish to resolve the conceptual confusion. This proposition provides the key to revealing how much real art actually exists, without official recognition, in many "purely technological" objects. And all too frequently, how little art can be found, on the other hand, despite the artists' signatures, salesmen's publicity, or journalists' reviews, in the products of "industrial art" or "applied art." In other words, how often in the first instance we face objects with perfect order and serene harmony between form and function, and in the latter merely clumsy attempts to add to the price by using "artistic" accretions, ornamentation, or contrived forms.

Art is order.

Beauty above all

has been the motto for the last half century. Today it has an obsolescent sound. The time has come to change the subject. It was believed that the rapid and brutal breakthrough of industrialism, the harsh expansion of what was viewed as a low form of culture, if not actually hostility to culture, had to be counteracted by championing "refined" culture: philosophy, religion, art. While practical life is today characterized by its optimism and desire to push ahead, the aestheticism of "cultural preservation" is increasingly turning into a downright defensive movement. In this way we may even end up distinguishing between two different types of people—those who can be described as living practically, and those viewed as cultural.

Down with beauty.

But the culture of the machine is incontestably conquering the world, while the struggle for beauty has lost its way in impracticable aestheticism. The concept of beauty adopted by advocates of culture during the transitional period is now hindering us in our efforts to find appropriate forms for our age and our circumstances; it prevents our spontaneous sense of reality. That is why we are now tempted to declare "Down with beauty, let us speak less of beauty for a while."

"Too much beauty" could be adopted as the motto for the cultural life of the last decades. Beauty as the hallmark of culture, the cult of beauty as a characteristic of personality, and—perhaps above all—beauty as the stamp of quality for a social upper class.

Order above all,

the motto for this new era, applies no less to building-art and the industrial arts as to politics, economics, and industry.

Building-art is behind the times. No industry is on the whole as badly organized as the building industry. No production is on the whole as poorly rationalized as building production. Yet if we include the industries that produce building materials, next to food this is our largest area of production.

Where form is concerned too, order is the highest expression demanded by modern building-art. Order made visible, one might add. We are no longer so pretentious as our forebears that we require every building to have eternal artistic values ("even as a ruin a building should still evince imperishable beauty," as someone once said). Our requirements are more modest but at the same time more responsible: buildings, furniture, drinking glasses may well be consumer items that we can destroy without regret after they have served for some short or long period, but while we use them we expect them to fulfill their role and serve us perfectly, so perfectly that we can also derive aesthetic enjoyment from observing them in use.

Style.

One might say that we are in the process of acquiring a new style, the style of our age. Some claim firmly that this is already with us, fully developed, in certain of the products of engineering. It is also possible to claim that our age not only lacks style, but that its only possibility for development lies in a lack of style.

Of course this all depends on what is meant by style. This is a dangerous word that has led to a great deal of discussion without result. It is therefore wise to first clarify the different meanings usually attached to it.

The most frequent is to use style to refer to a certain stock of ready-made forms. This is the more superficial, historically colored concept of style. In everyday language Rococo means curlicues, Empire a lot of stiff ornamentation, and Baroque a collection of bombastic forms.

In this superficial sense we can well say that our age lacks a style or, more correctly, that its "style" consists of its lack of style. Artistic eclecticism finally seems to have bankrupted itself after unsuccessful attempts to realize clearly pasted together or more or less "modernized" versions of all the forms of preceding cultures, or to invent new styles analogous to these, i.e., styles consisting of a series of approved forms. We must therefore face the fact that it is impossible for our culture to bring forth a style in this sense. We cannot embrace a certain form for any length of time and for its own sake. Our general approach is relativistic; no style can any longer be anything absolute for us.

On the other hand there can be no doubt that our age, in its desire for objectivity, to allow things to be what they are, to shape everything logically according to its function, has its specific characteristics. It is also fairly obvious that from an aesthetic point of view this perception of form as expressing function is itself one of the preconditions for a style of the times. But then style must be conceived in a way that differs from that described above.

By style we must then mean the ways and forms in which the needs of the age and the way in which people live find adequate expression. It can well be asked whether this definition of style is not more correct than the one recently cited. And here one must recognize that what has been said not only offers a possibility of developing our own style, because we live and think in ways that characterize us, but also that many excellent examples of this style already exist. Hitherto they have mainly been created by engineers. But now architects can also take their turn. Why are the works of engineers so often self-evidently beautiful? Because they have not been created with any specific aesthetic pretensions but with undivided attention to logical form.

The press box at the Stockholm Exhibition.

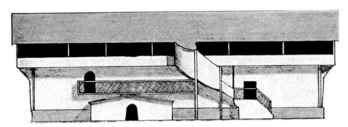

**A new "funkis building"? No, Ornässtugan.
There is not a big difference!**

It is the arrogant pretensions of architecture that have to be excised. That is what holds us back. To "organize" means to organize practically and aesthetically in the same breath.

When we have come so far that we no longer conceive of the aesthetic as something that comes from above to merge with the technical, which is of lower origin, but regard every form that does not offer a satisfactory expression of its function as quite simply deficient—then we will have provided the conditions for a general style for our times.

Construction, materials, and style.

Appropriate form-giving is the goal; materials, structure, and the like are merely means to attain it.

The style of our times is the product of our will, of our power to shape form. We use the means that have existed in the past and also create new ones.

It is a common misconception that the building style of our age should evolve "organically" from the mere existence of certain materials and methods, such as reinforced concrete. Naturally, no development can be as automatic as that. Concrete has been pressed into the service of "motif architecture" in providing all sorts of irrational forms. It is not until there is a purposeful will to find the logically appropriate form that we can achieve a style. Only then will the specific possibilities of different materials contribute in a natural way to giving form an assured character. And then the specific possibilities offered by various materials will play a natural role in giving the form a stamp of its own.

**Some blooms from the
garden of "motif architecture."**

**Top and above:
Goetheanum in
Dornach, the spiritual
school and heating
plant attached to it—
literary-symbolic
architecture.**

**Left: Cubistic interior
decoration—mundane-
picturesque quasi-
modernism.**

Fashions come and fashions go . . .

To counter the pessimistic approach that finds expression in this phrase and uses it to dismiss the entire modern movement we are discussing here, one can propose another approach, which uses exactly the same words to express an optimistic view of culture.

One must not underestimate the value of fashion as an expression of the age in the areas in which it rules.

And where would one draw the distinction between fashion and style, between transient fashion and enduring style?[35] Fashion need not, in principle, be worth less because it involves shorter periods of time. We cannot explain why a new fashion in shoes or hats can have such a liberating effect on us, like a word said at the right psychological moment. Of course, it is of little importance that the fashion in hats changes somewhat illogically and certainly does not always suit us, but feels more like an unpleasant decree we must obey merely because of some inscrutable mass psychosis. The main thing is that fashion can be valuable for the attitude that sees life and move-ment as pleasurable, that has abandoned faith in the absolute, a relic of religions and philosophies, to think and feel in less pretentious and more human terms.

There is nothing wrong therefore in preferring to call the new architecture a fash-ion instead of a style. One must merely express the reservation that the more stable areas of production, like building, are certainly less susceptible to small variations in decisive respects, if not perhaps the odd insignificant detail, and that it is unlikely that we can expect any new fashion for the next few years at least . . .

If we consider this more closely we will become even more certain that we should not view modern building-art as a passing fancy. As we pointed out earlier, its prime characteristic lies in its will to form its materials into an appropriate tool for our lives. If it is to be able to adhere to this principle, its manifestations should not therefore change more frequently or more rapidly than the way in which we live. And, after all, this changes slowly in the more important elements. In addition, modern building-art intends to visibly express the function of things. This too gives us no reason to conclude that the process will be rapid. It is unlikely that our way of seeing and experiencing the expression of function will change significantly in a short period of time.

Finally, we must not overlook the fact that a change in attitude and ways of think-ing has taken place in principle, not merely in our taste for forms. Without forcing the comparison, we could say that in aesthetic terms we are now undergoing the same revolution in our very ways of thinking as science did when it liberated itself from its dependence on religion.

It must be acknowledged that the "fashion" that can be characterized by its ability to adapt effortlessly to our needs, and therefore also involves continual adaptation to changes in these needs—this fashion contains little of what normally corresponds to the concept of fashion.

**A home: simple, cheap standardized furniture—
good art on the walls.**

Nonetheless, it cannot be denied that in today's architectural production we can observe a predilection for certain specific forms that are treated as more or less fixed stylistic elements. It is evident that the enthusiasm that seized architects all over the world upon discovering that our age can create its own form will find expression among many less independent practitioners acting in uncritical admiration of, for instance, Le Corbusier and his work. Architects take up half the program and all the seductive formal language, or perhaps only the language, and sit designing "modern" buildings for all they are worth . . .

But just as certainly as there will always be pale imitations, it is equally certain that forms with no rational grounds will vanish. The new spirit in building-art has a firm moral backbone.

New and old.

During the last century new and old have been mixed together to form a kind of hodgepodge, with the result that we cannot easily discriminate the one from the other. Our fine old buildings are not alone in seeming old, but have to put up with many recent imitations. Modern building-art is not allowed to look new and contemporary, but has to be based on something old. The old buildings we have restored and the new ones that are covered in patina therefore appear to be of a similar old age. Culture suffers greatly if the progression of time does not appear naturally and clearly. The invigorating charm of cultural change is lost. The multiplicity of ages in our environment, with the genuinely old and the genuinely new, is valuable, adding richness to our lives in the same way as the differences between the ages of people themselves.

It would be a great advantage if between new and old there were nothing that acted older than its years.

Building-art as an element of general culture.

Old buildings also offer a great deal of pleasure and stimulation today. Not just because of the atmosphere they can provide as entire buildings or fragments of formal beauty. They are stimulating and instructive above all in affirming the close and natural ties between the architecture of earlier periods and other aspects of their cultures. The splendid palace architecture of the Renaissance was matched by the same magnificence and luster of the life inside them, in the garments and the furniture; the Rococo imparted the same graceful character to a facade, a chair, and a shoe as to the individuals themselves; in Sweden old rural building-art was as natural, down-to-earth, and primitive as the rural population itself.

In the past culture was unified in character.

Building-art today has, on the other hand, not acquired its character from our age and its people. Our century, which is also the age of major technological progress,

Walking, then and now.

sport, and widespread popular movements, our open-minded, unsentimental age, is matched by buildings composed of a variety of old architectural fragments which, in a few decades, have ranged across the entire gamut of styles from the medieval to the neoclassical.

But inside these new imitations of the Renaissance, the Baroque, or the neoclassical, we encounter none other than our unsentimental and unceremonious contemporaries in jackets or sweaters. We do not tramp into our imitation farmers' cottages in farmer's boots, nor do we pirouette decoratively around each other amid our imitation Rococo and Gustavian furniture.

We move with a "straightforward" and natural, totally modern gait. The historicized environments we often create are out of step with the lives we live.

Culture is no longer unified.

As has already been said, it is popularly believed that style consists merely of the forms themselves. But if one can imagine a Gothic or Renaissance building stripped of its formal details, we will find that the skeleton of the building that remains still clearly represents the Gothic or the Renaissance. This means that style does not merely reside in a building's formal idiom but in its very plan and construction. If this interpretation of the concept of style is correct, it then follows that the formal details cannot create style on their own.

Diagrams of Renaissance and Gothic structures.

But let us continue. The Gothic is not merely an architectural style, it is the name we give to the culture of an entire epoch, in the same way Renaissance refers both to an enduring humanistic cultural movement and the expression it took in building-art and applied art. One cannot therefore consider architectural style as an isolated cultural phenomenon. We have previously stressed the intimate correspondence between style and the other aspects of human culture during past epochs. It is not possible to separate them.

Let us try to imagine a jumbled combination of the people of one period and the settings of another. If we conjure up the impossible vision of toga-clad Romans in a Rococo environment, we are approaching the lighthearted world of farce. If we reverse the experiment and place Rococo individuals in a Roman palace, the image will be just as confusing and out of character.

And if we invoke the image of a sympathetic and rather plump democrat in an overcoat against the background of the magnificent luster of the gold mosaic in the Golden Hall of Stockholms stadshus [Stockholm town hall] we will find that—either because of the lack of mystery about the former or the lack of contemporary relevance in the latter—they belong to two widely differing cultures.[36]

The culture of an era only comes into being when the environment is shaped by a natural congruence of building-art, applied art, and general culture.

As it is inconceivable that the contemporary general culture in which we live, shaped by industrialism and democracy, can deliberately change in order to correspond to our external environment, then it ought to be the environment or "style" that gradually adapts to the general culture.

Carl Malmsten was correct when he said: "The work of developing human society, the emergence of new forms for the now neglected spiritual education, the adaptation of society to the situation to which it has been reduced by industrialization and its ensuing revolutionary changes, and the search for a new balance must all take place at the same time as a new external unitary culture arises."[37]

The adaptation of this society, this new balance, means a new culture to some extent. It will not agree in everything with the old ideals, but this does not mean that it can be called decadent.

We recently talked to an English professor of archaeology who had built a very advanced modern concrete house.[38]

We therefore asked him if he liked modern building-art and received this answer:

"Yes, of course, indeed as a professor of archaeology I have to approve of the contemporary, of the agreement between an age and its external setting."

True or false building-art.

The self-evident form we mentioned earlier, the natural relationship between form and content, is characteristic of all the good architecture of the past—it is not something we have discovered only recently.

But the great upheavals of the nineteenth century brought with them—as we all know and have previously suggested—a segregation of building-art into the architectural and the practical. The architects mainly devoted their interest to exteriors and were commissioned only to devise facades; the practical work, floor plans, and interior proportions became a separate task. Form was imposed regardless of the building's purpose, the exterior without reference to what went on inside. The architecture was not the building itself but its exterior. In Stockholm our older apartment blocks of the kind found in Östermalm, Danviks hospital, and the 1909 industrial art exhibition were typical examples of this concept of architecture.[39]

In the decades that have followed there has been continuous development toward greater authenticity.

The architects working during this period performed a great feat in eradicating the earlier, somewhat superficial approach to architecture. No longer was the architect a decorator, but a thoroughly trained and active building professional. And as greater truth to

Gas station, not "gas empire."

Sport cabin, not "Swiss chalet style."

materials was demanded, there arose the requirement that buildings should evolve organically. There was more and more concern about the practical and the technological.

Building-art during this period, which was characterized by major artistic talents, was therefore in some respects the forerunner of modern architecture, to which it bequeathed a great deal of knowledge, sound professional training, and great professional ambitions.

But during this period (in which the authors of this publication were also involved) architecture also suffered a deficiency—the lack of natural agreement between form and content.

Indeed, let us acknowledge this: there have been two factors at work in the creation of our buildings, not merely the objective and structural conditions but also our aesthetic reminiscences. But these two aspects draw us in different directions; they do not sit easily with each other, and after a violent conflict between form and content the outcome is often neither adequate expression of the building's function nor something that in any way can measure up to the aesthetic charm of its predecessors.

A fairly good architect once built a school. He was enamored of the beautiful, rural eighteenth-century Baroque and wanted his building to incorporate this style. The school required large windows in its facade and enormous dormer windows in its tiled roof. The style required small windows and an unbroken stretch of roof. The result was a compromise that was neither a really good school nor really good eighteenth-century Baroque.

From the outset, this kind of twofold approach results in a poor compromise. We must admit that we have often decided on the architectural character of a new commission on the basis of earlier works that we love instead of using contemporary solutions to fit the purpose and characteristics of the new building.

Therefore Göteborgs konstmuseum [The Göteborg museum of art] does not have the natural clarity of Liljevalchs konsthall [Liljevalch art gallery] in Stockholm, but conceals its purpose behind the lineaments of a heavy, bricked-up Roman aqueduct.[40]

The public library in Stockholm, a very democratic institution, takes the external form of a classical fortress.[41]

In its main architectural feature, the central courtyard, Tändsticksbolaget [The Swedish match building] in Stockholm, the head office of an international trust, reflects the character of a Renaissance palace.[42]

The residential area erected for the Lidingö exhibition in 1925 bears the inappropriate guise for private homes of a row of mill worker's cottages.[43]

A lavatory chimney in the shape of a stone column with a stone capital, transformer stations that look like steeples. A crematorium designed to look like a lime kiln, another in the shape of a pyramid.

Stockholm's town hall has been described by a Swiss visitor as a "geniale Lösung einer unmöglichen Aufgabe" ["gifted solution to an impossible task"]. The impossible lies in the original pretense that the building has a past, has been made to look as if it is one of Stockholm's most time-honored buildings. The many facades and interiors in different styles, the

Department store.

bricked-up window openings, give the impression of a building history that spans centuries. There is something irritating about this affected historical romanticism that cannot be disguised by its brilliant positioning in the townscape, by its rhythmic felicity, the wonderfully beautiful garden. The Town Hall is the work of a contemporary architect who is among the most gifted in the use of form, and in an unusually munificent city, it is the climax of lengthy development and can leave nobody unmoved. But the new generation of architects can be forgiven for not seeing it as a natural expression of the twentieth century and its culture, and that as such they cannot continue in the same spirit.

We have been burdened by too many reminiscences of the architecture of earlier eras, we have leafed through too many volumes of fine copperplates, *Suecia antiqva* [Ancient Sweden], *Rome moderne*, *Gamla svenska städer* [Old Swedish towns].[44] We have allowed ourselves to be led astray and believe that by starting from beautiful and atmospheric old architecture we will attain the same aesthetic values in a new building.

Reality has given the lie to our beliefs.

All these excursions into different elements of style seem to be temporary whims of fashion. But that is not all they are. It is no coincidence that interest in the architecture of the Vasa period was followed by interest in seventeenth- and eighteenth-century architecture, in neoclassicism and the nineteenth century, and that these stylistic forms were replaced by modern architecture.[45] This is a consistent development, based on the ability of each newly adopted stylistic form to offer greater possibilities than its predecessor to meet the increasing demands for clarity and natural contemporaneity in planning and construction, to provide good form for the new needs and new construction methods of a new age. Form has undoubtedly slowly but surely approached the natural expression of content. Interest in "styles" has to the same extent increasingly declined among architects of all ages, not least in Sweden. And the transition to modern architecture is natural and logical.

We are not claiming that modern architecture always displays adequate agreement between content or purpose and form; at times it undoubtedly fails in this respect. But the endeavors of modern architecture to allow purpose itself to direct architectural form are correct and cannot be questioned. **A building should give expression to its content rather than to its architect**.

In his bill proposing the demolition of Stockholm's beautiful courthouse, Carl Lindhagen added the consoling words: "In any case it will still be possible in the future to build a copy in some other place in the capital for some other public need."[46]

This belief that architecture is some form of ancient receptacle into which anything can be poured is probably no longer shared by the general public. The attitude to architecture indicated in the words of Gottfried Semper is more correct and healthy: "Nur einen Herrn kennt die Kunst, das Bedürfnis. Sie artet aus, wo sie der Laune des Künstlers, mehr doch, wo sie mächtigen Kunstbeschützern gehorcht" ["Art serves only one master, necessity. When it obeys the mood of the artist, or mighty patrons, art becomes excessive"].[47]

A sideways glance at the concept of culture.

Someone once said that culture aims to transform the struggle for existence into a collaboration for existence. And this is a good way of putting it.

But images reveal something else, a popular view of the concept of culture:

"Culture"
is what is old.

"Un-culture" is what is new.

Many of the special guardians of culture consider

that this is good culture: "architecture," "art"	and this is un-culture: "machine culture," "soulless technology"
old wrought-iron Swedish chair	modern German tubular steel chair
Cloaca Maxima in Rome	modern sewage systems
Roman concrete (opus incertum, opus reticulatum)	modern concrete
sawn timber	rolled-iron girders
painted commercial signs, shopping streets, Pompeii	modern advertising
old-fashioned waltzes, the Boston	jazz
scent of manure from a meadow	smell of petrol
old flat roofs	new flat roofs
old tools	new tools, etc.

Why?

Our sense of history and our experience tell us, however, that all these new objects will, in fifty or one hundred years, be included in "good old-fashioned culture."

Justifiable and unjustifiable tradition.

Traditions, our inherited customs about how to lead our lives and do things in a certain manner, are the elements that link the old with the new.

Tradition has extraordinary power over the customs and habits of people. The changing conditions of the time lead to many changes in the way we live, but at the same time we want to cling to much of what we have learned and experienced in our childhood years. As not only the present and the future are of value to us but also our memories of the past, we want again and again to experience old events anew, to celebrate old festivals, meet old friends. Because deep within our humanity, hardly changed by time, tradition has its justification, and is highly valued by us all.

Traditionalism in building-art allows some degree of development—actually, throughout the ages development has been an established tradition. The variation in styles over time offers proof of how development overrides tradition.

Every style has emerged, almost with the power of an elemental force, as the ripe fruit of some general cultural movement, and tradition has had to give way or leap forward.

The Gothic, with its demands for light, airiness, and expressive structures, coincided to some extent with modern aspirations and shattered the Romanesque tradition of massive, fortresslike construction. The ostentatious architecture of the Renaissance suddenly emerged as the result of humanist study of antiquity and crushed medieval traditions.

In Sweden development has made similar leaps forward as the result of constant impulses from abroad. The introduction of the Renaissance style by the two Tessins marked a deliberate breach with the Vasa tradition;[48] neoclassicism after Gustav III's travels in Italy also broke suddenly and firmly with the traditions of the eighteenth century.[49] Our plain, unadorned early nineteenth-century facades were eclipsed by the plaster and stucco extravagance of late nineteenth-century international Baroque. This style was again abandoned at the beginning of our century for forms and stylistic features from the Middle Ages, the Vasa period, and the Renaissance, which had been ignored by tradition for a couple of centuries.

For us these interruptions in development may not seem so great, partly because we view them from a great distance and also because the patina of age links everything together, but there is no doubt that they were as apparent to their contemporaries as the explicit new architectural directions being adopted today.

Formal traditions in building-art and applied art can only be justified within a specific period of time, long or short, that is characterized by the same given culture.

Carl G. Laurin has given us the following felicitous characterization of the Empire style: "The strict, rectangular forms of the Empire style offer an admirable background for top-booted generals, who could recognize in the eagles clutching thunderbolts and bombs that supported the tables, in the classical fasces and axes that decorated the furniture, some element of their own gruff spirit."

The Empire period survived for several decades with these stylistic features and motifs, which developed slowly. During these decades, this formal tradition was natural and justified, because there was no significant shift of direction within general human and social culture.

But then? Was it natural for Empire traits to survive as a tradition when the period was no longer characterized by these top-booted generals, but by democratic and industrial populations with simpler footwear?

In every area of human life, nonetheless, traditional forms endure for a time during revolutionary cultural development.

**The first automobile and
the last Landau.**

**Factory in Rotterdam and employment office in Altona,
where form follows modern construction.**

When hansom cabs or carriages were replaced by automobiles, automobiles were initially given the same traditional form and fittings, a form that did not suit their purpose and a structure that we now view with a smile. It took several years before the unjustifiable traditional carriage form could be dispensed with and the automobile given a fairly natural form adapted to its own requirements. And not until today, when this form has been established for automobiles, can we see that the development of this type is one example of a justifiable tradition.

Undoubtedly, building-art has undergone enormous technical and material developments during the last fifty years. Building-art today differs in these respects from previous eras as motors do from horses. But if we also consider the treatment of form, up until recently building-art has made no more progress than automobiles did in the early years of their development.

It is true that development is not always the same as improvement, and we do not know whether horsepower is better or worse for human life and happiness than the horse. But building-art, like applied art, cannot decide such questions; it is a servant that has to accept the prevailing culture and base what it does on it.

We can see therefore that the technical and material aspects of building-art have kept up with the rapid development of the age, that planning endeavors to adapt to modern needs and construction to modern technology while its formal language belongs to the past, that is, tries to dress itself up with a little of the tradition and features of the current "style." This kind of form tradition is unjustified.

When we construct a building with a structural frame of iron and paste onto it a classicized facade of pilasters resting on heavy Palladian plinths (Skand[inaviska] Kreditbolgets hus [Scandinavian credit company building], Gustav Adolfs torg, Stockholm), when in other words the structure and the articulation of the facade are based on totally different static and architectural principles—then our architecture is not true but false.[50]

And just as certainly as in earlier cultural eras **the contemporary development of all aspects of building-art** was a tradition—and a tradition worth retaining—it is equally certain that yesterday's building-art was anything but emphatic about tradition.

It is only those who seek through their design work to give expression to contemporary existence and to the same prevailing culture that gives us our technology who maintain a genuine and justifiable tradition.

Form traditionalist (anxiously): Your opinions are merely cold, intractable logic. Why can't we keep the pleasure, the comfort and well-being that traditional trappings offer after all?

A gentleman: "You seem to place no value in the artistic way of life."[51]

A gentleman: "The powerful divinity of comfort is expelled with an ingenious electrical vacuum cleaner."[52]

A gentleman: "Are human beings utilitarian-mechanical (chemical-technical?), practical beings or the bearers of spiritual values? Is utility our servant or our aim?"[53]

We: Servant!

A gentleman: "We ask for values and you answer in kilowatts."

We: We also ask for values and are answered with ornaments, decorations, side issues.

Mr. Traditionalist: Decorations are not a side issue. Art is the bloom of life. We need to dispel the gloom with a little decoration, a little culture.

We: Decoration and culture, be careful not to equate them. But listen:

Stylistic trappings no longer suit us.

Gentlemen, you wear modern suits, as we can see. Fine, attractive fabrics, natural, fairly practical in cut. Are you ready to put on some traditional garb, a seventeenth-century business suit for instance? Or lace cuffs with your overalls?

Mr. T.: That would turn into a masquerade.

We: Precisely. But isn't it just as much a masquerade if we fix a few bits and pieces from the dress-up box, pilasters, surrounds, festoons, rosettes, friezes, and the like on our contemporary buildings, planned and constructed for today with normal, natural contemporary people living in them?

Mr. T.: Yes, but these elements of architecture also develop, after all, and they become modern.

We: Yes, they do develop, attempts are made to make them a little more personal and modern. Ornamentation is simplified for economic reasons, it is placed more sparsely, as "restrained decor," which adds to pretentiousness in a risky kind of way. Columns of even thickness are produced, surfaces smoothed, classical profiles flattened out, the legs of Rococo chairs curved in only one direction to make them easier to machine. Money now has greater sway over ornamentation than imagination or feeling for form.

But this development, which only means dilution, flattening, general vulgarization—

Mr. T.: —fits in well with our "marvelous" era!

We: Oh no, Mr. Irony, let us not advocate the bad for that reason. The difference between us is that you judge the age on its bad points, we on its good ones. You have to understand us: we see its vigor, clear-sightedness, and enterprising dynamism and do not feel it suitable to dress it up in something half-dead.

And moreover—the progressive weakening of stylistic ornamentation will lead, by circuitous routes, to the same goal as ours: its elimination.

We cannot go on using stylistic trappings,

nine times out of ten the results are very bad. We have tried—and failed.

Ornamentation is an art that has declined century by century in Europe. We cannot avoid the fact that classical, medieval, Renaissance, Baroque, and Rococo describe a process of continual decline. The nineteenth century, which was outstanding for its literature, painting, and music, has left us little of value in ornamentation and decoration. The Empire style, which was in itself a secondhand style, used extremely formulaic ornamentation.

Today we are working with **thirdhand styles** and the result is accordingly diluted. It is a gloomy but inescapable fact that 90 percent of the style-architecture of the last fifty to sixty years is rubbish. It does not matter how diligently our best architects consult their books, make sketches, erase charcoal drawings, and make fine models of their frills and flourishes, their stylistic trappings cannot measure up to those of their predecessors. What is the reason for this?

The architectural idioms of the past were cultivated in totally different, calmer, more autocratic working conditions than those of today. Today's working conditions will be the death of style-architecture. To make up for the rising costs of building, we now have to simplify and hasten the process. We therefore usually have neither the time nor the money to use the more old-fashioned working methods of handicraft—and stylistic trappings, which if they are to be good, demand these methods, will be poor when produced under our working conditions.

And above all: stylistic trappings no longer suit us, they do not inspire us, they are a dying art. Even if we had plenty of time and money at our disposal we would be

Swimming area
and villa in
Switzerland;
modern archi-
tecture that
suits us well.

unable to summon up the interest in them. The result of all this is poor quality. Are we to content ourselves with the second-rate?

Mr. T.: No, but then why not create modern ornamentation that you can take an interest in, that is based on modern working conditions?

We: Modern ornamentation—for the same time and money we could probably make some kind of cheap, standardized ornamentation, cast in artificial stone or iron. But would it give us any pleasure? All of these wretched modernistic attempts, with their confusions of pointed, slanted, acute-angled surfaces and lines, are highly off-putting.

Is not our era beginning to prefer clean surfaces? Look at a couple of modern buildings (for instance the house on page [293], the Barcelona pavilion on page [310]). Surely you would not like any ornamental finery on their beautiful, smooth facades?

Stylistic trappings are no longer interesting.

All the gentlemen vehemently protest.

We: That is how it is. This interest in styles can be found in a very highly educated group who know their art history and undoubtedly entertain both a genuine and honest love of good old-fashioned culture, as well as among a large group of people who in affirming the continued existence of traditional style-culture believe that they are participating in it, in other words, that they are "refined," just as refined as the racketeer who buys antiques.

But the general public does not share this interest, this need. You spoke of dispelling gloom with a little decoration. But today's imitated decorations, which nine times out of ten are bad, are where this gloom lies, in the dreariness of something making the best of itself to no effect, the dreariness of failure or indifference. The general public finds no joy in pilasters, moldings, and rosettes. They observe swarming crowds and shops, they find enjoyment and pleasure in open cityscapes and in parks. For them there is no joy in overdecorated palatial apartment blocks or the "restrained decor" of the newer ones.

We learn from both the old and new that decoration is not the same as pleasure, and that simplification is not the equivalent of dreariness.

The vast majority live for today and follow fashion, the style of the times. And we all do so when it comes to our clothes, our necessities, our means of communication.

We must move forward, follow the path our age itself shows us. Where does it lead?

We are not interested in the trappings of tradition, the relics of styles that were once structural elements but have now degenerated into decorative devices, suitable concealment for architectural jerry-building. The architectural essentials—walls, windows, doors, staircases, balconies, roofs, and chimneys—provide our means. The age seeks simplification, paring down, calm lines, beautiful flat surfaces. We make conscious use, but with greater freedom than in the past, of the contrast of light and

Delaware River Bridge, Philadelphia.

Monumentality dictated by the construction.

shade, openness and enclosure, between flat and contoured surfaces, between straight and curved lines, between hard materials and soft fabrics, between colors.

A gentleman: "You abdicate your artistic role."

A gentleman: "Total bankruptcy of the imagination."

A gentleman: "Did you go to the exhibition? Did you see Asplund's boxes? The stranded ocean liner?"[54]

We: — —

Mr. T.: What an impoverished, inartistic, tedious program!

Bandstand, Stockholm Exhibition.

Form dictated by purpose.

We: No, gentlemen, a rich program. Far richer, far more appealing and stimulating than anything tightly corseted in stylistic stays. Release them and the natural forms appear, our cheeks will regain their color. No longer tethered to style, imagination will have far greater possibilities for action and will be able to focus on essentials, on translating needs into realities. Do you believe that imagination, artistry will be written off as architecture alters and refines its forms? No, on the contrary, the simple, the functionally natural and beautiful requires just as much imagination, just as much artistry as traditional decoration. And in the search for modern form, in

German pavilion, Barcelona Exhibition.

Refined, modern elegance.

all our contemporary requirements, in the inspiration from modern technology, we have wonderful means of achieving such widely differing architectural expression, of achieving beauty that is perhaps not new, but stamped with modernity.

Mr. T.: And Art?

We: The new architecture needs the help of the fine arts. Painting and sculpture must become more prominent within the framework of architecture. But not in a subservient, "decorative" form, subordinate to architecture, not therefore as some intermediary between decorative architecture and sculpture in the way it is often used today and which does not appear to inspire our contemporary artists. But as free, autonomous art.

We believe that art and sculpture, liberated from far too rigid architectural constraints and from the same stylistic shackles as architecture, will flourish once more and perhaps in a renewed form.

Instead of the one hundred ornaments at twenty kronor apiece and the five decorations at two hundred kronor each that we now distribute equitably throughout a house we should marshal our resources and acquire a genuine, modern work of art that suits us.

Free, autonomous, living works of art instead of dainty, worthless decorations, instead of "tastefulness."

Painting and sculpture, which today calmly cultivate their great wisdom, will perhaps tomorrow, when they have been engaged by a more vigorous view of the time and space we live in, give us what we long for.

We see many hesitant attempts toward a new art in connection with modern architecture. Still we are left wondering whether they lead forward. Architecture that verges on sculpture and painting was a danger; perhaps painting and sculpture that approach architecture are also dangerous?

Profuse, rich modern art as a contrast to modern architecture?

Mr. T.: *(Exits right).*

"—the rhythm of the organic."

The amphitheater in Verona.

"The amphitheater lay half in light and half in shadow; broad and resonant, the beautiful oval extended itself through light and shadow.

As if at one stroke, more recent architecture sinks out of view. It is hardly possible anymore to pay attention to the Renaissance. This classical structure does not really triumph through its greater architectonic beauties, as indeed hardly any of them have survived; all that one can see is a great building mass, a ruin on the outside, unadorned on the inside. But irresistibly triumphant is the impression made by its enormous objectivity and purposeful simplicity, its grandiose manifestation of reason, the power of its will and the self-evident character of its form. One is gripped—at this one spot in Verona—by the rhythm of the organic. Involuntarily one imagines this wonderfully proportioned curved oval with all its stone ledges filled by people and sees in the mind's eye how the architectonic whole endows the masses with order and with tempo. Involuntarily one links this building with life and movement, while one always links Renaissance architecture to historical ideas alone. A totally new purpose for building becomes apparent to us. Renaissance architects took models as their starting point; the master of this arena started with the facts themselves, with the monumental perception of need. The former strove for beauty; the latter attempted to derive his style from necessity.

The beauty of the arena is, at least today, when only the skeleton of the building remains, the beauty of brilliant engineering. Therefore great anonymity, audacious impersonality, is inherent in it; it suggests the idea of an entire people, while on the contrary all other structures in the city make one think of social groupings, individuals, institutions, and special interests. In this spirit of antiquity there is spontaneity, there is unity."

(Karl Scheffler: *Italien*)[55]

Straightforward, sober, inviting—our tradition.

Today's architects have no desire to follow the line of development that is defined by variations in form traditions, by some sort of self-absorbed "architectural athletics," be it colonnades, anxious Baroque grandeur, rigid Empire elegance, or a modernistic orgy of free-floating slabs of concrete.

They want to follow the line of development that is called straightforwardness, and which is illustrated by the amphitheater in Verona and its "grandiose manifestation of reason"; by a windmill, whose entire form is based on the desire to capture the energy of the wind; by an old Swedish farmhouse that has evolved naturally from the time of its origin around the farmer and his way of life.

We do not subscribe to the perpetual survival of traditional forms but to our old tradition of straightforwardness, moderation, and friendliness, which we would like to believe is Swedish and which can find expression in widely differing forms.

Provincial—national—international,

three words that describe different phases of cultural development and perhaps different attitudes to culture as well.

Our standards change, the limits of our own cultural areas are widened—"the world is growing, the world is shrinking."[56]

The provincial, restricted to a county or a smaller area, has developed on the basis of its own needs and material conditions with no forceful impulses from outside. This was an admirable form of culture in the past that existed naturally and unconsciously. When the isolation of different provinces was ended by the major development of communications, provincial forms of culture ceased to exist as well. To a greater and greater extent the differences between provincial cultures have been leveled out as more and more of their characteristic features have been ousted by new ones common to all.

And so the provincial, where the distinctive once held sway, is slowly dying out.

The national is the provincial on a larger scale. But the more we extend the boundaries of a cultural area, the more vague its distinctive features become. Swedish national architecture that includes Västerbotten, Dalarna, Stockholm, and Skåne does not have features that are as distinctive as those of the architecture of Dalarna alone.

In culture the national is a nuance of the international. Our own circumstances and conditions, our landscape, climate, and material resources, our dispersed population, our temperament, our poverty, the way we live, all these have given our culture, which rests on an international foundation, its local color, its character.

In our architecture and our applied art, which absorbed abundant and direct impulses from elsewhere through the Vikings, monks, warriors, and travelers, this character has been obvious. We have no national Swedish "style." Our log

Classical Greece, which we cannot imitate.

houses have their counterparts in all forested countries, our Gothic, Renaissance, and Louis XVI styles are closely related to those of Germany, France, England, and Denmark. But in our buildings there is at any rate something of a specifically Swedish character.

The dimensions of our cultural domain today are international. More and more, relationships are being forged between the epicenters of nations all over our revolving globe. Ideas and professional problems connect people despite national boundaries.

Between periods of international struggle we have more and more international cooperation for survival. The same overwhelming and multifaceted array of international learning, inventions, and ideas comes to all nations more rapidly and to a greater extent than before.

What characterized the provincial was local by nature and subject to little change with the passing of time; on the other hand the distinctive characteristics of the international are more related to time than to place. International culture changes more rapidly, lives with a stronger pulse, but spreads more uniformly across countries than older forms of culture did.

The special character of the national therefore becomes less distinct. But it will not vanish; we can see national features in modern French, Russian, German, and Dutch architecture. And we can see them, or will be able to, in Swedish architecture as well.

But even if the national characteristics were, despite our desires and assumptions, to disappear completely, this would not be the same as a general degeneration of artistic culture. Has it become vulgarized because the layman cannot distinguish the architecture of the Russian Rococo, for instance, from the German or French? Or neoclassicism in Germany from the same style in other countries? Personalities and their acolytes mean much more than national characteristics for cultural profusion and variety. The individual differences between two modern architects from the same country, for instance Gropius and Mendelsohn in Germany, can be very significant. Modern architecture is based to a much greater extent than the older styles on formal freedom, and this allows greater possibilities of variation, perhaps also for national expression. Modern architecture also embodies a wealth of divergences, wit and poetic charm, imaginativeness, sober objectivity, and refined elegance.

A gentleman: "Modern architecture—a German import!"

We: Yes, perhaps it is, or at least a French-German-Czech-Austrian-Dutch import. Just as Baroque was an Italian import, or Rococo a French import. And just as much as our Gothic is—a German import.

But let us not go on talking about national architecture. What about the builders who developed our Swedish building-art in the cottages, palaces, and churches they erected—do you believe they thought or spoke of being national?

No, they did what we have to do: respect objective demands and contemporary natural conditions. **We cannot preach the national into existence, it has to develop of its own accord.**

Someone shouts: A national building-art is valuable for tourism. "Beauty pays."

We respond: The unconsciously national is a virtue, the contrived, deliberate, pasted-on national form is an evil. We are not working for those who ferret around for national characteristics. We cannot conjure a national bloom from the soil. Our building-art merely seeks its natural goal, it has no commercial ends in sight, will not provide souvenirs for tourists.

The Norwegian painter Chr[istian] Krogh: "All national art is bad, all good art is national."[57]

England.   **School in Welwyn.**

France.   **Villa Savoye.**

Holland.   **School in Hilversum.**

Project for a Lenin Institute.

Russia.

USSR Pavilion in Paris 1925.

Sweden.

Hammarforsens Power
Plant.

S. L. T. office and factory
building, Stockholm.

Cottage, Stockholm
Exhibition, 1930.

U. S. A.

Skyscraper.

Finland.

Newspaper building, Turku.

Norway. The Artists' House, Oslo.

Denmark. House, Hellebæk.

Row houses, Dammerstock.

Germany.

Vacation resort, Urach.

The city.

Public interest and the way forward.

An old, historical city is about to disappear. It is little consolation that a historical city is **continually** disappearing—that it did so in 1830, 1730, 1630. Sorrow
at the turn progress is taking is constant among local patriots, as constant as development itself.

How can we attain something that is both new and good to replace the old and
good that we are losing?

The great public interest, which finds expression in complaints about the dissipa-
tion of values, in the constant anxiety conveyed in newspapers for the vanishing past
and the approaching new—these individual and general declarations, motions, the
hubbub of disparate desires, all this moving interest, which is a declaration of love,
must really gratify us all.

Interest has a value in itself.

But often it is too negative and the negative is of no help to us.

Sometimes it is right to preserve the old and avoid the new. But no reasonable
person, not even our archaeologists, merely wants to "preserve" and "avoid," wants
to prevent the natural renewal of the city. The negative approach is only revealed in
answer to the question, "What do we want the new to look like?"

Many respond by renouncing the age in which they live, by referring to the old. A
city of reproductions, or at least imitations, is their answer. They believe that everything old is good, everything new bad. They want to obstruct the modern, in other
words what is true to its time, or banish it to the outskirts (where anything goes).
Some want to submit architecture to restrictive statutes, some want to call in foreign
experts to provide them with old Swedish architecture!

THE NEW IS ALWAYS WRONG.
Dedicated to those who are always grizzling about the "unsightliness" of our beautiful petrol pumps.

From the *Evening Standard*.

"The new is always wrong."

We are battling with a formidable force: the age itself and its will.

Forces that exert energy in different directions cancel each other out, either entirely or in part. Industrialism, democracy, and the entire spirit of the age work forward; the motto for cultural forces that insist on the dear old form traditions of centuries past is "focus backward."

In the ceaseless and wearying tug-of-war between forward and backward, in our taxing bicameral cultural system, lies the basis of the confusion of today, of the perils that threaten the beauty of our city.

Today's tug-of-war, the often merely backward-looking and negative interests, the constant anxiety and divided atmosphere in the city, can ultimately lead to nothing good.

What we need now—as during the great cultural epochs—is to combine the positive endeavors, sustained by conviction and enthusiasm, of laymen as well as professionals, toward the same end and on the basis of our own time, without which we will never achieve any new good to take the place of the old good that must disappear.

Art, not least building-art, after a time of general preparation, appears more or less suddenly in a new guise. This new form, which emerges from the circumstances of the age, evolves into a "style" and triumphs all over the world. It is a process of this kind that we are experiencing in building-art right now.

Is the city a work of art or a living organism?

The value of a building cannot be judged merely by its impact on the cityscape, its treatment of the exterior and interior, but above all on how it meets the needs of some form of work or living.

Nor can a cityscape be seen as a more or less deliberately balanced rhythmic and picturesque creation, like a painting composed of architectural motifs. "The city as a work of art" is a dangerous concept. The city does not possess eternally static beauty like a sculpture or a painting. It originates from real needs, whose changing nature it must satisfy. The city is an expression of movement, work, life in a thousand different forms—it is a living organism. Like everything that has life, all of its parts develop from birth to death. The milieu is, and must be, subject to change.

The living milieu is completely changed.

The usual and obvious principle is that a city must be allowed to grow. With a population of five hundred thousand it cannot wear the same "costume," or a larger size of the same costume, as when it housed two hundred thousand people.

The city grows when new areas are added to its periphery, and consequently the old city center is also affected. Streets need widening and new roads must be constructed as traffic increases; buildings also become higher.

And for a long time a revolutionary reorganization has been taking place in all major cities in the formation of central commercial areas, downtown, and outlying housing areas.

It is these circumstances and not a new architectural idiom that are decisive in changing the milieu of a city in its entirety.

Smaller-scale places, streets and squares, also change, gradually and without resistance.

An old-fashioned milieu cannot be maintained artificially in a progressive city. The ongoing human, social, and economic developments inevitably entail new types of buildings among the old. And the old facades, where the ground floors have been rebuilt for shops and where stylistic details are covered or obscured by showcases and display windows, undergo a radical change of character.

The atmosphere of the old streets vanishes completely: no children play, no flocks of sparrows on the pavement, nobody giving their mother a ride on their kick-sled—as we used to—to go shopping on Main Street.

We have definitely abandoned our small-town idyll. The street is no longer a living room. There, overwhelming movement rules. It is crowded with people, automobiles, buses, streetcars, and the neon lights and display windows "cry out" their wares.

The street is dominated by the hustle and bustle that always accompanies commerce. The continual hum of traffic, noise, the movement of people, give the street a new character.

The conclusion is this: we can no longer stand in the middle of traffic to gaze at details of the facades; neither we ourselves nor our eyes can find the repose to do so. Interest has more or less shifted downward from the street's facades to the street itself.

The living milieu in our modern streets has changed completely, and architecture, which has to base its work on life, will also be different.

The modern clothes people wear, the smooth shiny surfaces of automobiles, buses, and streetcars, asphalt, large display windows of glass, shimmering neon lights—these are some of the features of our new environment.

Still Stockholm.

Let us turn here to the attitude of modern architecture toward the problems of the old city and let us concentrate our observations on Stockholm, which is undergoing the urban development we sketched out above.

We need not be afraid of placing modern buildings among the old ones that survive. Our predecessors did the same, setting the style of their time directly next to the old.

On Skeppsbron the seventeenth century built its modern Hanseatic stepped-gable buildings amid the smaller medieval ones, and the eighteenth century placed its modern classicizing styles among the stepped-gabled buildings—nobody ever thought of using stepped gables again. Today, however, when the old buildings are replaced one after another by new ones, we are not given architecture that belongs to the present; once again we get Skeppsbron's styles in scarcely improved versions. Development has halted to the detriment of our culture.

Everything new must clash with the old—this is the very nature of development, just as a child, full of lust for life, is jarring next to the elderly.

Look at Stockholms slott [Stockholm royal palace], which, when it was new, as a strictly modern creation, must have "clashed" with the saturated ambience of the seventeenth century.[58] And as a new building in the 1770s, the stock exchange must have offered a palpable contrast to the old buildings surrounding it on Stortorget.[59] Consider the Carolinian sepulchral chapel built in the Baroque style by the Tessins in the Gothic Riddarholmenskyrkan [Riddarholmen church] and the Baroque tower on

Berlingske building, Copenhagen.

Modern amid the old.

Commercial building, Drottninggatan,
Stockholm.

the Gothic Storkyrkan [Stockholm cathedral].[60] These are bold contrasts. But they evolved with the disarming, unquestioning acceptance and strong self-awareness possessed by previous eras, but which our time seems to lack.

We assert that we have the same rights and obligations as our predecessors to show the physiognomy of our age in our architecture, to express the living environment that is accepted by all.

Respect is a necessary social concept. A building must show respect for its neighbors, which can be expected to endure longer. Respect does not mean stylistic imitation—we mean respect for the surrounding architectural scale, proportions, grouping, and color.

Carl Lindhagen is undoubtedly correct that the printing house of Norstedt & Söner (where a celebrated custodian of culture is at work) and the Riksarkivet [National archives] (where our memories are preserved) constitute an act of vandalism in their lack of respect for one of the most beautiful and memorable spots in the city.[61] And we consider the modernistic color scheme of brutal yellow and red, which was applied without objection to a modern apartment block on Norr Mälarstrand, as equally lacking in respect.

Changeability in the city environment—that is the logic. But life is not merely logic. At times we want to break the rational rule with an irrational exception; at times we don't want to follow the voice of reason, but we want to retain a piece of the old environment, a venerable, purposeless building, a couple of ancient trees that are not too much in the way.

The way we feel about a certain monumental, or old, picturesque part of the city is natural. We have seen it since our childhood, we know its history and it has a charm of its own. If it has to go, we will miss it like an old friend, even though we know that nature also ordains that our friend must in the end depart.

We do not hesitate to preserve a valuable milieu with totally viable buildings and with adequate routes for traffic. But in exceptional cases there are also parts of the city or buildings that have such historic significance for the city or such outstanding features that they should be preserved as well, even if this involves major practical or economic sacrifice.

Stockholm is a city of incomparably flourishing and varying appeal. Nature has bestowed this upon us; it is not of our doing. The water that stretches between the islands, the wide views across them, the invigorating elements of almost untouched nature, the rhythm of hills, ridges, and low-lying land, some of the buildings along the waterfronts and the soaring spires—these are our assets.

But many buildings, particularly in the central areas, do not offer the same attractive environs and in many places lack both architectural beauty and appeal.

From these opposing points of view we all, even those of us who are not afraid of the process of development, can arrive at some definite requirements:

to preserve the open water intact and inviolate; to preserve what remains in the heart of the city of free vegetation and natural shoreline; to preserve the city's undulating topography; to preserve as far as possible its outstanding architectural settings; to preserve to some extent buildings of particularly valuable architectural or historical importance.

When the decision has been made to preserve an old building or an area that is no longer completely viable, let us clearly recognize that this is a direct concession to historical interests, which in an old city are both natural and extensive, and that we

The city from the garden of the Stockholm Town Hall.

are working on the same principles as a museum. This is a dangerous principle in a growing city, but is correct in the rare cases when for powerful historical and purely aesthetic reasons it takes precedence over demands for natural development.

But otherwise: it still remains Stockholm, still natural development with demands for the highest standards of quality.

Standard criticism and popular clichés.

Modern architecture, like everything else in this world, needs a great deal of criticism and is not harmed by it.

When criticism is sound, when it is slightly positive, then we are influenced by it. Like the schoolboy above, who in the fall of 1930, after an enthusiastic presentation on modern architecture, took a drubbing from an older pupil.

"Functionalism will disappear by itself."

Our modern architecture, which has not yet matured, and is certainly not yet ripe to disappear, will develop toward greater certainty, clarity, expressiveness, and refinement. It will not revert to the ideas of the 1920s. Let us all unite in pleasure at this kind of disappearance.

"The new style has an external vulgarity that is dreadful."

Simplicity is not vulgarity, except to officious aesthetes.

The vast majority of buildings in our city date from the mid-nineteenth century and later. A mess of stucco and plaster Baroque, pointless small corner towers, narrow gables, false fronts, oriel windows, an occasional dreadfully disruptive pyramid roof (on the Nationalmuseum [The national museum of fine arts]), and some equally disruptive (artistic?) mansard roofs (Gustaf Adolfs torg)—this is the semi-old architecture we can see in Stockholm at the moment, as it really appears.[62]

No one has taken up cudgels against this vulgarity and no champion of culture calls us "to arms" when today we repeat the worst of what was being done twenty, thirty years ago.

For there is a kind of ugliness that is so insipid, so customary, that everyone considers it natural. Nobody condemns the unintentionally ugly. Relatively high quality is required before a building comes in for strong criticism.

In the realm of art, unfortunately, the perfect work is the exception. "The new style" has the same "right" as the old to leave us with some ugly buildings. No one can demand that everything new should be good—nor are many of the "functionalist" buildings good. Even a modern architect can be wrong, can make a mistake, just as an old-fashioned one, just as a critic, can.

But honest people judge a movement by its best works. The simplicity of the new style is not vulgarity; at its best it offers expressive beauty, much as the simple art of building-art did in the past.

"Functionalism is an indication of the crassest materialism, it ignores all deeper values and is therefore hostile to culture."

Two times two, as someone once said, can be calculated fairly approximately as four units plus a one-hundred-thousandth.

With the same degree of approximation this opinion is incorrect.

We are looking for forms that are suitable and natural for our age, we are looking for a close link with the fine arts and with the finest gifts of nature, we want to give people the better homes they need, which will leave them with some energy to cultivate their intellectual gifts.

Is it not possible with reasonable approximation to describe this materialism as—idealism?

**What Stockholm
should look like.**

"Last summer's exhibition gave us a foretaste of what Stockholm will look like if functionalism spreads."[63]

Is Stockholm an exhibition, a summer fairy tale?

A poet turns to Architecture and sings the following (which for some reason has been laid out as a four-line stanza):

"And I feel that you expect of me
a rectangular, right-angled inner life
that you can set against a drafting triangle
to determine: Straight."

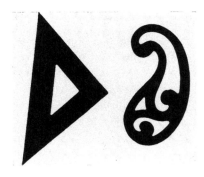

**Drafting triangle or French
curve?**

"Machine for living."

This expression, which was coined by Le Corbusier, was to become for many opponents of the new building-art a *gefundenes Fressen* [gift from the gods].

"They want us to live in a machine, these deranged modernists, but no thank-you, I prefer a house that stands still," and so on.

It may be less inflammatory to consider what the author really meant with this expression. All he is saying is that a dwelling should function effectively for its intended needs—and who could disagree with that? By another analogy he calls a painting *une machine à émouvoir* ["a machine for stirring emotion"].[64]

It is psychologically interesting to observe how machine is a word that automatically enrages the "cultural" public.

"Machine romanticism."

As has been pointed out, this epithet is an invention of one or two artistic connoisseurs, who use it so often and warn against it.

Only one question can be asked: If our age is to feel any romance, is it not better to direct our feelings toward things that are closely linked to our own lives and their creations, instead of trying to sustain the specific infatuations of the past? Whether we rate them higher or lower, is there any reason for valuing the romantic nature of Lindberg's flight across the Atlantic or the powerful performance of a giant dynamo on a different scale from the one we use for a young maiden's amorous dreams among the birch groves or anywhere else you like? If not, then perhaps infatuation with the creations of human will and organizational ability should be placed highest.

"The building looks like a box."

Now the foremost builder in this country has said (our readers must certainly have observed on several occasions that our unshakeable determination to be objective is more than compatible with the right to seize on the quotations that suit us) that a building is a box, that it should be a box. And therefore everyone should be content . . .[65]

This method of always comparing something with something else, by the way, merely betrays the inherent uncertainty of the appraiser. He cannot take each thing for what it is and what it wants to be. He must constantly have clichés ready to pigeonhole things under the false impression that he is rendering them familiar.

This is acknowledged as a bad, if not to say dishonest, method in literary criticism. That it should somehow be justifiable in architecture is difficult to grasp.

The Royal Palace, Stockholm. Just a box as well.

Accept.

These arguments against the new spirit in building-art and industrial art come from a variety of sources.

But they all share an attitude to reality: the skeptical onlooker's.

They can take the form of the noblest and finest criticism, worldly-wise gestures, and postures of skeptical defensiveness, on down to mere journalistic wit.

Another attitude to reality: the doers.

The opposition between the onlooker and the doer is expressed in the following quotations from two men who have each, in their own way, had great influence on society.

> *Gustaf Steffen*:   "There is a danger in all that exists, since every-
> where its viability is challenged.
> There is a danger in all that is to come, since its
> viability has not yet been tested."[66]

> *Henry Ford*:   "One who fears the future, who fears failure, limits
> his activities. Failure is only the opportunity more intel-
> ligently to begin again. There is no disgrace in honest
> failure; there is disgrace in fearing to fail."[67]

How much simpler it is to adopt the attitude of the former.

How much greater the difficulty in acting like the latter.

How easy it is to make fun of the aberrations of our age and in this way avoid the difficulties reflected in them.

How hard to sustain the demand that spiritual and material culture should be one. But how necessary.

From this necessity evolves this moral imperative:

accept

the reality that exists—only in that way have we any prospect of mastering it, taking it in hand, and altering it to create culture that offers an adaptable tool for life.

We have no need for outworn forms from earlier cultures to sustain our self-respect.

We cannot tiptoe backward away from our own era.

Nor can we skip past what troubles and confuses us into a utopian future.

We can only look reality in the eye and accept it to be able to master it.

There has never been any real doubt in cultural life today about our means or our ends. Only the weary and pessimistic claim that we are in the process of creating a mechanical culture that is an end in itself. The organization of the world's resources and the improvement and stabilization of the living conditions of individuals are what we are working toward. But these are merely means to enable richer lives to be led. If that end is distant, we have to make even greater endeavors to perfect the means.

If our cities have become outmoded, if more than half of their populations live in cramped conditions, if a horde of practical needs are unresolved, then we must first devote all our energy to solving them.

Anyone who cannot accept is withdrawing from participation in the development of culture. He will fade away in a meaningless pose of embittered heroism or worldly-wise skepticism.

What is important above all in this divided age is to clarify concepts so that we do not destroy each other with words whose content and truth value have not been tested. Instead we must unite all the forces that fundamentally seek the same ends and work together to create the culture that we need.

Translated from the Swedish by David Jones.

Notes

Acceptera was first published in 1931 by Tiden, the publishing arm of the Swedish Social Democratic Party. With the addition of an afterword by Anders Åman, it was reissued as a facsimile edition in 1980 (Stockholm: Tiden, 1980). In 1932 the chapter "Form" was extracted, redesigned, and published as *Form: ett kapital ur acceptera* (Stockholm: Skolan för bokhantverk, 1932). A long extract from the chapter "Staden" (The city) was translated into Italian and included in Stefano Ray, *Il contributo svedese all'architettura contemporanea e l'opera di Sven Markelius* (Rome: Officina, 1969).

Despite the fact that *acceptera* has never been translated into English before, it is often referred to in English-language scholarship, usually in connection to Gunnar Asplund, the most well known of the authors outside Sweden and the subject of numerous English-language publications. To some extent *acceptera* has also come to the attention of the English-speaking world through the influence of its authors on the Finnish architect Alvar Aalto, who remains a central and much-researched figure in English-language scholarship on twentieth-century architecture. In common English usage, the book is already spoken of as *acceptera*, and not by a translation of that word. This familiarity has led the editors of this volume to leave the title untranslated. Further, literal translations such as "accept" or "to accept," seem to diminish something of the force of the title in its original language without adding appreciably to an English speaker's ability to pronounce or understand the meaning of the word.

In *acceptera* the authors make numerous references to buildings, places, people, utterances, and articles without giving full details or referencing their sources. Where it has been possible to identify the references in question, the editors have done so in the following notes; a few of these references remain unidentified, as they were in the original of 1931. Likewise, the *acceptera* captions are often loosely descriptive. The editors' elaborations on those images for which further identification could be found appear on pages 345 to 347, following our notes on the text itself.

1. Sw. *byggnadskonst*: lit. "the art of building," here rendered as "building-art" following recent translations of the related German word *Baukunst*. See Hermann Muthesius, *Style-Architecture and Building-Art: Transformations of Architecture in the Nineteenth Century and Its Present Condition*, introduction and translation by Stanford Anderson (Santa Monica, CA: Getty Research Institute, 1994). Like Muthesius, the authors of *acceptera* seem to prefer "building-art" over the Latin-derived *arkitektur*. They were probably influenced by Muthesius's distinction between a more objective and contemporary "building-art" and the frivolous "style-architecture" of the past. See Anderson, Introduction, pp. 1–2. See also *acceptera* authors' discussion of "stylistic trappings," p. 305. Sw. *konstindustri*: translated here as "industrial art," and in other contexts as the more general "applied art."

2. Lewis Henry Morgan (1818–1881), American lawyer, ethnographer, and anthropologist, was the author of *Ancient Society, or Researches in the Lines of Human Progress from Savagery Through Barbarism to Civilization* (New York: H. Holt & Co., 1877).

3. Edvard Westermarck (1862–1939) was a Swedish-speaking Finnish philosopher and sociologist, noted social anthropologist, professor at Helsinki University, (1906–18), Åbo Akademi (1918–32), and London School of Economics (1907–30), and author of *The History of Human Marriage* (London: Macmillan, 1891).

4. Robert Briffault (1876–1948), a French-born doctor, historian, social anthropologist, novelist, and author of *The Mothers: A Study of the Origins of Sentiments and Institutions* (New York: Macmillan, 1927), was educated in New Zealand and active as a writer in England after the First World War.

5. Ger. *Siedlungen*: developments of small, functionally designed apartments and row houses intended for low-income families, supported by public funding and built by leading modern architects in many of Weimar Germany's larger cities. For the influence of these developments on the authors of *acceptera*, see Creagh, Introduction, p. 131 and n. 25.

6. Sw. *Folkets hus*: lit. "house of the people," assembly halls and community centers set up after the 1890s by local societies associated with the Swedish labor movement.

7. Sw. *saklig gestaltning*: here, "objective embodiment." The *acceptera* authors use these two words, cognates of the German words *sachlich* and *Gestaltung*, throughout the text and in similar ways to discourses in Germany at around this time. In this translation derivatives of Sw. *sak* (thing, object), such as *saklig* and *saklighet*, have been translated as "objective," "factual," "down-to-earth," "matter-of-fact," "straightforward," and "purposeful." Sw. *gestaltning* from *gestalta* (to give form to, to shape, to embody) has been rendered as "shaping form," "form-giving," "embodiment," "design," and as "giving visible expression."

8. The *acceptera* authors noted here: "Francis Delaisi, *Les deux Europes*, Paris 1929, from which the following presentation has been taken." In *Les deux Europes: Europe industrielle et Europe agricole* (Paris: Payot, 1929), the French journalist and economist coined the terms the authors adopt: "A-Europe" and "B-Europe."

9. Sw. *stationssamhälle*: small communities that sprang up around stops on Sweden's rapidly expanding railroads in the late 1800s.

10. Karl Key-Åberg, *Af Stockholms stadsfullmäktige beslutad undersökning af arbetarnes bostadsförhållanden i Stockholm* (Stockholm: K. L. Beckmans boktryckeri, 1897).

11. Henri Dubreuil, *Standards* (Paris: Bernard Grasset, 1929), p. 94.

12. Magdalena Sophia (Malla) Silfverstolpe (1782–1861), Swedish author, held a famous literary salon in her Uppsala home.

13. Hagaparken, a large park located in the northern Stockholm district of Solna, originally a royal estate, was developed in the 1780s by Frederik Magnus Piper along the lines of the English picturesque garden.

14. Sw. *Jorden krymper–jorden växer*: almost certainly a reference to the collected essays of the Finnish architect Sigurd Frosterus, *Jorden krymper,*

jorden växer (Stockholm: Schildt, 1930), in which, under the influence of German historian Oswald Spengler, he ponders the nature of contemporary Western civilization through the dualism of technological progress and ecological degradation.

15. Sw. *studiecirkel*: "study circle." Influenced by the nineteenth-century movements for adult education in Britain and the United States, study circles were introduced to Sweden in 1902 by Oscar Olsson (1877–1950), Good Templar, social democrat, and member of parliament (1913–48). Study circles were key to the educational ambitions of the labor and cooperative movements and played an important role in "taste education" through organizations such as Svenska Slöjdföreningen (The Swedish arts and crafts society) and Kooperativa Förbundet (The Swedish cooperative wholesale society).

16. The original text cites 250,000 million kronor per year; the editors' research indicates that this was a misprint and the actual expenditure was closer to 250 million kronor.

17. See Carl G. Laurin, "post funkis," *Svenska Dagbladet*, September 25 and 26, 1930. On Laurin, see Lane, Introduction, n. 34.

18. Sw. *genomgående lägenhet*: an apartment that runs the full depth of a building, with two apartments on each floor and windows at front and back, providing improved ventilation and natural light.

19. Sw. *egna hem*: a small, detached owner-occupied home, strongly associated with *egnahemsrörelsen*, the Swedish movement for home ownership that began in the 1890s. Geared toward stemming the tide of emigration, the movement promoted the construction of owner-occupied homes for low-income rural households, though it quickly expanded to accommodate workers in towns and cities and soon became a national concern, with the state administering special loans to foster home ownership. In the 1910s architects such as Torben Grut and Ragnar Östberg drew plans for *egna hem* that reflected rural building traditions (see Lane, Introduction, n. 51). The homes took on a simpler form as standardized house types were later developed. See Eva Eriksson, "International Impulses and National Tradition 1900–15," in *20th Century Architecture: Sweden*, eds. Claes Caldenby, Jöran Lindvall, and Wilfried Wang (Munich: Prestel, 1998), pp. 42–44.

20. Sw. *familjehotell*: "family hotel," a term of American origin, though not as commonly used in the United States as its equivalents "apartment hotel" and "residential hotel." Family hotels, which first appeared in the U.S. in the latter half of the nineteenth century, featured private apartments complemented by shared services and facilities, and were promoted as a solution to the increasing expense of retaining servants. The term seems to come into use in Sweden around 1920, although buildings with central kitchens had been erected in Stockholm on European models as early as 1907. By the 1930s, particularly through the work of Sven Markelius and Alva Myrdal, the term "family hotel" had become somewhat interchangeable with *kollektivhus* (collective house) and *centralhem* (housing with shared facilities), but it retained a sense of its origins in the American capitalist system in being considered a profit-making rather than cooperative venture. The emphasis here on "family" seems to be important, as the *acceptera* authors, and later Myrdal, would propose this form of housing as a response to the changed nature of the family as an economic unit. In the 1950s the term "family hotel" would be used again, in an attempt to distance certain collective housing arrangements from the radical left-leaning implications of the *kollektivhus*. See Creagh, Introduction, pp. 135–136.

21. Sw. *hall*: an entry hall or vestibule, but also in some Swedish apartments of the time a significantly larger, wider room that connected an entry vestibule to other rooms in the apartment.

22. Sw. *typisering*: derived from Ger. *Typisierung*, the development, creation, or formation of types. See Paulsson, in the present volume, n. 11.

23. The *acceptera* authors noted here: "Ford: 'Today and Tomorrow.'" Henry Ford in collaboration with Samuel Crowther, *Today and Tomorrow* (London: William Heinemann Ltd., 1926), pp. 80–81.

24. Stockholm stads småstugebyrå (The Stockholm municipal small cottage bureau) was established in 1927 to further promote the *egna hem* principle by facilitating, through loans and practical assistance, small owner-built dwellings. The bureau developed standardized house types, provided prospective owner-builders with drawings and instruction, and delivered materials cut to size or in prefabricated building components. In the case of Enskede (1907) and Bromma (1913), two suburbs set out on garden city principles, these cottages were constructed on land leased to the home owner by the municipality.

25. Sw. *funkis*: derived from *funktionalism* (functionalism), with no English equivalent in this form. A slang word coined by the press at the time of the Stockholm Exhibition, *funkis* was often used in a derogatory sense. The authors of *acceptera* considered it an overused word describing a set of stylistic features with no connection to the broad social and architectural intentions of their work.

26. Carl Malmsten (1888–1972) was an architect, furniture designer, and educator. After winning a competition in 1916 to design furniture for Stockholms stadshus (The Stockholm town hall), he went on to exhibit alongside Gunnar Asplund and Uno Åhrén at Hemutställningen (The home exhibition) in 1917. Interiors and furniture for some of the most important buildings of the 1920s followed, including Ivar Tengbom's Stockholms Konserthus (The Stockholm concert hall), 1928, and Tändstickbolaget (The Swedish match company), 1928. His writings from this period include *Om svensk karaktär inom konstkulturen* (Stockholm: Bonnier, 1916) and *Skönhet och trevnad i hemmet* (Stockholm: Natur och Kultur, 1924). After 1927 Malmsten founded adult education schools for arts, crafts, and industrial design. Active in Svenska Slöjdföreningen, he exhibited furniture at the Stockholm Exhibition of 1930, while remaining a vocal opponent of the exhibition's program and functionalism in general. Malmsten discussed the symmetrical, "pyramidal" grouping of furniture and artworks mentioned here in "Hemtrevnad," Birgit Kewenter, ed., *Hem och hushåll årsbok för 1924* (Stockholm: Kooperativa förbundets förlag, 1924), pp. 38–40. See also Creagh, Introduction, p. 130.

27. Sw. *hemindustri*: lit. "home industry," or cottage industry in the older sense of the word, whereby handicraft products are manufactured in the home using materials or semi-finished goods supplied by an agent or merchant, to whom the finished goods are returned for sale. Synonymous with the protoindustrial Sw. *förlagssystem*, Ger. *Verlagssystem*, or "putting-out system," home industries emerged in Sweden toward the end of the eighteenth century.

28. Karl-Erik Forsslund (1872–1941), a Swedish author, journalist, poet, and educator, was a key figure in the Swedish adult education, local heritage, and nature conservation movements. Complex in his views, he combined radical political beliefs with a conservative attitude to traditional culture and was vehemently opposed to both metropolitanism and modern art and architecture. The home was a central conception in his work, and his most important book, the bestseller *Storgården: En bok om ett hem* (Stockholm: Wahlström & Widstrand, 1900), describes an idyllic life in a traditional, red-painted farmhouse in the Dalarna countryside. See Creagh, Introduction, p. 130.

29. Stuart Chase (1888–1985), American economist, has been credited with originating the term "New Deal" in 1932. *Men and Machines* (New York: Macmillan, 1929).

30. Sw. *hemslöjd*: lit. "home-crafts," though this word is translated variously today, as "handcraft" and "handicraft," for example. (In this volume the Sw. *hantverk* has been translated as "handicraft.") Before the eighteenth century, all craft production carried out in the Swedish home was referred to as *hemslöjd*. By the beginning of the twentieth century however, the term was mostly associated with the commercial production of traditional handmade goods (textiles, furniture, pottery, woodwork, wrought-iron work) organized through bodies such as Föreningen Svensk Hemslöjd (The association of Swedish home-crafts) and Svenska Hemslöjdsföreningarnas Riksförbund (The national league of Swedish home-crafts associations). The translation of *hemslöjd* as "home-crafts" to indicate a specific type of refined handicraft based on traditional Swedish models follows the example of publications in English by these organizations circa 1931. See Key, in the present volume, n. 28.

31. Here, a reference to the program for the manufacture of better and affordable everyday goods launched by Svenska Slöjdföreningen and outlined in 1919 by Gregor Paulsson in *Vackrare Vardagsvara* (*Better Things for Everyday Life*), which appears in the present volume. As the authors concede, the collaborations between artists and industry that Svenska Slöjdföreningen brokered in the 1920s generally produced luxury items, such as those displayed at a number of international exhibitions in the latter half of the decade. It would not be until well into the 1930s, with changes in public taste and the advent of foreign competition, that Swedish companies seriously reassessed the way household goods were designed and manufactured for the mass market.

32. Thorsten Odhe (1892–1965), author of many books on consumer cooperation and the economy, was active in the Kooperativa Förbundet (The Swedish cooperative wholesale society). The editors' efforts to determine the source of the summary of his views here were unsuccessful.

33. Thorn, previously in East Prussia, has been part of Poland since 1918; just south of Gdansk, it is now known as Torun. The guild ordinance was part of Emperor Sigismund's Reformatio Sigismundi of 1523, which helped to protect local craftsmen from competition from Gdansk and elsewhere. The warning against innovation was not atypical of late medieval guild ordinances throughout Europe.

34. Probably a reference to the essay "Building" by Hannes Meyer (1889–1954), radical Swiss architect and controversial director of the Bauhaus from 1928 to 1930. Meyer described building as "giving shape to the functions of life" and as "deliberate organization of the processes of life," concluding that "building is simply organization: social, technical, psychic organization." Hannes Meyer, "bauen," in *bauhaus, zeitschrift für gestaltung*, vol. 4 (Dessau: Bauhaus, 1928), pp. 118–20. There may also be an echo here of Ernst May (1886–1970), Frankfurt city architect and overseer of city planning between 1925 and 1930, and his exhortation to architects to "create something decisively new out of today's vital conditions of life." "Das neue Frankfurt," in *Das neue Frankfurt*, vol. 1, no. 1 (1926–27): p. 6.

35. The original reads "enduring fashion and transient style," presumably a misprint, given the following discussion.

36. Stockholms stadshus, by Ragnar Östberg, 1909–23, executed in warm red brick, granite, and marble, "modern" in its asymmetry, is often described as the height of Swedish National Romanticism in architecture. It is also internationally known for its dramatic site, turrets, historical imagery, and lavish decoration, including Einar Forseth's "Golden Hall," with its glittering mosaic walls. In the first decades of the twentieth century, Östberg (1866–1945) was one of Sweden's leading architects, the author of a book on small house design, and a follower of Ellen Key (see Lane, Introduction, n. 51). He designed a number of important buildings including Villa Pauli, 1905; Villa Ekarne, 1905; Yngve Larsson House, 1907; the Carl Eldh Studio, 1918; Östra Real School (Eastern senior high school, Stockholm, 1906–10); Villa Bonnier, 1924–27; the Helsingborg Crematorium, 1929; and the Sjöhistoriska muséet (Museum of maritime history, Stockholm, 1933–35).

37. The *acceptera* authors are quoting from an article by Malmsten ("Genmäle av arkitekt Carl Malmsten," *Tidskrift för Hembygdsvård*, no. 4, 1930, p. 105), in which Malmsten quotes himself from *Om Svensk karaktär inom konstkulturen*.

38. Bernard Ashmole (1894–1988), Yates Professor of Archaeology, University College London, built the highly controversial reinforced concrete house "High and Over" in Amersham, Buckinghamshire, 1928–30, hiring as his architect New Zealander Amyas Connell (1901–1980), soon a principal member of the firm Connell, Ward & Lucas.

39. Östermalm, a Stockholm neighborhood developed in the late nineteenth century, was dominated by large apartment buildings in various historical and eclectic styles, with colorful facade architecture of the sort reformers criticized. Danviks hospital, originally founded in 1551 by King Gustavus Vasa, was rehoused in a new building

by architect Aron Johansson, 1902–15, in a monumental, medieval style. The 1909 Allmänna svenska utställningen för konsthantverk och konstindustri (National Swedish exhibition of applied and industrial art) in Stockholm, nicknamed "The White City" after the 1893 World's Columbian Exposition in Chicago, was organized by Svenska Slöjdföreningen (The Swedish arts and crafts society). Ferdinand Boberg (1860–1946), an important designer of some of Sweden's most innovative buildings around the turn of the century, supervised the exhibition. His temporary exhibition buildings, faced in white stucco, included a domed exhibition hall and towers topped by Secession-like gilded balls.

40. Göteborgs konstmuseum, by Arvid Bjerke, R. O. Swensson, Ernst Torulf, and Sigfrid Ericson, 1916–23, a monumental neoclassical building, is the focal point of Kungsportsavenyn, the main avenue in Göteborg. On Liljevalchs konsthall, see Kåberg, Introduction, p. 65.

41. Stockholms stadsbibliotek (The Stockholm public library), by Gunnar Asplund, 1920–28, additions 1928–31. This and the following unfavorable mention of the Lidingö exhibition, which was largely the work of acceptera co-author Sven Markelius, seem to be good-humored attempts at self-critique.

42. Tändsticksbolaget (The Swedish match company headquarters), by Ivar Tengbom, inaugurated 1928. Interior design and textiles by Elsa Gullberg, furniture by Carl Malmsten, light fixtures by Orrefors glasbruk and artist Simon Gate, murals by artist Isaac Grünewald, and sculptures by Carl Milles.

43. In 1925 Sven Markelius laid out a garden city neighborhood of one- and two-family houses for the Bygge och Bo (Building and Home) exhibition, Lidingö. See Maria Perers, "The Building and Home Exhibitions: Forerunner to the 1930 Stockholm Exhibition," Scandinavian Journal of Design History, vol. 11 (2001): pp. 74–97.

44. From the late nineteenth century to the 1920s these publications and others like them were used as a reference by both practicing Swedish architects and students at Kungliga tekniska högskolan and Konstakademin. Erik Dahlbergh, Suecia antiqva et hodierna (Det forna

och nuvarande Sverige) (Stockholm: E. J. Dahlbergh, at the expense of the King, 1667–1716), a collection of over four hundred engravings depicting Sweden as a great power, its towns, castles, and important estates. Paul Marie Letarouilly, Édifices de Rome moderne; ou, Recueil des palais, maisons, églises, couvents et autres monuments publics et particuliers les plus remarquables de la ville de Rome (Paris: F. Didot, 1840–57), extensive collection of measured drawings of Roman buildings from the Renaissance and Baroque periods. Svenska teknologföreningens afdelning för husbyggnadskonst, eds., Gamla svenska städer: gator och gränder, hus och gårdar. Samlingsverk i bilder jämte förklarande text (Stockholm: Generalstabens litografiska anstalts förlag, 1908–30), a series of publications illustrating old Swedish towns, streets, and buildings, collected by, among others, Sigurd Curman, Carl Westman, and Ragnar Östberg.

45. The Vasa period began with the rule of King Gustav Vasa (1496–1560)–the first Swedish king, who was elected after defeating the Danes and ruled Sweden from 1523 to 1560–and ended with the abdication of Queen Kristina in 1654. In the nineteenth century the first king of Sweden was used as a symbolic reference in strengthening the idea of nationhood, and the style of the Vasa period was revived in art and architecture, for example at Danviks hospital, mentioned in n. 39 above.

46. Carl Lindhagen (1860–1946), lawyer, politician, and member of parliament, 1897–1917, 1919–40, was mayor of Stockholm from 1903 to 1930; see also n. 51 below. The building referred to is Bondeska palatset (Bonde palace), 1662–67, Nicodemus Tessin the elder and Jean de la Vallée, architects; some later additions by Johan Eberhard Carlberg, 1753; renovations by Ivar Tengbom, 1949. Served as Stockholm's town hall and municipal courthouse between 1753 and 1916. Motion to Stockholm city council by Mayor Carl Lindhagen, 1928, overruled 1929. See Claes G. Ellehag, Bondeska Palatset (Stockholm: Stockholmia förlag, 1989), pp. 7, 87.

47. The sentences quoted here from the architect and theorist Gottfried Semper (1803–1879) were well-known

in architectural debates. Otto Wagner adopted the first sentence (in Latin, "Artis sola domina necessitas") as the cornerstone of his functionalist theory. They come originally from Semper's Vorläufige Bemerkungen über bemalte Architektur und Plastik bei den Alten (Altona: Johann Friedrich Hammerich, 1834), reprinted in Kleine Schriften, Manfred and Hans Semper, eds. (Berlin: W. Spemann, 1884), p. 218.

48. Nicodemus Tessin the elder (1615–1681) took study trips from 1651 to 1653 to Italy, France, Germany, and the Netherlands and introduced Sweden to Roman and French classicism. The architect behind the original design for the monumental Drottningholms slott (Drottningholm palace), begun in 1662, he also designed private palaces in Stockholm and its surrounds. His son, Nicodemus Tessin the younger (1654–1728), count and leading architect of his time, continued his father's work on Drottningholms slott and designed Stockholms slott (The royal palace), 1690–1704, and Tessinska palatset (Tessin palace), 1692–97. On study trips to Rome from 1673 to 1678 he was influenced by Bernini and studied with Carlo Fontana.

49. King Gustav III made a trip to Italy in 1783 and 1784. Experiencing the remains of antiquity and the monuments of the Italian Renaissance firsthand had a great impact on him. Gustavian style before the king's Italian voyage, known as early Gustavian style, was neoclassical and still reminiscent of Rococo, while the late Gustavian style is more angular and antiquarian.

50. Skandinaviska kreditaktiebolaget (from 1939, Skandinaviska banken), by Erik Josephson, 1914–16, Stockholm.

51. The acceptera authors have slightly amended a quote from Stockholm Mayor Carl Lindhagen, the original of which was "Functionalism seems to place no value in the artistic way of life." It comes from a motion to the Stockholm city council in 1930 in which Lindhagen proposed that important city buildings should not be permitted in the functionalist style, but should be reserved for commercial architecture or for building on the outskirts. Stockholms stadsfullmäktige. Motioner 1930, nr. 12, here taken from

Per Råberg, *Funktionalistiskt genombrott* (Stockholm: P. A. Norstedt & Söner, 1972), p. 223, p. 358 nn. 9, 10.

52. Laurin, "post funkis."

53. The *acceptera* authors inserted "(chemical-technical)," into this quote from Malmsten, "Genmäle," p. 101.

54. A reference to the Stockholm Exhibition of 1930, for which Gunnar Asplund was the chief architect. The negative reference to the exhibition pavilions as "boxes" was probably first made by Carl Malmsten toward the end of August 1929, just as the pavilions were going up. See n. 65 below. Disparaging references to functionalist buildings as "ocean liners" or "steam ships" were common in the press from 1929 to 1931. Here it is likely the authors are referring to an article by the critic Torsten Fogelqvist, who in "The Boxes on Djurgården" declares that the "entire flotilla of steam ships"—the exhibition buildings under construction—should be torn down in order to start again. "Lådorna på Djurgården," *Dagens Nyheter*, August 26, 1929.

55. Karl Scheffler, *Italien: Tagebuch einer Reise* (Leipzig: Insel, 1916), pp. 37–38. Scheffler (1869–1951) was editor of *Kunst und Künstler*, the leading art critic for the important Berlin newspaper *Vossische Zeitung*, and author of many popular books on art.

56. See n. 14 above.

57. Christian Krohg (1852–1925) was a Norwegian artist, critic, and journalist with radical, individualist, urban, and internationalist views. It is unclear whether Krohg uttered these words or the quote is an oral myth. Nevertheless it captures Krogh's view as expressed in "Fædrelandsbekymrede Kunstnere" and "Det nationale i Kunsten," both 1902; reprinted in Krohg, *Kampen for tilværelsen*, vol. 1 (Copenhagen: Gyldendal, 1920–21), pp. 68–72 and 73–76.

58. Stockholms slott, by Nicodemus Tessin the younger, 1690–1704 (see n. 48 above), completed by Carl Hårleman.

59. Börshuset, by Erik Palmstedt, 1773–76, restored by Ove Hidemark, 1982.

60. Gothic church with Baroque burial chapel for royalty and nobility, c. 1280–1310; extended in the fifteenth century.

61. P. A. Norstedt & Söner, publishing house and printing press, by Magnus Isæus, 1882–91, located on the waterfront of Riddarholmen adjacent to the old Riksarkivet by Axel Fredrik Nyström, 1887–90, a cast-iron framed structure clad to look like a Venetian Gothic palazzo. The "celebrated custodian of culture" to whom the authors refer is probably Carl G. Laurin, who was employed at Norstedt, his family's company, from 1893. On Laurin, see Lane, Introduction, n. 34.

62. Nationalmuseum, by Friedrich August Stüler, 1846–66, a Florentine/Venetian Renaissance–style palazzo, on the waterfront across from Stockholms slott.

63. A reference to the Stockholm Exhibition, May–September, 1930.

64. Le Corbusier's collaborator, Amédée Ozenfant, was probably the first to say "L'oeuvre d'art est une machine à émouvoir," sometime during the mid-1910s. Le Corbusier later used the phrase to describe the Parthenon. See Daniel Naegele, "Savoye Space: the Sensation of the Object," *Harvard Design Magazine*, Fall 2001, pp. 5, 12, n. 11.

65. The "foremost builder" in question is the architect Ivar Tengbom (1878–1968). In 1929 Tengbom gave an interview to a Stockholm newspaper in which he reprimanded Malmsten for his critique of the Stockholm Exhibition and its buildings as "boxes": "Architect Malmsten criticizes the exhibition's 'boxes.' But in controversies surrounding architecture, isn't it an old and worn-out weapon to call buildings 'boxes'? A building *must* be a box, but a box with proportions." "Ett hus skall vara en låda, men en låda med proportioner," *Aftonbladet*, August 24, 1929.

66. Gustaf Steffen (1864–1929) was a prominent Swedish political economist. See Lane, Introduction, p. 22 and n. 26.

67. Henry Ford, *My Life and Work*, p. 23.

Annotations to the Illustrations

The following annotations, which expand on *acceptera*'s captions where possible, are based on a list compiled by Anders Åman, with the help of Eva Rudberg and Björn Linn, for the facsimile edition of *acceptera* (Stockholm: Tiden, 1980), pp. 206–208. Included here (with additions and amendments by the editors of this volume) courtesy of Anders Åman.

p. 140. The cover of the original 1931 edition of *acceptera*, seen here, includes an excerpt of the closing paragraphs of the book, beginning with the phrase "the reality that exists."

p. 153. Office of Sven Wallander, founder and president of Hyresgästernas Sparkassa och Byggnadsförening (The national federation of tenants' savings and building societies; hereafter abbreviated as HSB). Belkingegatan, Stockholm. 1929.

p. 172, top. Adolf von Menzel. *Eisenwalzwerk* (The iron-rolling mill). 1872–75. Oil on canvas, 62 ¼ x 100" (158 x 254 cm). Alte Nationalgalerie, Berlin.

p. 189. Graph from Uno Åhrén's investigation of housing conditions for the Stockholm Exhibition of 1930. The key at the top reads: "workers, lower civil servant, higher civil servant, all/total, liberal professions, manufacturers/businessmen."

p. 190. Cyrillus Johansson. Apartment building, Norr Mälarstrand and Jakob Westinsgatan, Stockholm. Mid-1920s.

p. 192. Drawings showing town plan development. Published in Uno Åhrén, "Byggandet som konst och politik," *Spektrum* 1 (1931): p. 16.

p. 193. Midtown view of New York; in left foreground: Sugarman & Berger. The New Yorker Hotel, 481 Eighth Avenue. 1930.

p. 194. Stadshagen district plan by Stockholms stads stadsplanekontor (Stockholm municipal planning office), 1930.

p. 195, top. Georg Scherman. Apartment buildings for Ladugårdsgärdet district, Stockholm. Student project, 1929.

p. 195, bottom. Diagram from Uno Åhrén's study of housing conditions for the Stockholm Exhibition of 1930, *Katalog över bostadsavdelningen* (Stockholm: Utställningsförlaget, 1930), p. 38.

p. 196. Walter Gropius. "High-rise apartments on the Wannsee," fifteen eleven-story blocks planned for six hundred families, Berlin. 1931.

p. 197. August Künzel in cooperation with Paul Artaria and Hans Schmidt. Row houses for large families, Siedlung Schorenmatte, Basel. 1929. At right, an apartment building built for the 1930 Swiss Housing Exhibition.

p. 201. Max Ernst Haefeli and Werner M. Moser. Apartment living room, "Model Houses on the Wasserwerkstrasse," Rotach-Häuser, Zurich. 1927–28. Ernst Kadler-Vögeli and Max Ernst Haefeli. Cane chair. 1926. Mfr.: A.-G. Möbelfabrik Horgen-Glarus, Horgen.

p. 202. Living room with MR20 Armchair by Ludwig Mies van der Rohe. 1927. Tubular steel and cane. Mfr.: Berliner Metallgewerbe Joseph Müller, Berlin. See also p. 299, upper right.

p. 203. Erik Friberger. Model apartment no. 1 for a household of three to four people, Stockholm Exhibition, 1930. Erik Friberger and Nils Enström. Living and dining room furniture. Mfr.: AB Ferdinand Lundqvist, Göteborg.

p. 204 Sven Wallander's office, HSB. HSB model apartment no. 2 for the Stockholm Exhibition, 1930.

p. 205. Sven Markelius's house, Nockeby, Stockholm. 1930. See also p. 243.

p. 206. Kurt von Schmalensee. Model apartment no. 6 for a household of four to six people, Stockholm Exhibition, 1930. Erik Chambert, AB Chamberts Möbelfabrik, Norrköping. Interior design and furniture. Table lamp. Mfr.: AB Arvid Böhlmarks Lampfabrik, Stockholm. Carpets. Mfr.: Kasthalls Mattfabrik, Kinna. See also p. 210.

p. 208. Sven Wallander's office, HSB. HSB model apartment no. 1 for the Stockholm Exhibition, 1930.

p. 210. Kurt von Schmalensee. Model apartment no. 6 for a household of four to six people, Stockholm Exhibition, 1930. View of living room and plans. See also p. 206.

p. 213, top. American apartment unit, described as an "efficiency apartment" and published in *Architectural Forum*, November 1924, p. 253.

P. 213, bottom. The text at left reads: "lesser talented students to housing cells"; at right, "talented students to the university."

p. 214. Sven Wallander's office, HSB. Playroom in an HSB-built apartment building, Svarvargatan, Stockholm. 1930.

p. 215. Frits Schlegel and Edvard Thomsen. Houses, Skovshoved district, Copenhagen, 1929.

p. 216, top. Birger Jonson. House no. 52 for a household of two to four people, Stockholm Exhibition, 1930.

p. 216, bottom. Eskil Sundahl and Olof Thunström, Kooperativa Förbundets arkitektkontor (The Swedish cooperative wholesale society architects' office; hereafter abbreviated as KFs arkitektkontor). Row houses, Hästholmen (now Kvarnholmen), Stockholm, 1930. See also p. 237.

p. 218. Thorkild Henningsen. Row house, plan and view from a window, Fuglebakken, Fredriksberg, Copenhagen. 1928.

p. 222. Collage with books, medieval church at Dalhem, Gotland (early thirteenth century, restored 1899–1914), Doric temple (temple of Poseidon, Paestum, c. 450 BCE), and 1929 Nash "Advanced Six" sedan, manufactured in Kenosha, Wisconsin.

p. 224. Stockholms stads småstugebyrå (Stockholm municipal small cottage bureau). "Small-cottage" type III being assembled, Olovslund, Bromma. 1928.

pp. 226–27. Paul Artaria and Hans Schmidt. House on the Wenkenhalde, from construction to completion, Riehen (Basel), Switzerland. 1927.

p. 228, top. Construction, Siedlung Mammolshainerstrasse, Frankfurt am Main, published in *Das neue Frankfurt*, 1928.

p. 228, bottom. Construction, Siedlung Westhausen, Frankfurt am Main, published in *Das neue Frankfurt*, 1930.

p. 229. Ernst May and staff. Siedlung Praunheim, Frankfurt am Main, view from the Nidda Valley. 1926–28.

pp. 230–32. Walter Gropius. Row houses (layout, construction, and model), Siedlung Törten, Dessau, Germany. 1926–28.

p. 235. Ludwig Mies van der Rohe. Apartment building plans, Weissenhof Siedlung, Stuttgart. 1927.

p. 237. Eskil Sundahl and Olof Thunström, KFs arkitektkontor, apartment building and row houses, aerial view, 1930. See also p. 216, bottom.

p. 238. Real estate advertisements: "5 room villa in mansion style" and "Charming 7 room Ornäs villa with magnificent view of Lake Mälaren."

p. 243. Living room, Sven Markelius's house, Nockeby, Stockholm, 1930. See also p. 205. Johan Petter Johansson. "Triplexpendel" ceiling light. 1926. AB Enköpings Verkstäder, Enköping (Johansson's own workshop). Marcel Breuer. Table. 1925–26. Tubular steel and lacquered plywood. Mfr.: Gebrüder Thonet, Vienna.

p. 252. Artur von Schmalensee, KFs arkitektkontor. Oatmeal mill (interior), Kvarnholmen, Stockholm. 1928.

p. 258. Sigurd Lewerentz. General Motors bus. 1930. Mfr.: AB Hägglund & Söner, Örnsköldsvik. Exhibited at the Stockholm Exhibition, 1930.

p. 259. Uno Åhrén. Light fixtures. c. 1930. Mfr.: Nordiska kompaniet, Stockholm. Standard chair. 1930. Mfr.: AB Svenska Möbelfabrikerna, Bodafors.

p. 260. Standardized door handle, published in *Das neue Frankfurt*, 1928. Gustav Dalén. AGA stove (Aktiebolaget Gasaccumulator). 1931. Enameled cast-iron and chromium alloy. First manufactured in the UK, 1931. Carl Hörvik, Sven Malm, Olle Nyman, Kalle Lodén, and Georg

Scherman. Glassware. Mfr.: Målerås glasbruk; distr: Kooperativa Förbundet (The Swedish cooperative wholesale society). Exhibited at the Stockholm Exhibition, 1930.

p. 261. Marguerite Friedlaender. Coffee service. 1930. Mfr.: Staatliche Porzellanmanufaktur Berlin.

p. 264. Simon Gate. Optic-blown footed vase. 1930. Executed by Gustav Bergqvist. Mfr.: Orrefors glasbruk. Exhibited at the Stockholm Exhibition, 1930. Dag Ribbing. Combined record player and radio, with detached speaker. 1930. Mfr.: AB C.A.V. Lundholm, Stockholm. Exhibited at the Stockholm Exhibition, 1930.

p. 273. John Browning. 9mm Browning semi-automatic pistol with shortened barrel, model M/07. Mfr. in Sweden: Husqvarna, Huskvarna, 1916–40.

p. 274. Alphonse Tellier. "Tellier 1" monoplane with parasol wings. 1926. Mfr.: Nieuport-Delage, Nieuport, France. Telephone. 1929. Mfr.: H. Fuld & Co., Frankfurt am Main.

p. 275. Robert Maillart. Aqueduct over Eau-Noire, Châtelard, Switzerland. 1925.

p. 276. Otto G. Carslund, unidentified painting, c. 1930.

p. 277. W. M. Dudok, et al. De Bijenkorf department store, Rotterdam. 1930.

p. 278. Wilken Wilkenson, Röjeråsen tower, Rättvik. 1928.

p. 280. J. A. Brinkman and L. C. van der Vlugt/Mart Stam. Van Nelle Tobacco Company Factory, Rotterdam. 1928. See also p. 302.

p. 283. Gunnar Asplund. Press box for the Stockholm Exhibition, 1930.

p. 284. Illustration of Ornässtugan after Viking Göransson, published in *Stockholms Dagblad*, October 1, 1930. Ornässtugan (Ornäs cottage), sixteenth-century log house in Dalarna, famous retreat of Gustav Vasa while at war with the Danes, was also well known from the copy exhibited at the Paris Exposition Universelle of 1867, and then relocated to the grounds of the Royal Residence at Ulriksdal.

p. 285, top. Rudolf Steiner. Second Goetheanum. 1924–28.

p. 285, middle. Rudolf Steiner. District heating plant, Dornach, Switzerland. 1913.

p. 287. Uno Åhrén's apartment, Drottninggatan, Stockholm. Armchair Model No. 6009, later B9. c. 1904. Steam-bent beechwood. Mfr.: Gebrüder Thonet, Vienna. Paintings or prints by Hilding Linnqvist and Pablo Picasso.

p. 290. Pehr Hillerström the elder. *Spelparti hos stassekreterar Elis Schröderheim* (Card party in the home of Elias Schröderheim). 1782. Oil on canvas, 43 3/4 x 54 3/8" (111 x 138 cm), Nationalmuseum, Stockholm.

p. 291, bottom. Diagrams from Auguste Choisy, *Histoire de l'architecture* (Paris: Gauthier-Villars, 1899), vol. 2: Ducal Palace, Urbino, p. 675; Church of St. Jacobius, Toulouse, p. 465.

p. 293. Lois Welzenbacher. Westphalia House, Recklinghausen, Germany. c. 1930.

p. 294, bottom. Hans Leuzinger. Swiss Alpine Club cabin. 1929–30.

p. 296. Erich Mendelsohn. Schocken department store, Chemnitz, Germany. 1928.

p. 298, top. Traditional farmhouse and attached barns, Skåne.

p. 298, bottom. Richard Döcker. House at Weissenhof Siedlung, Stuttgart. 1927.

p. 299, top left, right. Wrought-iron Swedish chair probably mid-nineteenth century. Ludwig Mies van der Rohe. MR20 Armchair. 1927. See also p. 202.

p. 302, top. J. A. Brinkman and L. C. van der Vlugt/Mart Stam. Van Nelle Tobacco Company Factory, Rotterdam. 1928. See also p. 280.

p. 302, bottom. Gustav Oelsner, et al. Employment office, Altona (Hamburg), Germany. 1927.

p. 304. Photograph with ruff and feather painted on the man's costume by Gunnar Asplund.

p. 306. Max Ernst Haefeli. House in Wollishofen, Zurich. c. 1930.

p. 308. Paul P. Cret and Ralph Modjeski. Delaware River Bridge (now Benjamin Franklin Bridge), Philadelphia. 1920–27.

p. 309. Nils Einar Eriksson. Bandstand for the Stockholm Exhibition, 1930.

p. 310. Ludwig Mies van der Rohe. German pavilion for the Barcelona Exhibition, 1929.

pp. 312–13. Roman amphitheater, Verona, Italy. First century CE.

p. 318. Louis de Soissons. Handside Lane School, Applecroft Road, Welwyn Garden City, UK. View from gardens and playing fields. 1922–23.

p. 319, top. Le Corbusier. Villa Savoye, Poissy, France. 1930.

p. 319, bottom. W. M. Dudok. School, Hilversum, Netherlands. 1929.

p. 320, top. Ivan Leonidov. Unexecuted project for Lenin Institute and Library, Moscow. 1927.

p. 320, bottom. Konstantin Melnikov. USSR pavilion for the Exposition internationale des arts décoratifs et industriels modernes, Paris, 1925.

p. 321, top. Osvald Almqvist and Kreuger & Toll. Hammarforsen power plant, Ragunda municipality, Hammarstrand. 1928.

p. 321, middle. Ivar Tengbom and Nils Ahrbom. Model, S. L. T. (Esselte) office building, Vasagatan, Stockholm. View from the rear. 1928.

p. 321, bottom. Sigurd Lewerentz. House no. 47 for a household of four to five people. Stockholm Exhibition, 1930.

p. 322, bottom. Alvar Aalto. *Turun Sanomat* newspaper building, Turku, Finland. 1930.

p. 323, top. Gudolf Blakstad and Herman Munthe-Kaas. Kunstnernes hus (Artists' House), Oslo. 1930.

p. 323, bottom: Kay Fisker. Summerhouse, Sjölunsvej, Hellebaek, Denmark. 1926.

p. 324, top. Alfred Fischer and Walter Merz. Row houses, Dammerstock Siedlung, Karlsruhe, Germany. 1929.

p. 324, bottom. Adolf G. Schneck. "House on the Alb" vacation resort, Urach, Germany. 1930.

p. 329, top. Bengt Helweg-Møller. *Berlingske Tidendes* newspaper building, Pilstræde, Copenhagen. 1930.

p. 329, bottom. Wolter Gahn. Office building, Drottninggatan 14, Stockholm. 1929.

p. 331. Stockholm, aerial view from the east. The Royal Palace appears at the lower right corner of the central island, Gamla stan (Old town). See also p. 336.

p. 333. Uno Åhrén. Collage of newspaper clippings critical of the 1930 Stockholm Exhibition. From "Till Pressen," *Byggmästaren*, no. 10 (1929): p. 160. Headlines here read: "unswedish," "Boxes," "the latest fashion," "imported goods!" "Functionalism does not suit us," "real scandal," "steamboat funnel–what are you doing?" "beauty pays," and "-ism of the day."

p. 335, top. Gunnar Asplund. Paradise restaurant, Stockholm Exhibition, 1930.

p. 336. Nicodemus Tessin the younger. The Royal Palace, Stockholm. 1697.

Selected Bibliography

Ahlberg, Hakon. *Swedish Architecture of the Twentieth Century.* Edited by F. R. Yerbury. London: Ernst Benn, 1925.

Åhrén, Uno. "Brytningar" (Turning points). *Svenska Slöjdföreningens Årsbok*, 1925, pp. 7–36. In *Nordic Architects Write*, edited by Michael Asgaard Andersen. London: Routledge, 2008.

Ambjörnsson, Ronny. "Family Ideas in Sweden and the Tradition of Ellen Key." In *Traditional Thought and Ideological Change: Sweden and Japan in the Age of Industrialism*, edited by S. Cho and N. Runeby. Stockholm: University of Stockholm, 1988.

Andresen, Sabine, and Meike Sophia Baader. *Wege aus dem Jahrhundert des Kindes: Tradition und Utopie bei Ellen Key* (Paths from the *Century of the Child*: tradition and utopia in Ellen Key). Neuwied: Luchterhand, 1998.

Asplund, Gunnar, "Vår arkitektoniska rumsuppfattning" (Our architectonic understanding of space). *Byggmästaren*, no. 12 (1931): pp. 203–210. In *Nordic Architects Write*, edited by Michael Asgaard Andersen. London: Routledge, 2008.

Baagøe, Thomas, and Barbro Ilvemo. *From Ellen Key to Ikea: The Arts and Crafts of Industrial Design of the Twentieth Century.* Göteborg: Röhss Museum of Arts and Crafts, 1991.

Blundell-Jones, Peter. *Gunnar Asplund.* London: Phaidon, 2006.

Brunnström, Lisa. *Det svenska folkhemsbygget: om Kooperativa Förbundets arkitektkontor* (Building the Swedish welfare state: Regarding the Swedish Co-operative Union and Wholesale Society's architectural office). Stockholm: Arkitektur förlag, 2004. With summary in English, pp. 326–27.

Caldenby, Claes, Jöran Lindvall, and Wilfried Wang, eds. *20th Century Architecture: Sweden.* Munich: Prestel, 1998.

Carlson, Alan. *The Swedish Experiment in Family Politics: The Myrdals and the Interwar Population Crisis.* New Brunswick, NJ: Transaction, 1990.

Creagh, Lucy. "Asger Jorn and the 'Apollo and Dionysus Debate,' 1946–48." In *Architecture + Art: New Visions, New Strategies,* edited by Eeva-Liisa Pelkonen and Esa Laaksonen. Helsinki: Alvar Aalto Academy, 2007.

De Angelis, Ronald. "Ellen Key: A Biography of the Swedish Social Reformer." Dissertation, University of Connecticut, 1978.

De Maré, Eric. "The New Empiricism: Antecedents and Origins of Sweden's Latest Style." *Architectural Review*, January 1948, pp. 9–11.

Dräbing, Reinhard. *Der Traum vom "Jahrhundert des Kindes"* (The dream of a "Century of the Child"). Frankfurt am Main: Peter Lang, 1990.

Eriksson, Eva. *Mellan tradition och modernitet: arkitektur och arkitekturdebatt 1900–1930* (Between tradition and modernity: architecture and architectural debate 1900–1930). Dissertation, Department of Art History, Stockholm University. Stockholm: Ordfront, 2000. With summary in English, pp. 514–20.

Exhibition of Swedish Contemporary Decorative Arts. Exhibition catalogue. New York: The Metropolitan Museum of Art, 1927.

Facos, Michelle. *Nationalism and the Nordic Imagination: Swedish Art of the 1890s.* Berkeley, CA: University of California Press, 1998.

Frick, Gunilla. *Svenska Slöjdföreningen och konstindustrin före 1905* (The Swedish arts and crafts society and art industry before 1905). Dissertation, Department of Art History, Uppsala University. Stockholm: Nordiska museet, 1978. With summary in German, pp. 247–72.

——. "Furniture Art or a Machine to Sit on? Swedish Furniture Design and Radical Reforms." *Scandinavian Journal of Design History* 1 (1991): pp. 77–105.

Friedman, Alice T. "Frank Lloyd Wright and Feminism: Mamah Borthwick Cheney's letters to Ellen Key." *JSAH*, vol. 61:2 (June 2002): pp. 140–51.

Hall, Thomas. "Urban Planning in Sweden." In *Planning and Urban Growth in the Nordic Countries*, edited by Thomas Hall. London: E & FN Spon, 1991.

Isacson, Maths, and Lars Magnusson. *Proto-Industrialisation in Scandinavia.* Leamington Spa, UK: Berg. 1987.

Ivanov, Gunnela. *Vackrare vardagsvara–design för alla? Gregor Paulsson och Svenska Slöjdföreningen 1915–1925* (Better things for everyday life–design for everybody? Gregor Paulsson and the Swedish society of arts and crafts 1915–1925). Dissertation, Department of Historical Studies, Umeå University. Umeå: Umeå universitet, 2004. With summary in English, pp. 86–93.

Jacobson, Th. Plænge, and Sven Silow, eds. *Ten Lectures on Swedish Architecture.* With contributions by Sven Markelius, Eskil Sundahl, Alva Myrdal, Sven Wallander, et al. Stockholm: AB Tidskriften Byggmästaren, 1949.

Johannesson, Lena. "Ellen Key, Mamah Bouton Borthwick and Frank Lloyd Wright: Notes on the Historiography of Non-existing History." *Nova: Nordic Journal of Women's Studies*, vol. 3, no. 2 (1995): pp. 126–36.

Kåberg, Helena. *Rationell arkitektur: Företagskontor för massproduktion och masskommunikation* (Rational architecture: corporate offices for mass production and mass communication). Dissertation, Uppsala University. Uppsala: Acta Universitatis Upsaliensis, 2003. With summary in English, pp. 131–37.

Key, Ellen. *Individualism och socialism: Några tankar om de få och de många* (Individualism and socialism: thoughts about the few and the many). Studentföreningen Verdandis småskrifter, no. 55. Stockholm: Bonnier, 1895. (German: "Die Wenigen und die Vielen." In *Die Wenigen und die Vielen: Neue Essays.* Berlin: Fischer, 1901.)

——. *Missbrukad kvinnokraft* (The misuse of the power of woman). Stockholm: Bonnier, 1896. (German: *Missbrauchte Frauenkraft.* Paris: Langen, 1898.)

——. "Torpedo under arken." In *Henrik Ibsen: Festskrift i anledning af hans 70de fødelsdag.* Bergen: Grieg; and Stockholm: Beijer, 1898. (English: *The Torpedo under the Ark: "Ibsen and Women."* Translated by Mamah Bouton Borthwick. Chicago: Seymour, 1912.)

——. *Barnets århundrade.* Stockholm: Bonnier, 1900. (German: *Das Jahrhundert des Kindes.* Berlin: Fischer, 1902. English: *The Century of the Child.* New York: Putnam, 1909.)

——. *Lifslinjer* (Lifelines). 3 vols. Stockholm: Bonnier, 1903–1906. (German (vol. 1): *Über Liebe und Ehe.* Berlin: Fischer, 1906. English: *Love and Marriage.* New York: Putnam, 1909.)

———. *Kvinnorörelsen*. Stockholm: Bonnier, 1909. (German: *Die Frauenbewegung*. Frankfurt am Main: Rütten u. Loening, 1909. English: *The Woman Movement*. Translated by Mamah Bouton Borthwick. New York: Putnam, 1912.)

Klein, Barbro. "The Moral Content of Tradition: Homecraft, Ethnology, and Swedish Life in the Twentieth Century." *Western Folklore*, vol. 59, no. 2 (Spring 2000): pp. 171–95.

Koblik, Steven. *Sweden's Development from Poverty to Affluence, 1750–1970*. Minneapolis: University of Minnesota Press, 1975.

Lane, Barbara Miller, *National Romanticism and Modern Architecture in Germany and the Scandinavian Countries*. New York: Cambridge University Press, 2000.

Lengborn, Thorbjörn. "Ellen Key." *Prospects: The Quarterly Review of Comparative Education*, vol. XXIII, no. 3/4 (1993): pp. 825–37.

Lindén, Claudia. *Om kärlek: litteratur, sexualitet och politik hos Ellen Key* (On love–literature, sexuality and politics in Ellen Key). Dissertation, Department of Literature and History of Ideas, Stockholm University. Stockholm: Symposion, 2002. With summary in English, pp. 305–12.

Magnusson, Lars. *An Economic History of Sweden*. London: Routledge, 2000.

Markelius, Sven. "The Structure of Stockholm," and "Swedish Land Policy." In G. E. Kidder Smith, *Sweden Builds*. 2nd edition. New York: Reinhold Publishing, 1957.

McFadden, David R., ed. *Scandinavian Modern Design, 1880–1980*. Exhibition catalogue. Cooper-Hewitt Museum. New York: Abrams, 1982.

Nylén, Anna-Maja. *Hemslöjd*. Lund: Håkan Ohlssons Förlag, 1968. (English: *Swedish Handcraft*. Translated by Anne-Charlotte Hanes Harvey. Lund: Berlingska Boktryckeriet, 1976.)

Nyström-Hamilton, Louise. *Ellen Key: Her Life and Her Work*. New York: Putnam, 1913.

Ostergard, Derek E., and Nina Stritzler-Levine, eds. *The Brilliance of Swedish Glass 1918–1939: An Alliance of Art and Industry*. New York: The Bard Graduate Center for Studies in the Decorative Arts, Design, and Culture; and New Haven, CT: Yale University Press, 1996.

Paulsson, Gregor. "The Creative Element in Art: An Investigation of the Postulates of Individual Style." *Scandinavian Scientific Review*, vol. 2 (1923).

———. *Swedish Contemporary Decorative Arts*. New York: The Metropolitan Museum of Art, 1927.

———. *Design and Mass Production*. London: Design and Industries Association, ca. 1931.

———. "White Industry." *Architectural Review*, March 1931, pp. 78–84.

———. *Die soziale Dimension der Kunst* (The social dimension of art). Bern: Francke, 1955.

———. *The study of cities: notes about the hermeneutics of urban space*. Interdisciplinary Studies from the Scandinavian Summer University. Copenhagen: Munksgaard, 1959.

———. *Idea and form: studies in the history of art*. Stockholm: Almqvist & Wiksell, 1959.

Paulsson, Gregor, with Henry-Russell Hitchcock, William Holford, Sigfried Giedion, Walter Gropius, Lucio Costa, and Alfred Roth. "In Search of a New Monumentality: A Symposium," *Architectural Review*, September 1948, pp. 117–28.

Perers, Maria. "The Building and Home Exhibitions–Forerunner to the 1930 Stockholm Exhibition." *Scandinavian Journal of Design History* 11 (2001): pp. 74–97.

Pettersson, Hans. *Gregor Paulsson och den konsthistoriska tolkningens problem* (Gregor Paulsson and the problem of art historical interpretation). Dissertation, Department of Art History, Uppsala University. Stockholm: Brutus Östlings Bokförlag, 1997. With summary in English, pp. 203–07.

Pred, Alan. "Pure and Simple Lines, Future Lines of Vision: The Stockholm Exhibition of 1930." In Alan Pred, *Recognizing European Modernities: A Montage of the Present*. London: Routledge, 1995.

Råberg, Per. *Funktionalistiskt genombrott: radikal miljö och miljödebatt i Sverige, 1925–1931* (Functionalist breakthrough: radical environments and environmental debate in Sweden, 1925–1931), 2nd ed. Stockholm: Norstedt, 1972. With summary in English, pp. 332–47.

Ray, Stefano. *Contributo svedese all'architettura contemporanea e l'opera di Sven Markelius* (The Swedish contribution to contemporary architecture and the work of Sven Markelius). Rome: Officina, 1969.

Rudberg, Eva. *Sven Markelius: Architect*. Stockholm: Arkitektur förlag, 1989.

———. *The Stockholm Exhibition 1930: Modernism's Breakthrough in Modern Architecture*. Stockholm: Stockholmia förlag, 1999.

———. *Uno Åhrén: en föregångsman inom 1900-talets arkitektur och samhällsplanering* (Uno Åhrén: a pioneer in 20th-century architecture and town planning). Stockholm: Statens råd för byggnadsforskning, 1981. With summary in English, pp. 249–53.

Shand, P. Morton. "Stockholm, 1930." *Architectural Review*, August 1930, pp. 67–72.

Snodin, Michael, and Elisabet Stavenow-Hidemark, eds. *Carl and Karin Larsson: Creators of the Swedish Style*. Boston: Little, Brown, 1997.

The Stockholm exhibition 1930 of arts and crafts and home industries: Official guide. Stockholm: Utställningsförlaget, 1930.

Swedish Cooperative Wholesale Society's Architects' Office. Stockholm: Kooperativa Förbundet, 1935.

Swedish Cooperative Wholesale Society's Architects' Office. Part 1, 1935–1949; and Part 2, 1925–1949. Stockholm: Kooperativa Förbundet, 1949.

Tilton, Tim. *The Political Theory of Swedish Social Democracy*. Oxford: Clarendon Press, 1990.

Trägårdh, Lars. "Statist Individualism: On the Culturality of the Nordic Welfare State." In *The Cultural Construction of Norden*, edited by Øystein Sørensen and Bo Stråth. Oslo: Scandinavian University Press, 1997.

Varnedoe, Kirk. *Northern Light: Nordic Art at the Turn of the Century*. New Haven, CT: Yale University Press, 1988.

Vestbro, Dick Urban. "Collective Housing in Scandinavia: How Feminism Revised a Modernist Expression." *Journal of Architectural and Planning Research*, no. 14 (Winter): pp. 329–49.

Widenheim, Cecilia, ed. *Utopia & Reality: Modernity in Sweden 1900–1960*. New Haven, CT: Yale University Press, 2002.

Index of Names

Page references to illustrations appear in italics. *Accepta* illustrations may be identified beyond what their captions provide; see annotations on pp. 345–47.